Chicken Soup
for the Soul.

Chicken Soup for the Teenage Soul.

25th Anniversary Edition

Chicken Soup for the Teenage Soul 25th Anniversary Edition
An Update of the 1997 Classic
Jack Canfield, Mark Victor Hansen, Kimberly Kirberger and Amy Newmark

Published by Chicken Soup for the Soul, LLC www.chickensoup.com
Copyright ©2021 by Chicken Soup for the Soul, LLC. All Rights Reserved.

The publisher gratefully acknowledges the many publishers and individuals who granted Chicken Soup for the Soul permission to reprint the cited material.

Front and back cover illustrations courtesy of iStockphoto.com/OlgaYakovenko (©OlgaYakovenko)
Interior illustrations courtesy of iStockphoto.com/OlgaYakovenko (©OlgaYakovenko)

Cover and Interior by Daniel Zaccari

Distributed to the booktrade by Simon & Schuster. SAN: 200-2442

Publisher's Cataloging-In-Publication Data
(Prepared by The Donohue Group, Inc.)

Names: Canfield, Jack, 1944- compiler.
Title: Chicken soup for the teenage soul, 25th anniversary edition : an
    update of the 1997 classic / [compiled by] Jack Canfield [and 3
    others].
Other Titles: Chicken Soup for the Soul
Description: 25th anniversary edition. | Cos Cob, CT : Chicken Soup for
    the Soul, LLC, [2021] | Originally published: Deerfield Beach, FL :
    Health Communications, 1997. | Interest age level: 013-018. | Summary:
    "... new stories to help today's teens be the happiest, best versions
    of themselves"--Provided by publisher.
Identifiers: ISBN 9781611590814 | ISBN 9781611590821 (ebook)
Subjects: LCSH: Teenagers--Conduct of life--Literary collections--Juvenile
    literature. | Teenagers--Conduct of life--Anecdotes--Juvenile
    literature. | CYAC: Conduct of life--Literary collections. | Conduct of
    life--Anecdotes. | LCGFT: Anecdotes.
Classification: LCC BJ1661 .C17 2021 (print) | LCC BJ1661 (ebook) | DDC
    158.1/28/0835--dc23
Library of Congress Control Number: 2021937458

PRINTED IN THE UNITED STATES OF AMERICA
on acid∞free paper

30 29 28 27 26 25 24 23   03 04 05 06 07 08 09 10

Chicken Soup for the

Teenage Soul®

25th Anniversary Edition

An Update of the 1997 Classic

Jack Canfield, Mark Victor Hansen, Kimberly Kirberger and Amy Newmark

Chicken Soup for the Soul, LLC
Cos Cob, CT

Changing lives one story at a time®
www.chickensoup.com

Table of Contents

❶
~Relationships~

❷
~Friendship~

❸
~Family~

❹
~Love and Kindness~

❺
~Learning~

❻
~Tough Stuff~

❼
~Making a Difference~

❽
~Going for It~

Introduction

*Stop trying to be less of who you are. Let this time in
your life cut you open and drain all of the things that
are holding you back.*

~Jennifer Elisabeth, Born Ready

You've made it through your preteen years and grown accustomed to... growing up. This is your time to discover who you really are, including your strengths, your passions, and who you really want to have in your life. This is your time to feel empowered, to go for what you want, define how the world sees you, and become less judgmental about family and friends... and yourself.

You feel like one foot is out the door, but you still live very much at home and will for years. Sometimes that's frustrating, but if you're honest with yourself you know you're not ready to leave. This is your time to start making choices and figuring out how best to use the freedom (and responsibilities) that are coming down the road.

It's still mostly about people, isn't it? That's why we start this book with chapters on Relationships, Friendship, Family, and Love and Kindness. Then we move on to chapters about Learning, Tough Stuff, and Making a Difference. And finally, because you're looking to the future, we end with a chapter on Going for It.

The important thing is that you're not alone. When you read these stories about the experiences of other kids your age, you'll realize you share many experiences and emotions. That is so empowering and comforting.

And that's why this collection of stories for teenagers has become a classic, one of our most popular books ever. We published *Chicken Soup for the Teenage Soul* in 1997 and it sold millions of copies. Now we present it to you updated for its 25th anniversary. We've pulled out some stories that seem out of date these days. We added in ten stories that were in the original *Chicken Soup for the Preteen Soul* because we felt they were more suited for this book for teenagers. And we included 29 brand-new stories for you — ones about being a teenager during the pandemic, social media and technology, and many other modern-day issues.

We're excited to present this new collection to you, and we hope you'll sample some of our other books for teenagers as well. There's a wealth of inspiration, comfort, and great advice in them that will help you navigate these life-changing years.

Relationships

Relationships—of all kinds—are like sand held in your hand. Held loosely, with an open hand, the sand remains where it is. The minute you close your hand and squeeze tightly to hold on, the sand trickles through your fingers. You may hold on to some of it, but most will be spilled. A relationship is like that. Held loosely, with respect and freedom for the other person, it is likely to remain intact. But hold too tightly, too possessively, and the relationship slips away and is lost.
~Kaleel Jamison, The Nibble Theory and the Kernel of Power

A Best Friend Crush

Life is an adventure in forgiveness.

~Norman Cousins

When I was in kindergarten, I had a friend named Jacob. After grade one, he moved across town and went to a different school. Sometimes I saw him in town, but not often.

The summer I turned thirteen, I spent a lot of time at the beach, and Jacob was there every day. We became close friends again, often hanging out one-on-one or with other friends.

It felt like I was in a classic chick-flick movie, the one where your childhood friend comes back into your life and you start dating and fall in love. I even asked him to be my date for my grade eight graduation dance; we went together as friends. We slow-danced at lots of events, and we hung out with each other's families.

Except Jacob had already had girlfriends. I had never dated before. All my friends knew I had a crush on him, and soon enough, Jacob knew too. I found out though that he "just wanted to be friends," and he "didn't think of me that way."

For a while in grade nine, we were still friends. We messaged each other, and he told me that he still had feelings for his ex-girlfriend. I could empathize with him, because he felt the same way about his ex that I felt about him.

But even knowing that he liked someone else, my feelings for him didn't change. I tried to get my friends to set us up for the next school dance, but he took a different friend instead and I ended up going alone. He told my friends that he didn't want to ruin our friendship by dating me.

I didn't understand why he wouldn't even consider trying to date me, at least for a little bit. I believed our friendship would be strong enough to last no matter what. I wanted a "first kiss" so badly, and I wanted to share it with someone who meant a lot to me.

But after that school dance, things became really awkward. We hardly spoke. We never had lunch together, even though we were now at the same high school. He was keeping secrets from me and ignoring me. I was so hurt that I would shoot dirty looks at him when I thought he wasn't looking, and I told all my friends how he had betrayed our friendship, hoping it would get back to him and he would apologize. After "not wanting to ruin our friendship" by dating me, he chose instead to live his life without me in it at all.

We graduated high school and went our separate ways. Finally, when I was twenty, I looked back on how we had tried to pick up our childhood friendship, only to end up estranged from one another. I realized that as immature high school students, we had let our feelings get the best of us, and in the process had not always treated each other fairly. But I had no way to tell him how I felt, to apologize. I only had an old e-mail address that he didn't reply to, and none of my friends had his phone number.

Three years later, I ran into another friend I hadn't seen since high school. She was friends with Jacob's roommate, and through them, I was finally able to get his phone number. I sent him an apology, and to my surprise, he sent me an apology back. We both acknowledged the falling-out and shared the blame, finally bringing us to peace.

Our lives have taken us down separate paths. We only share a couple of texts a month, and I'm okay with that because I know we have at least moved past the pain from high school. I can look back at the old photos of us at age six and smile — because we haven't thrown everything away; we have each simply moved forward.

— Julia Tilson —

A Letter to My Sixteen-Year-Old Self

Respect yourself and others will respect you.
~Confucius

Dear Sixteen-year-old Me,

I know you're having a hard time. Your two best friends have ditched you, and you're feeling unmoored and wondering how everything could have unraveled so quickly. It wasn't one big fight, but rather a lot of little things that separated you from the two of them.

I know you feel confused and hurt and angry. School used to be filled with laughter and inside jokes, but now the social logistics of each day are a puzzle without an answer key. Where to sit at lunch? Who to talk to at cross-country practice? You've cried more over the loss of these two friends than you've ever cried over a boy.

It's hard to see this now, but listen: they do care about you, and your friendship with them was real. High school is messy and confusing and full of changes, and the three of you are in different places, wanting different things. And that's okay. Even though this is painful, it is better for you to let go of your friendship with them now, rather than stick around and feel bad about yourself all the time or turn into someone you don't want to be.

In six years, you will go to the wedding of one of these friends, and all the angst and hurt you are writing about in your journal right now will seem like a novel you read about someone else. The other friend will get married around the same time you do (yes, you are in fact going to get married — I'll get to that in a minute) and you will genuinely wish her well. You will wish both of these girls the utmost happiness.

I know you feel supremely uncool and unsure of yourself. But let me tell you something important, something true: there is nothing wrong with you. You don't need to be concerned about what the other kids at school think of you. (Besides, the other kids at school aren't thinking bad things about you — that's all in your head. The other kids, even the popular crowd, respect your straight-lacedness. Wait and see what nice things they write in your senior yearbook.)

Take a deep breath and lean into the parts of yourself that feel the most true and real and YOU. Those are the best parts of yourself. Those are the parts to cultivate, to nourish, to nurture. When you find sprouts of self-consciousness and comparison and shame, yank those roots out of your soil. Don't waste any time watering those weeds.

Want to know a secret? Want to know the silver lining to this painful period? When these two friends ditch you, it will open up your life for other friends to come in. You will become closer with people who accept you exactly as you are. Remember how close you and Erica were in middle school? Reach out to her again now. She is kind and steady and she truly cares about you. She is a lifelong friend. One day, she will be a bridesmaid in your wedding. Be grateful for her and soak up these everyday moments with her.

I want you to know that you are enough exactly as you are. Mom and Dad know what they are talking about. When they tell you that you are beautiful and kind and strong and worthy, when they tell you that you have no idea how loved you are, when they tell you that one day in the not-too-distant future you will indeed meet a boy who appreciates you for exactly the person you are — listen to them. They are right.

Sixteen-year-old self, your nose is not too big. Your hair is not frizzy. You are not the least bit overweight, and you never need to feel even the slightest twinge of guilt for eating two or three of Mom's famous chocolate-chip cookies.

Right now, I know it feels like you're never going to meet a boy who like-likes you, much less loves you. Here's what I want to tell you about love: it's bigger and better, more complex and yet more simple, more consuming and yet more ordinary, than you imagine it to be. Love is going to break you apart and put you back together again, stronger and braver and more content in your own individual wholeness. Love is going to take you by surprise and take your breath away.

Love isn't something you can map out. It's not a short story you can revise and revise again. It's not a physics problem you can solve. It will sweep into your heart without warning, announcing itself to you boldly, and even though you might feel a little bit scared or unready, you will not be able to ignore it. When love is right, it will continue to grow and grow inside of you, and you won't have to make excuses for it, and you won't have to twist yourself to fit into what doesn't fit. The right love will become a part of you, like your breath, and it will give you life in little moments every day, with you hardly even realizing it.

Right now you think that love means grand gestures and passionate kissing in the rain, but real love is in the ordinary, everyday moments that connect you to another person. When you feel seen and understood and accepted and cared for, little by little, day by day.

To be honest, sixteen-year-old me, your first kiss won't come for another couple of years, and it isn't going to be all that spectacular. But your first kiss with the guy who will become your husband? It will be worth the wait. Here's what I can tell you about your future husband: he will make you laugh every day; he will be a wonderful listener; and he will support you with all of his heart. He will be so handsome, and he will tell you that you are beautiful and he loves every detail about you. He will be better than any of the loves you imagined for yourself before you met him.

I know that deep down you realize how fortunate you are, and you're grateful for your parents and your brother, for Erica and your teachers and Gramps, for your books and your writing. Lean into those things that fill you up. Savor them.

As Mr. Enfield, the drama teacher, will tell you, life is ephemeral. It is always changing, and even those things that feel permanent about your life right now are fleeting. So soak it in, every day. Even the hard days. Be confident in the person you are now and the person you are becoming. Don't get lost in self-doubt or worry.

You have no idea how much you are going to grow, and stretch, and shine, and explore, and how big and wide and incredible the world is. You have no idea of the wonders waiting in your future, in this life you are building. Trust in me, your thirty-two-year-old-self. And trust in yourself, as you are here, now, at sixteen. Everything you need is already there inside of you.

Love,
Your Future Self

— Dallas Woodburn —

The Real Me

I think in life, you know when you meet your person.
~JoJo Siwa

When I was fifteen, I had a best friend. Dani and I had four classes together, shared a large friend group and were on the same sports teams. We spent a lot of time at each other's houses on the weekends doing normal fifteen-year-old things like baking cupcakes, watching scary movies, calling boys, and meeting our friends for backyard bonfires.

Then the day came when the two of us wanted to try alcohol for the first time. We called my aunt, who is three years older than me, and asked her to bring us a bottle. She didn't need much convincing.

I am not making a case for the splendors of underage drinking. I promise you that. In fact, when the liquor touched my lips, I immediately ran to the sink to spit it out. My aunt, her friends and Dani cracked up laughing. I couldn't understand it. Was I tasting the same thing they were? If so, how was it that they could swallow something so vile?

They poured about three shots into my Disney Fantasia cup. When everybody went to take their next communal sip, I just pretended to gulp down the liquor. Then I watched as they grew more intoxicated. I felt jealous, so I finally drank what remained in my cup.

Everyone but Dani left, and we went to my room to watch TV. Dani had just started seeing this boy, a star baseball player whose parents were highly regarded in our community. Dani was very excited to be his girlfriend. She told me this and then said, "I haven't kissed him yet."

That wasn't something that had concerned me with my own

short relationships with boyfriends. I always got bored and ended a relationship after a month anyway. It always seemed there had to be someone better for me; love had to be more.

Dani, however, did not feel the same way. I asked her why she hadn't kissed him yet. She laughed and shrugged, stating she didn't know if she was a good kisser or not. I told her "I'm sure you're a fine kisser and I bet he wouldn't even know it if you weren't." She shrugged. The most cringeworthy stereotypical thing happened next. She stared at her hands and twirled her fingers around each other before shyly asking, "Do you think you can tell me if I'm good or not?"

I laughed, not to embarrass her, but truly from shock. Then I thought, why not?

So, she leaned in close, and our lips touched, and we kissed. My mind felt like it was floating down a river of euphoria and the kiss went on a minute too long. Then I pulled away and after a brief silence we broke out laughing. I told her she was a fine kisser but maybe overdid the tongue part. She punched my arm and we laughed some more.

We turned on a movie and Dani fell asleep fast. I knew something bigger than I was willing to grasp had happened. I had never felt such strong feelings kissing anyone else before that. I was terrified of what this could mean. Instead of investigating the feelings, I turned away from them. There were more kisses after this, with both boys and girls, but I always needed liquor to kiss the girls — an excuse.

I wish I had learned then that although courage can be found in a bottle, acceptance and self-esteem cannot. Maybe then instead of feeling embarrassment in the morning over these kisses and blaming the bottle, I would have accepted the hard cold truth, I liked girls, and from what I can remember about those drunken nights, there were girls who liked me too.

It took a few too many years for me to accept the truth of that incident. Dani and I never talked about it. Maybe that was why I told myself it was nothing to get worked up about. I was a cheerleader and on the homecoming court. I didn't believe I fit the description of a woman who likes other women, and I had great relationships with men in the years following.

However, something always seemed not quite right about them; they were more like good friends in my opinion. It wasn't until after college that I accepted this reality.

Today I live in a quaint apartment in downtown San Diego with a woman who I love very much. I no longer need liquid courage to be the real me.

— Alyssa Rodriguez —

Losing the "Us"

When an emotional injury takes place, the body begins
a process as natural as the healing of a physical wound.
~Melba Colgrove, How to Survive the Loss of a Love

"So does this mean you want to break up?" I asked softly, hoping my question would go unanswered. That is how it all began, or I guess, ended. The months the two of us had shared were some of the happiest, hardest and most educational months I ever experienced. It seemed impossible that this was the last conversation we would have as Ben and Lia, the couple.

I had ignored the fact that the majority of high-school relationships do not last. I guess, in the back of my mind, I always thought that Ben was the only boy I would ever have these feelings for, that he was the only boy who would ever understand me. I never took into account that the last month of our relationship was one of the hardest times I had ever gone through. It just stopped being fun. It stopped being about us and started to be about everything that surrounded him and me.

The next day at school I tried looking great to make him see what he had given up. I even tried to talk to him like my heart wasn't aching, like I was better off and even happier. But inside I looked at him and could only see all the love and time I had given and all the hurt I had received. I walked around school in a complete daze and cried myself to sleep every night. He was the only thing I thought about, dreamt about and talked about. I drove my friends crazy by constantly analyzing the situation. *How could it have ended?* I found my other half when I was with him. I felt like something had been torn from me, like

I was no longer whole.

One night, I couldn't stand it. I gave up and called him. I didn't last five minutes before I broke down and started crying. I told him I had forgotten how to be by myself, and that I needed him. I didn't know how to be Lia without Ben. We had been through so much together that I could not imagine getting through this on my own. He told me that he would always care for me, but that it had become impossible to love me.

For weeks I couldn't see him with other girls without thinking that they were dating. I threw myself at different guys.

I don't know at exactly what point things started to change. I began spending time with my friends. I joined clubs and made after-school plans. I was doing all I could to stay busy.

Slowly I began to have fun by myself, without Ben. Beyond that, I discovered things I liked doing, ways I could be of help. I lent a sympathetic ear to others who were hurting.

I began to smile and, finally, to laugh again. Whole days would pass without a thought of Ben. I would see him at school and wave. I was not ready to be friends with him. I was still healing. But I know I didn't cover a big wound with a Band-Aid and forget about it. I let the wound heal itself and felt enough pain to know that I had truly cared for him.

In my rebound stage, I pursued a lot of guys. Once I healed, they pursued me. The wonderful thing that happened was that I learned how to be a whole person, not half a couple. I'm in a new relationship now, and eventually we will probably break up, and it will be hard, and I will cry and feel just as much, if not more, pain. But I had to ask myself if never caring for someone so that I wouldn't feel that hurt was worth it. I know now that the famous quote is true. "Better to have loved and lost than never to have loved at all." Because no matter what, loving yourself can heal anything.

— Lia Gay, 16 —

After a While

After a while you learn the subtle difference between holding a hand and chaining a soul,

And you learn that love doesn't mean leaning and company doesn't mean security,

And you begin to learn that kisses aren't contracts and presents aren't promises,

And you begin to accept your defeats with your head up and your eyes open, with the grace of an adult, not the grief of a child,

And you learn to build all your roads on today because tomorrow's ground is too uncertain for plans.

After a while you learn that even sunshine burns if you get too much.

So plant your own garden and decorate your own soul, instead of waiting for someone to bring you flowers.

And you learn that you really can endure…

that you really are strong,

and you really do have worth.

And you learn and you learn…

with every good-bye you learn…

— Veronica A. Shoffstall, 19 —

The Miss of a Great "Miss"

You never lose by loving.
You always lose by holding back.
~Barbara De Angelis

'll never forget the day I first saw "a dream walking." Her name was Susie Summers (name changed to protect the fantastic). Her smile, which sparkled beneath two twinkling eyes, was electric and made people who received it (especially guy people) feel very special.

While her physical beauty was astounding, it was her invisible beauty I shall always remember. She really cared about other people and was an extremely talented listener. Her sense of humor could brighten your entire day and her wise words were always exactly what you needed to hear. She was not only admired but also genuinely respected by members of both sexes. With everything in the world to be conceited about, she was extremely humble.

Needless to say, she was every guy's dream. Especially mine. I got to walk her to class once a day, and once I even got to eat lunch with her all by myself. I felt on the top of the world.

I would think, "If only I could have a girlfriend like Susie Summers, I'd never even look at another female." But I figured that someone this outstanding was probably dating someone far better than myself. Even though I was president of the student body, I just knew I didn't stand a ghost of a chance.

So at graduation, I said farewell to my first big crush.

A year later, I met her best friend in a shopping center and we had lunch together. With a lump in my throat, I asked how Susie was.

"Well, she got over you," was the reply.

"What are you talking about?" I asked.

"You were really cruel to her the way you led her on, always walking her to class and making her think you were interested. Do you remember the time you had lunch with her? Well, she stayed by the phone the entire weekend. She was sure you were going to call and ask her out."

I was so afraid of rejection, I never risked letting her know how I felt. Suppose I had asked her out and she'd said no? What's the worst thing that could have happened? I wouldn't have had a date with her. Well, guess what? I DIDN'T HAVE A DATE WITH HER ANYHOW! What makes it worse is that I probably could have.

— Jack Schlatter —

My First Kiss, and Then Some

I was a very shy teenager, and so was my first boyfriend. We were high school sophomores in a small town. We had been dating for about six months. A lot of sweaty hand-holding, actually *watching* movies, and talking about nothing in particular. We often came close to kissing — we both knew that we wanted to be kissed — but neither of us had the courage to make the first move.

Finally, while sitting on my living room couch, he decided to go for it. We talked about the weather (really), then he leaned forward. I put a pillow up to my face to block him! He kissed the pillow.

I wanted to be kissed sooooo badly, but I was too nervous to let him get close. So I moved away, down the couch. He moved closer. We talked about the movie (who cared!), he leaned forward again. I blocked him again.

I moved to the end of the couch. He followed, we talked. He leaned… I stood up! (I must have had a spasm in my legs.) I walked over near the front door and stood there, leaning against the wall with my arms crossed, and said impatiently, "Well, are you going to kiss me or not?"

"Yes," he said. So I stood tall, closed my eyes tight, puckered my lips and faced upwards. I waited… and waited. (Why wasn't he kissing me?) I opened my eyes; he was coming right at me. I smiled.

HE KISSED MY TEETH!

I could have died.

He left.

I wondered if he had told anyone about my clumsy behavior. Since I was so extremely and painfully shy, I practically hid for the next two years, causing me to never have another date all through high school. As a matter of fact, when I walked down the hallway at school, if I saw him or any other great guy walking toward me, I quickly stepped into the nearest room until he passed. And these were boys I had known since kindergarten.

The first year at college, I was determined not to be shy any longer. I wanted to learn how to kiss with confidence and grace. I did.

In the spring, I went home. I walked into the latest hangout, and who do you suppose I see sitting at the bar, but my old kissing partner. I walked over to his bar stool and tapped him on the shoulder. Without hesitation, I took him in my arms, dipped him back over his stool, and kissed him with my most assertive kiss. I sat him up, looked at him victoriously, and said, "So there!"

He pointed to the lady next to him and said to me, "Mary Jane, I'd like you to meet my wife."

— Mary Jane West-Delgado —

Changes in Life

I was 16 years old and a junior in high school, and the worst possible thing that could happen to me did. My parents decided to move our family from our Texas home to Arizona. I had two weeks to wrap up all of my "business" and move before school began. I had to leave my first job, my boyfriend and my best friend behind, and try to start a new life. I despised my parents for ruining my life.

I told everyone that I did not want to live in Arizona and would be returning to Texas the first chance I had. When I arrived in Arizona, I made sure everyone knew that I had a boyfriend and best friend waiting for me in Texas. I was determined to keep my distance from everyone; I would just be leaving soon anyway.

The first day of school came, and I was miserable. I could only think of my friends in Texas and how I wished I could be with them. For a while, I felt that my life was over. Eventually though, things got a little better.

It was in my second period accounting class where I first saw him. He was tall, trim and really good looking. He had the most beautiful blue eyes I had ever seen. He was sitting just three seats away from me in the same front row of class. Feeling I had nothing to lose, I decided to talk to him.

"Hi, my name is Sheila; what's yours?" I asked with a Texas drawl.

The guy next to him thought that I was asking *him*.

"Mike."

"Oh, hi, Mike," I humored him. "What's your name?" I asked again, focusing my attention on this blue-eyed boy.

He looked behind him, not believing that I could be asking him for his name. "Chris," he responded quietly.

"Hi, Chris!" I smiled. Then I went about my work.

Chris and I became friends. We enjoyed talking to each other in class. Chris was a jock, and I was in the school band; in high school, peer pressure demanded that the two groups did not mix socially. Our paths crossed occasionally at school functions; but for the most part, our friendship remained within the four classroom walls of accounting class.

Chris graduated that year, and we went our separate ways for a while. Then one day, he came to see me while I was working in a store in the mall. I was very happy to see him. He went on my breaks with me, and we started talking again. The pressure from his jock friends had subsided, and we became very close friends. My relationship with my boyfriend in Texas had become less important to me. I felt my bond with Chris growing stronger, taking the place of my relationship in Texas.

It had been a year since I moved from Texas, and Arizona was starting to feel like home. Chris escorted me to my senior prom; we triple-dated with two of his jock friends and their dates. The night of my prom changed our relationship forever; I was accepted by his friends, and that made Chris feel more comfortable. Finally, our relationship was in the open.

Chris was a very special person to me during such a difficult time in my life. Our relationship eventually blossomed into a very powerful love. I now understand that my parents did not move the family to Arizona to hurt me, although at the time, it sure felt as though they had. I now firmly believe that everything happens for a reason. For had I not moved to Arizona, I never would have met the man of my dreams.

— Sheila K. Reyman —

First Love

Truly loving another means letting go of all
expectations. It means full acceptance,
even celebration of another's personhood.
~Karen Casey

Michael and I were never really boyfriend and girlfriend. He was three-and-a-half years older than I, which was a lot when I still didn't need to wear a bathing suit top. We grew up around the pool and tennis courts of a country club. He was an excellent tennis player with sure, calm strides and a powerful stroke. When I had to take time out from swimming and diving because my lips had turned blue, I sat on the grass wrapped in a towel and watched the tennis matches. Later in the day, the guys would come to the pool and hoist the girls on their shoulders for water fights. I liked it best on Michael's shoulders, which were broad. I felt safe.

At 16 his parents allowed him to drive during the day, and he often brought me home in his gray Dodge. The autumn after I turned 14, he started asking if I wanted to go to a late-afternoon movie with him. I wanted to say yes, but then I would get this jumpy feeling in my stomach and always change my mind. His dark eyes looked into mine, both pleasing and frightening me.

Gradually I stayed longer in his car, talking about things that troubled me. My older sister had lots of boyfriends, and although I worshipped her, she mostly didn't want anything to do with me. Then there were the intrigues around who was dating whom and which friends I trusted and why. A lot of my pain centered around my relationship with my parents, who had divorced when I was 11 and remarried when I was 13. I didn't know anyone else with a broken family, and I felt ashamed and unsure of myself, like I wasn't as good as the other kids. I could talk with Michael about all this. He was reassuring, and I began to trust him.

As time passed, I was ready to go to the movies with him. We also enjoyed hanging out at my house, where we would go down to the television room in the basement. I loved to watch TV with Michael so that I could cuddle with him on the couch. We were a strange pair. He loved sports, while I loved the arts. My sister and others made fun of his sports obsession. I guess I would have preferred it if everyone thought he was cool or if he'd been more artistic, but no one else cared about me the way he did. When he kissed me for the first time, we were at his house during a thunderstorm, watching a baseball game on television. I ran up to my sister's room when I got home. I must have looked goofy as I stood in her doorway and announced, "Michael kissed me."

"So?" she said. "Was that the first time?"

"Yeah," I nodded.

"What have you guys been doing all this time?" she demanded.

Michael dated other girls, and I went out with other boys. But I hated their sweaty palms and was horrified when a blind date tried to put his tongue in my mouth. Only Michael understood that I needed to move slowly, and he was always very patient with me. Even though Michael reassured me many times that our relationship was special by saying, "It doesn't matter whether or not I have a girlfriend or you have a boyfriend; I will always be there for you," I still got jealous when I saw him interested in someone else.

Michael got engaged to a girl from out of town when I was 19. I was the only unmarried, unrelated girl at the wedding. As the bride and groom said good-bye to everyone, Michael came over to me and kissed me on the cheek.

"I love you," he said.

He remained true to his word. When I needed to talk to someone, he was there. I got jealous sometimes when I thought of him loving and being romantic with his wife, but that changed as she and I became friends. I moved across the country and only saw Michael occasionally, at the club when I returned to visit my family. Now we sat at the pool and watched his kids swimming. Our lives were very different. I thought I probably wouldn't have much more than a half hour's worth of conversation to share with him, but I always felt a current of love go through me when I saw him.

When I was 38, my father died. The morning before his funeral, I thought to myself, *I wonder if Michael knows.* We hadn't seen each other or spoken for years. After the service the next day, as I was talking with the many friends and family who had come for the funeral, I felt a hand on my shoulder. I turned and saw those dark eyes.

"Are you alright?" he asked. I nodded. Putting both hands on my shoulders, he held me, looking into my eyes.

No one had ever understood the bond between us. I'm not sure that we did. But it was, and will always be, there.

— Mary Ellen Klee —

A High School Love Not Forgotten

When they saw him walking across our high school campus, most students couldn't help but notice Bruce. Tall and lanky, he was a thinner replica of James Dean, his hair flipped back above his forehead, and his eyebrows always cocked upward when he was in deep conversation. He was tender, thoughtful and profound. He would never hurt anyone.

I was scared of him.

I was just breaking up with my not-so-smart boyfriend, the one you stayed with and went back to 30 times out of bad habit, when Bruce headed me off at a campus pass one morning to walk with me. He helped me carry my books and made me laugh a dozen times with giddiness. I liked him. I really liked him.

He scared me because he was brilliant. But in the end, I realized I was more scared of myself than of him.

We started to walk together more at school. I would peer up at him from my stuffed locker, my heart beating rapidly, wondering if he would ever kiss me. We'd been seeing each other for several weeks and he still hadn't tried to kiss me.

Instead, he'd hold my hand, put his arm around me and send me off with one of my books to class. When I opened it, a handwritten note in his highly stylized writing would be there, speaking of love and passion in a deeper sense than I could understand at 17.

He would send me books, cards, notes, and would sit with me at my house for hours listening to music. He especially liked me to listen to the song, "You Brought Some Joy Inside My Tears," by Stevie Wonder. At work one day I received a card from him that said, "I miss you when I'm sad. I miss you when I'm lonely. But most of all, I miss you when I'm happy."

I remember walking down the street of our small village, cars honking, the warm lights from stores beckoning strollers to come in from the cold, and all I could think about was, "Bruce misses me most when he's happy. What a strange thing."

I felt deeply uncomfortable to have such a romantic spirit by my side, a boy — really a man at 17 — who thought his words out wisely, listened to every side of an argument, read poetry deep into the night and weighed his decisions carefully. I sensed a deep sadness in him but couldn't understand it. Looking back, I now think the sadness stemmed from being a person who really didn't fit into the high school plan.

Our relationship was so different from the one I'd had with my prior boyfriend. Our lives had been mostly movies and popcorn and gossip. We broke up routinely and dated other people. At times, it seemed like the whole campus was focused on the drama of our breakups, which were always intense and grand entertainment for our friends to discuss. A good soap opera.

I talked to Bruce about these things and with each story, he'd respond by putting his arm around me and telling me he'd wait while I sorted things out. And then he would read to me. He gave me the book, with these words underlined: "It's only in thy mind's eye that one can see rightly."

In response — the only way I knew how — I wrote passionate letters of love and poetry to him with an intensity I never knew before. But still I kept my walls up, keeping him at bay because I was always afraid that he'd discover I was fake, not nearly as intelligent or as deep a thinker as I found him to be.

I wanted the old habits of popcorn, movies and gossip back. It was so much easier. I remember well the day when Bruce and I stood outside in the cold and I told him I was going back to my old boyfriend. "He needs me more," I said in my girlish voice. "Old habits die hard."

Bruce looked at me with sadness, more for me than himself. He knew, and I knew then, I was making a mistake.

Years went by. Bruce went off to college first; then I did. Every time I came home for Christmas, I looked him up and went over for a visit with him and his family. I always loved his family — the warm greetings they gave me when they ushered me into their house, always happy to see me. I knew just by the way his family behaved that Bruce had forgiven me for my mistake.

One Christmas, Bruce said to me: "You were always a good writer. You were so good."

"Yes." His mother nodded in agreement. "You wrote beautifully. I hope you'll never give up your writing."

"But how do you know my writing?" I asked his mom.

"Oh, Bruce shared all the letters you wrote him with me," she said. "He and I could never get over how beautifully you wrote."

Then I saw his father's head nod, too. I sank back in my chair and blushed deeply. What exactly had I written in those letters?

I never knew Bruce had admired my writing as much as I had his intelligence.

Over the years, we lost touch. The last I heard from his father, Bruce had gone off to San Francisco and was thinking about becoming a chef. I went through dozens of bad relationships until I finally married a wonderful man — also very smart. I was more mature by then and could handle my husband's intelligence — especially when he'd remind me I had my own.

There's not one other boyfriend I ever think about with any interest, except for Bruce. Most of all, I hope he is happy. He deserves it. In many ways, I think he helped shape me, helped me learn how to accept the side of myself I refused to see amid movies, popcorn and gossip. He taught me how to see my spirit and my writer inside.

— Diana L. Chapman —

First Kiss — First Lesson

It's all right letting yourself go,
as long as you can get yourself back.
~Mick Jagger

The night of my first real kiss was also the night of the worst fight I ever had with my mother. I'd had my eye on Jon Glass forever, and suddenly out of nowhere I spied him at the party that my best friend, Lara, and I had finally gathered the courage to stop by. The guy throwing the party lived in a skinny brick house on a crazy steep hill in San Francisco. Light from the kitchen and a streetlight down the block spilled into the little backyard garden, not quite reaching the corner where Jon was standing in a cluster of people. I was wearing my favorite pink shirt and Levi's with patches I'd sewn onto the knees. Lara smoothed my hair and told me to smile and pushed me out the door of the kitchen and into the garden. The next thing I knew, Jon and I were talking and then we were the only people still in the garden and then we were leaving the party together and walking hand in hand up and up the steep street and then we kissed and I felt like I was living someone else's life, I was so happy.

The party was only a couple of blocks from my school, so I knew the streets we walked along as well as I knew the ones in my own neighborhood. But as I held Jon's hand and we walked and stopped and kissed, I felt like I was seeing the houses and the trees and the world for the first time. In a way I felt as if I were seeing Jon for the first time. Like, before he was just this guy — okay, a very nice guy with amazing pale blue eyes who helped me with my calculus homework and played soccer as if he were born with cleats on his feet — but now here he was picking me a flower off a tree in someone's front yard. We meandered to a nearby park and sat on the swings and looked at the stars. Of course I lost track of time as we roamed around, and when Jon finally dropped me off at my house, the sky was starting to turn light blue and pink with the dawn.

My key had barely hit the lock on the front door when my mother pulled it open and said in her most dangerous and quiet voice, "Where is he?" Just like that — deadpan. Each word equally weighted, equally heavy: "Where is he?" I stood on the stoop in the early-morning spring cold, yearning to bolt the 10 feet — so close, so far — between me and the safety of my room.

I tried to play dumb. "Who are you talking about, Mom?"

But she just stood there blocking the doorway — hands on hips, face contorted with anger — and said; "You're untrustworthy, you're irresponsible, and you're a disappointment."

Later that day, Lara told me my mom had freaked out and called her at home in the middle of the night. Lara didn't have any idea where I'd gone after I left the party, but she tried to cover for me by saying she was sure I was fine; after all, I was just hanging out with Jon. But that just made my mother worry more ("Jon? Who is Jon?"), and by the time I got home, her worry and stress and churning imagination — combined with her fatigue and relief that I was home safely (no longer wandering the streets in the middle of the night with some strange boy) — finally boiled over, and she exploded at me. I was so shocked at her harsh reaction — shouldn't she be happy that I was actually safe and would no longer have to cope with the shame of never having kissed a boy? — that I screamed right back at her and, after she let me in off the stoop, I slammed my door and flung myself face down on my bed and cried and cried at the grand injustice that was my life.

The next morning at breakfast, I could barely eat. My mom didn't yell anymore — she just told me I couldn't go to the formal citywide dance I'd been looking forward to for months. So I didn't yell anymore, either. I just got up from the table and went to my room and called Lara and made plans to have her pick me up for the dance at 7 P.M.

that Friday. I didn't care what my mother said. I was going anyway.

The week passed perfectly pleasantly. I went to school, I raced home in time to see *Days of Our Lives,* I fussed around pretending to study, my mom got home late from work, we ate spaghetti and salad, and I silently cleared the table without her asking. When Friday night rolled around, I gathered my formal dress and my favorite heels and my stockings and shoved them into a bag. Then, as soon as the headlights from Lara's car swept into my window as she swung into the driveway, I slipped out the front door and softly pulled it closed behind me. Free.

Jon didn't show up at the dance but some other cute boys did, and a couple of them talked to me and I was complimented on my purple silk dress and my purple suede shoes and I made sure to stand next to Lara, who looked stunning in something backless and red and short. But I was so racked with guilt for having taken it out on my mother that I just couldn't have the time of my life like I'd anticipated. Afterward, I was scared to go home and face the music, so Lara and I just drove the dark streets of San Francisco aimlessly, with the radio on way too loud, and ended up eating slightly stale muffins at Dunkin' Donuts with a couple of worn-out cops who looked at us like we were crazy delinquents for not being home in bed at such a late hour.

I finally went home and crept under the covers, and in the morning my mother looked upset and didn't really talk to me. In fact, she hadn't really talked to me since our big fight. I guess she didn't know what to do, so she put me on the phone with my father, who was living in Los Angeles at the time. He didn't lose his temper. He just asked, "Why didn't you talk to her about it? Ask her again if you could go to the dance? Tell her you were sorry you were late? Call when you knew you'd be out with Jon?" In other words, why didn't I just think about what I was doing and realize my actions affected other people?

Uh, good question. And I wish I could say that I had a big talk with my mother right after I got off the phone with my father, but I didn't. And the situation got worse before it got better.

The next time I saw Jon outside of school was when I walked into a party just in time to see him disappear into a bedroom with another girl. Her name was Michele, and she was a year younger than me and had a reputation for going too far with too many people. Standing there in the middle of some stranger's sunken living room where people were dancing. I started crying. In a burst of boldness, Lara tried the door of the room Jon and Michele occupied ("I'll interrupt them, and then he'll feel bad and come out," she promised) — but the door was locked. I had lost him. I had never had him.

While I sat in another bedroom and cried and imagined what the two of them were doing together, girls from the party came in and sat with me and told me raunchy men-are-jerks jokes. ("A man asked a genie to make him a billion times smarter than any other man on earth. The genie turned him into a woman.") Eventually, after Jon had finally emerged from the locked bedroom, I confronted him by a swing set in the backyard and made him tell me to my face that he was sorry.

I listened to him say that he didn't want a girlfriend and had a problem with commitment, and I listened to the litany of crimes against his soul: his parents' divorce, the death of his dog, the difficulty of his chemistry class, living in the shadow of his older brother. All the excuses he used to forgive himself for harming me. Everything he said seemed pretty lame and beside the point, to tell the truth. In fact, what he offered wasn't an apology at all, and it didn't make me feel any better because nothing really could. (Although, I must admit, I was not unhappy the next week at school when all the girls snubbed Jon because they knew everything that had happened. And I was willing to listen when his cousin cornered me in an empty classroom and told me that she thought I was too cool for him anyway.)

So things with Jon obviously didn't end perfectly or even anywhere near how I would have liked, but at least I tried to settle things with him and gave him the benefit of listening to his side of the story. It kills me that I cornered Jon — who had betrayed me — and made him talk to me, but I never even gave my mom that chance. So how could I expect her to understand what was at stake for me in staying out late that night, in going to the dance? I owed her — and she owed me — a conversation. But that meant we each would have to articulate what we wanted, we each would have to deal with the other person's needs, and at the time I thought I couldn't deal.

A conversation is a slippery creature. A conversation is a risk. A real conversation changes the people who have it. It's about exchanging ideas, considering other opinions, shifting positions. That's why conversations are so difficult: You risk changing yourself, admitting you were wrong, coming to appreciate the other person's perspective. My mother and I were afraid to have an honest conversation because then she would have to admit her daughter was no longer a baby, was old enough to kiss a boy, wanted to kiss boys. And I would have to admit I was wrong not to call. That I was way later coming home than I'd ever been before. That even though I wanted to kiss boys, I still needed my mom.

Sometimes the whole story replays in my mind like a movie, and I know exactly what to do. Outside by the swing set, I calmly tell Jon how hurt I am, how I feel that he misled and betrayed me, and that I'm sorry about all the stuff he's been through in his life, but it's really no excuse for the way he acted. And instead of being silent at breakfast, I tell my mom how sorry I am to make her worry, but I also tell her why I like Jon so much. I describe how he sits next to me in history class and leans over and doodles on the edge of my notebook and how his shoes are always scuffed and his socks almost never match, and my mom and I laugh together. I mean, what mom's heart isn't going to melt when you tell her about a guy who saves you a seat in class and waves as the boys' soccer team runs by the girls' practice field? And in the new movie, I listen to my mom's side of the story and try to see the situation from her point of view.

It's not like I just settle for everything she tells me, either. When she says that I can't go to the dance, I persist. Ask again. Think about why she says I can't go, reevaluate the situation using my new understanding of where she's coming from, revise my approach and ask again. When it comes out in our conversation that she doesn't think I deserve to go out because I rarely help out around the house, I do extra chores and ask again. Bring home an A on a tough test and ask again.

What I really wanted in the end wasn't Jon, specifically — obviously, he turned out to be a jerk — but the kind of life where Jon was possible, where my mom wouldn't freak out when I missed curfew, where I could go out with boys without causing a major crisis. And what my mother ultimately wanted wasn't a daughter who blindly obeyed her every rule, but a daughter she could rely on and trust and not stay up half the night worrying about. And what I know now is this: If my mom and I had done that deceptively simple thing, talking, negotiating, compromising until we agreed on a set of privileges, then we both would have gotten something we wanted.

—Jennifer Braunschweiger—

Chapter 2

Friendship

Some people come into our lives and quickly go. Some stay for a while and leave footprints on our hearts. And we are never, ever the same.
~Flavia Weedn

The Power of Empathy

You have a right to your thoughts and feelings.
Your feelings are always valid.
~Iyanla Vanzant

My older brother posted an infographic on his Instagram story last week. I clicked on it and the name Quawan Charles took up my screen. He was a fifteen-year-old whose body was found in a sugar cane field in rural Louisiana. I was immediately shocked. My younger brother is fifteen, and I cannot wrap my head around the thought of this happening to him. I couldn't comprehend this happening to anyone.

That Black teenager's face was beaten to the point that it was almost unrecognizable. His body was not found until three days after he went missing, three days after his parents reported that he hadn't come home. Their concerns were shrugged aside. They were told he was probably at a football game.

The infographic didn't have much information related to the case, so I searched his name. I found the GoFundMe that was created to raise money for a private autopsy report. A black and white photo of Quawan Charles' distorted face took up the top spread of the page. The skin on one side of his face was so damaged my skin crawled just looking at it. His lips were so destroyed that his teeth were visible. I felt physically ill.

At the moment I saw the picture, I was sitting with a new friend. She's very nice, but she's white, as are the majority of the kids at my new school. White or Asian. So as nice as she was, I didn't feel comfortable talking about this with her. I wanted to talk about it with someone who could relate to the feeling. The awful feeling.

I started crying. I usually don't cry, especially in public. But this reaction was raw, and in no way was I embarrassed about it. It was actually good, because this happens so often that I'd become desensitized to hearing stories about the violent ways in which Black people are killed. Before it became noticeable, I stood up and left the table. I called one of my closest girlfriends back home, who is Black, and told her what I'd seen and read. As I talked about it my tears of sorrow turned into tears of rage.

I was so angry that my hands started shaking. So angry that a little boy was murdered in such a horrific way. Angry that the authorities didn't take this family seriously when they reported him missing. I was angry that there was little to no publicity about this child's life lost, that it seemed as if no one cared. I was so angry that this type of thing happens often enough that it was no longer a surprise to me. And I was angry that I couldn't talk about it with anyone near me, at least not someone who looks like me. I was unbelievably angry.

When I went home that day, I didn't mention it to my parents. Just like my new friend, they're white; they could sympathize, but not empathize. They can't relate to the fact that after hearing that this happened in 2020, I'm considering not having children. They can't relate to how tired I am of having race constantly on my mind.

At that moment I wanted someone to be angry with me, scared with me — someone who could understand my feeling of hopelessness.

When we had lived in Atlanta I was surrounded by a mix of racial groups. My friends were diverse, but my closest ones were mostly Black. I felt comfortable discussing the world we live in with someone whose perspective was like mine. I never had to worry about whether I would be perceived as a stereotype, even with those who I was close with. I never felt awkward bringing up racism, because I knew they would agree to some extent and share their own similar experiences. But with my white friends, or with other racial groups, these topics didn't feel as natural. Like I said earlier, someone's sympathy isn't the same as empathy. This difference between sympathy and empathy is a barrier that means something.

But then we moved to Thailand. I'd never lived somewhere with so few Black people. I knew this move would be a change, but I didn't know how it would feel. After the move, there has been a lack of emotional support that I'd always had access to before and this new experience has been weird for me. To be fair, part of the problem is because I'm new and don't know everybody yet. But still, if there had been one other Black person I was at least familiar with, I would have run to them.

Until that terrible moment in the cafeteria, I hadn't understood how strong the relationship between my sisters back home and me was. I could talk about what happened and didn't feel stupid crying. I was able to express my emotions unfiltered without having to worry about stepping on toes. I appreciated hearing something other than "that's terrible," "I'm so sorry," "I can't imagine." The support that I get from Black friends, Black teachers, Black coaches, Black mentors, is on another level that isn't present or shared with others outside of the community.

It's the automatic recognition that we share something, and it's deeper than our skin. The ability to relate to each other's experiences and views is an amazing thing that I get to experience. No matter what, there will always be people in the Black community that are there to support you and root for you when others aren't. I'm a part of an amazing group that calls each other Black queens and kings, for the sole purpose of bringing one another up.

Even though I am not physically with this community, it doesn't take much to receive their comfort. I'm able to text or call my friends whenever I need their support. This unwavering support is something I look forward to when I am back in the States for college, surrounded again by my brothers and sisters. This connection is the safe space where we all want to see each other succeed, where there's a safety net for all of us when needed.

— Amara Dynes —

Best Moms Ever

Step-parents are not around to replace biological
parents, rather to augment a child's life experience.
~Azriel Johnson

Most kids are lucky if they get a great mom. I've been blessed more than most because I have two great moms.

My mother and father met in the military. After ten years, when my brother was seven and I was two, they divorced. When I was four, I got a new stepmom, Tina. I was a brat about it and throughout most of my childhood I didn't treat her well. Somewhere inside me a voice said, "She can't take the place of Mom. She's not my mom; she can't tell me what to do."

When I was about twelve my father gave me a rude awakening. One day, after I had been particularly awful to Tina, he took me aside and said something like, "Do you think that when you come here I'm the one who goes to the store and buys your favorite foods? Do you think that I plan fun things like going to the movies, pool, and Kings Island? Do you think I go out and buy you clothes and toys? Well, I don't. Tina is the one who does all those things. It's time that you start respecting her."

I was bewildered and flabbergasted. Could this be true? Instantly I was filled with guilt and shame. How awful it must have been for her to put time, energy, and love into a brat who pushed her buttons.

Something clicked for me that day. A wave of appreciation and love came over me. That day I started calling her Mommy Tina. By the age of fourteen, when I moved in with my dad, I dropped the Tina and called her Mom.

Most stepchildren don't understand what a stepparent goes through, especially a stepmom. They try to love this child who is horrible to them. They make sacrifices to feed, clothe, and provide for this child who isn't even their blood. Tina had no obligation to do any of those things for me, but she did.

I didn't grow in her stomach, but she grew in my heart. Now I'm writing this at age twenty-five and I have so much love, affection, and appreciation for this woman who came into my life. She has loved me, supported me, sacrificed for me, provided for me, given me advice, and shown me unconditional love and forgiveness. It is because of her that I love the way I do. You don't have to share DNA to love someone. I will always be grateful for this strong, beautiful woman who was brought into my life. I am also thankful that I have a mother who understands the love I have for Tina.

I only hope that I am a fraction as good as the two moms I've been blessed with. And I hope that any stepchild reading this knows that there is room in your heart for two moms. Don't take stepmoms for granted. Don't spend your time in bitterness when you could be building a relationship to last a lifetime. For the stepmoms out there, don't give up hope. Sometimes it takes us a long time to get there but most of us do.

— Stephanie Simmonds —

Learning to Accept Help

Courage starts with showing up
and letting ourselves be seen.
~Brené Brown

I didn't even scratch the surface!" I whispered out loud to myself in panicked confusion. Since my school had shut down for COVID-19, I was expected to work at home. Unfortunately, I had little to no motivation to do any schoolwork. Whenever I sat down, my mind would wander off to other things. I had no focus and finals were coming up. I had more than enough work on my plate without this new assignment.

How could I possibly do this in one week? My hands started trembling and it was hard to breathe. My heart was pounding and tears were rolling down my face. I stood up to get some water. Bad decision. My ears began to ring so loudly I couldn't hear anything, not even my own voice. My head felt heavier and heavier, dragging my body down to the ground as I started swaying back and forth and then plummeted towards the floor. I couldn't see and I felt like I was slipping in and out of consciousness.

I don't know how long I lay on the ground unable to get up. When I snapped out of it, I got up, took some ibuprofen, and never told anyone. I knew exactly what had happened — I had just had a panic attack. I'd battled anxiety since I was twelve, and, because of the increasing isolation due to COVID-19, my symptoms were worsening. I had experienced panic attacks before, though never as extreme as this one.

I convinced myself that if I just got some rest, things would be better in the morning. Unfortunately, it did not get better. I went through the summer and then when August came around, and orientation day was looming, it stimulated my social anxiety. I wasn't ready to step into a room full of people who I didn't know, people who would judge me. The first day of in-person class wasn't any better, as my heart pounded every time I spoke, my mind second guessing every word that came out of my mouth. Every day was a new day for anxiety to take its toll on my physical and mental health.

The first real panic attack I had at school happened around the end of lunch. I ran to the bathroom and isolated myself in a stall for a whole period. I was afraid to walk into my classroom because of how red and puffy my eyes were, but I powered through it. I got to the point where I had to stay home from school for a week because of how anxious I got even stepping through the door. I felt alone, yet it hurt to be around people. I didn't know who to talk to, or even if I should open up to people about it. The whole week I stayed home, I felt more centered, I could focus more, and I was calmer. However, all good things must come to an end, and when Monday rolled around, I had to go back.

The first hour or so back at school was okay, I had to come up with excuses to explain my absence and re-assess any missing work I had. But then a hurricane of anxiety came crashing into me, destroying any hope of having a good day. I ran through the bustling halls to the bathroom and closed myself into the last stall, hoping this attack would pass quickly.

But this time something was different; this time I wasn't alone. I saw two shoes underneath the stall doors and recognized who they belonged to. They were my friend Morgan's shoes. "Are you okay?" she asked, "I saw you run in here crying."

"Y-yeah," I stuttered, "I'm fine."

"Really, because you're crying on the bathroom floor," she replied.

"Really, I-I'm okay."

It was quiet for a moment before Morgan responded sweetly, "It's okay to cry, but you don't have to do it alone."

She sat outside the stall until I was ready to come out. Neither of us said a word, and we didn't need to; it was comforting just to be with someone. When I came out, she wrapped me up in a hug, and I instantly melted, not realizing how tense I was. I knew I had to go to class, but I was less scared knowing that she was with me, right by my side.

I wasn't magically cured of my anxiety after this, nor did my panic attacks cease. I still struggle with anxiety today. I have good days and bad days. But I know that on the bad days, I have someone to hold my hand, and that makes me feel less lonely.

I learned that it's okay to get help. I began therapy and started getting more comfortable talking about my issues in a safe space. Our natural instinct is to hide our feelings and never talk about them, lest we be labeled overdramatic or weak. But reaching out to others is very critical and very helpful. The most important thing I've learned in spite of all the anxiety is that I'm not alone. You are not alone either. Or at least, you don't have to be.

—E. K. Bannon—

The Girl Who Never Talked

Find out who you are and do it on purpose.
~Dolly Parton

I never really felt like I fit in. I was a freshman in high school and my only close friend was Sabella, who I had known since kindergarten. Bella is and always will be one of my best friends, but she had other close friends too, and I didn't. I was on the volleyball team, and on the court I knew exactly who I was and where I was supposed to be. I loved all of my teammates, but when we were sitting in the bleachers before and after games I would just sit there quietly, totally unsure of myself.

At school, it seems like the only time anyone talked to me was just to jokingly say, "You are so quiet... do you ever talk?" I wanted to talk; I just couldn't find the words. I never felt like I knew what to say in a big group of people.

One Saturday after our game Bella was supposed to come over and spend the night at my house. We always had a lot of fun together. I wished that I could talk to the other girls the way I talked to her. But before we left the gym that day, some of the other volleyball girls invited her to go to the movies with them. Since Bella had already made plans with me, they asked if I would like to go to movies with them too.

One of the moms drove us, and we all piled into the back seat of her Suburban — Rhiannon, Destinee, Christine, Sabella, and me. I was kind of nervous at first, but once it was just us five, I came out of my shell. For the first time in my life, I really felt like I was a part of the conversation, instead of just sitting there listening. Turns out I had a lot to say.

That was a night that would change my life. All the way there, and all the way back, we talked and laughed, and notice I said "we." I even told a few jokes and was so glad I did. By the end of the night, one of them turned around and yelled enthusiastically, laughing at something I said: "I don't think I've really ever heard you talk before! You are hilarious! You are so fun to be around!"

Another one of the girls added, "I can't believe we've never hung out before!"

I felt like I would cry, but I couldn't, because I was too busy smiling. Finally, I had friends too, as in plural. We all spent the night at Rhiannon's house, but I don't think we slept a wink. We drank way too many sodas, ate all the junk food in the house, and shared all our secrets. By the end of the night, we all knew who had a crush on which guys. Christine was the only one who had really been allowed to date, and she told us all about it. By 2-3 a.m. we must have prank called every cute boy we knew, and some who we didn't know. Destinee was the master at prank calling. We had the time of our lives. I laughed until my chest hurt.

At school on Monday, they all raved about how much fun shy little Kayleen was. We had so much fun that weekend, that we tried to repeat it many times, but it was never quite as much fun as it was that first time. I guess we all needed a good friend more than any of us realized.

A few weeks later, one of the parents took us all to Six Flags, and we had little friendship bracelets made. They had a tiny piece of glass with a little piece of rice inside that had all our names printed on it.

I was one of the first ones to turn sixteen, and when I got a truck, the first thing I wanted to do was take my friends back to the movie theater.

Destinee didn't have a car, so I picked her up for school every morning, and we jammed out to loud country music all the way there. We became inseparable. When Destinee's mom wouldn't let her go out on the weekends, I would pull into her driveway with my headlights turned off, and she would climb out her bedroom window. (Sorry Mrs. W!)

Now I had two best friends. Most weekends, we would cruise around town in Sabella's candy-apple red truck with the radio turned up way too loud. We had a lot of fun "mudding" in my old truck at my ranch and playing pool and sitting in the hot tub at Sabella's.

When I got my first boyfriend, at the age of sixteen, I spent a lot of time in a neighboring town, and his cousin Scarlet also became a really close friend of mine.

I had been just a lonely high school freshman, who "never talked to anyone" at school. But before I knew it, I had four best friends, who gave me more love and confidence than I knew what to do with. I also ended up reconnecting with another childhood friend, Lauren.

My friends are all total opposites. They are a little wild and totally outgoing, and I am totally cautious and shy. But they made sure I had fun, and I made sure they didn't get into too much trouble!

We are all grown up now, and hardly ever see each other, as we are busy with jobs and our families.

The more I grew up, the more I realized that even when I felt "left out" or like I "didn't fit in" at school, I always had three best friends who were right there at home all along, my mama and my two sisters. I spend most of my time getting into trouble with them nowadays.

I haven't seen that little best friends' bracelet in years. But even now, seventeen years later, I know my girls Destinee, Scarlet, Sabella, and Lauren will always be there for me, anytime I need them… or anytime I just need to talk!

— Kayleen Kitty Holder —

Beyond the Scarf

I am what time, circumstance, history, have made of me,
certainly, but I am, also, much more than that.
So are we all.
~James Baldwin

t keeps moving around my face. The cool fabric turns hot on my skin by afternoon. My hair peeks out despite my desperate attempts to contain it. Everybody knows me as the funny girl in class who furiously readjusts her hijab every five minutes. And that's on a normal day. It's an absolute nightmare on gym class days. Once, I was so blinded by my untamable scarf that I tripped on the track and nearly collided into someone.

I decided to wear a hijab full-time freshman year to connect with my faith more. I didn't anticipate the struggles it would bring in a new environment, high school, where everyone else seemed so polished. For a while, I thought I was doomed to be the only hijabi who didn't know how to wrap her hijab properly.

At some point, I realized my insecurities stemmed from my fear of misrepresenting other Muslims. My mom warned me beforehand of the implications of wearing a hijab — it extended beyond providing modesty. With a scarf around my head, it was clear as day what I represented to others when I stepped into public spaces. I wanted to be confident in appearance, yes, but also in my identity. Instead, the imperfections and the pressure to be a model Muslim made it even harder to step out of my shell.

During freshman year, my history teacher asked a question about how Islam regarded religious scholars and regular people. No one responded. Instead, everyone looked at me, the girl in the bright pink hijab. I was upset. I knew my teacher wanted me to answer, and I didn't want to be the spokesperson for my religion. I didn't want to risk changing someone's perception negatively. Eventually, I willed myself to speak and then got upset at myself for shying away. For being an imperfect representation of my community. Why couldn't I be like my other Muslim classmates? Like the activists I saw on TV? Why was it so hard to speak?

Incidents like these and my seemingly inherent inability to wrap my hijab gave way to lots of self-loathing. If I couldn't stand tall and confident in who I was, then why was I even wearing a hijab? Despite my original intention to connect with my religion, I felt even more distant from it.

One day in the girl's bathroom, I struck up a conversation with an upperclassman adjusting her hijab in the mirror. To my surprise, she didn't judge me when I told her my struggles. Instead, she recounted her first time wearing a hijab and how it wasn't nearly as polished as it is now. It was a relief to hear I wasn't the only one who had experienced hiccups. Eventually, I got comfortable enough to join the other girls in front of the mirrors. The conversations slowly shifted from styles of hijab to more complex topics, such as cultural traditions of our faith, and the news and how it affected us.

It was in the girl's bathroom that I found a community among young Muslim girls like me. We were all trying to maintain our Muslim identity in a world that was increasingly Islamophobic. It was in our conversations that I felt the most understood, by people who shared common traits, upbringings, and struggles. To me, the hijabis in the bathroom represented community: a group of people who could empathize with others, rather than simply sympathize.

Eventually, I learned that it was okay to love my identity, to wear it proudly, and still be reserved about it. It's okay to feel angry when people look to you for all the answers. I found strength in my friends. I found strength within myself. I no longer pressure myself to be the perfect Muslim because that notion does not exist. Now, I connect to

Islam in my own way. To others, my hijab might signify a fundamental aspect of my identity, but to me, it's just another part of me — nothing profound, just me.

— Maisha Sheikh —

The Gossiper

A woman repeated a bit of gossip about a neighbor. Within a few days the whole community knew the story. The person it concerned was deeply hurt and offended. Later, the woman responsible for spreading the rumor learned that it was completely untrue. She was very sorry and went to a wise old sage to find out what she could do to repair the damage.

"Go to the marketplace." he said, "and purchase a chicken, and have it killed. Then on your way home, pluck its feathers and drop them one by one along the road." Although surprised by this advice, the woman did what she was told.

The next day the wise man said, "Now, go and collect all those feathers you dropped yesterday and bring them back to me."

The woman followed the same road, but to her dismay the wind had blown all the feathers away. After searching for hours, she returned with only three in her hand. "You see," said the old sage, "it's easy to drop them, but it's impossible to get them back. So it is with gossip. It doesn't take much to spread a rumor, but once you do, you can never completely undo the wrong."

— Author Unknown —
Submitted by Helen Hazinski

A Simple Christmas Card

A friend is a gift you give yourself.
~Robert Louis Stevenson

Abbie, shy and reserved, started ninth grade in the big-city high school in the center of town. It never occurred to her that she would be lonely. But soon she found herself dreaming of her old eighth-grade class. It had been small and friendly. This new school was much too cold and unfriendly.

No one at this school seemed to care if Abbie felt welcome or not. She was a very caring person, but her shyness interfered with making friends. Oh, she had those occasional buddies — you know, the kind that took advantage of her kindness by cheating off her.

She walked the halls every day almost invisible; no one spoke to her, so her voice was never heard. It reached the point where she believed that her thoughts weren't good enough to be heard. So she continued to stay quiet, almost mute.

Her parents were very worried about her, for they feared she'd never make friends. And since they were divorced, she probably needed to talk with a friend very badly. Her parents tried everything they could to help her fit in. They bought her the clothes and the CDs, but it still didn't work.

Unfortunately, Abbie's parents didn't know Abbie was thinking of ending her life. She often cried herself to sleep, believing that no one would ever love her enough to be her real friend.

Her new pal Tammy used her to do her homework by pretending to need help. Even worse, Tammy was leaving Abbie out of the fun she was having. This only pushed Abbie closer to the edge.

Things worsened over the summer; Abbie was all alone with nothing to do but let her mind run wild. She let herself believe that this was all that life was cracked up to be. From Abbie's point of view, it wasn't worth living.

She started the tenth grade and joined a Christian youth group at a local church, hoping to make friends. She met people who on the outside seemed to welcome her, but who on the inside wished she'd stay out of their group.

By Christmastime Abbie was so upset that she was taking sleeping pills to help her sleep. It seemed as though she was slipping away from the world.

Finally, she decided that she would jump off the local bridge on Christmas Eve, while her parents were at a party. As she left her warm house for the long walk to the bridge, she decided to leave her parents a note in the mailbox. When she pulled down the door to the mailbox, she found letters already there.

She pulled the letters out to see who they were from. There was one from Grandma and Grandpa Knight, a couple from the neighbors… and then she saw one addressed to her. She tore it open. It was a card from one of the guys in the youth group.

> Dear Abbie,
> I want to apologize for not talking with you sooner, but my parents are in the middle of a divorce, so I didn't have a chance to talk with anyone. I was hoping you could help me with some questions I have about divorced kids. I think we could become friends and help each other. See you at Youth Group on Sunday!
> Sincerely your friend,
> Wesley Hill

She stared at the card for a while, reading it over and over again. "Become friends," she smiled, realizing that someone cared about her life and wanted plain, quiet Abbie Knight as a friend. She felt so special.

She turned around and went back to her house. As soon as she walked in the door, she called Wesley. I guess you could say he was a Christmas miracle, because friendship is the best gift you can give anyone.

— Theresa Peterson —

Please Listen

When I ask you to listen to me
and you start giving me advice,
you have not done what I asked.
When I ask you to listen to me
and you begin to tell me why
I shouldn't feel that way,
you are trampling on my feelings.
When I ask you to listen to me
and you feel you have to do something
to solve my problem,
you have failed me,
strange as that may seem.
Listen! All I ask is that you listen.
Don't talk or do — just hear me.
Advice is cheap; 20 cents will get
you both Dear Abby and Billy Graham
in the same newspaper.
And I can do for myself; I am not helpless.
Maybe discouraged and faltering,
but not helpless.
When you do something for me that I can
and need to do for myself,
you contribute to my fear and
inadequacy.
But when you accept as a simple fact
that I feel what I feel,

no matter how irrational, then I can stop trying to convince you and
get about this business of understanding what's behind this irrational
feeling.
And when that's clear, the answers are
obvious and I don't need advice.
Irrational feelings make sense when
we understand what's behind them.
Perhaps that's why prayer works, sometimes,
for some people — because God is mute,
and he doesn't give advice or try
to fix things.
God just listens and lets you work
 it out for yourself.
So please listen, and just hear me.
And if you want to talk, wait a minute
for your turn — and I will listen to you.

— Stacia Gilmer —

She Told Me
It Was Okay to Cry

*It takes a lot of understanding, time and trust to gain a
close friendship with someone. As I approach
a time of my life of complete uncertainty,
my friends are my most precious asset.*
~Erynn Miller, age 18

I saw her last night for the first time in years. She was miserable. She had bleached her hair, trying to hide its true color, just as her rough front hid her deep unhappiness. She needed to talk, so we went for a walk. While I thought about my future, the college applications that had recently arrived, she thought about her past, the home she had recently left. Then she spoke. She told me about her love — and I saw a dependent relationship with a dominating man. She told me about the drugs — and I saw that they were her escape. She told me about her goals — and I saw unrealistic material dreams. She told me she needed a friend — and I saw hope, because at least I could give her that.

We had met in the second grade. She was missing a tooth, I was missing my friends. I had just moved across the continent to find cold metal swings and cold smirking faces outside the foreboding doors of P.S. 174, my new school. I asked her if I could see her Archie comic book, even though I didn't really like comics; she said yes, even though she didn't really like to share. Maybe we were both looking for a smile. And we found it. We found someone to giggle with late at night, someone to slurp hot chocolate with on the cold winter days when school was canceled and we would sit together by the bay window, watching the snow endlessly falling.

In the summer, at the pool, I got stung by a bee. She held my hand and told me that she was there and that it was okay to cry — so I did. In the fall, we raked the leaves into piles and took turns jumping, never afraid because we knew that the multicolored bed would break our fall.

Only now, she had fallen and there was no one to catch her. We hadn't spoken in months, we hadn't seen each other in years. I had moved to California, she had moved out of the house. Our experiences were miles apart, making our hearts much farther away from each other than the continent she had just traversed. Through her words I was alienated, but through her eyes I felt her yearning. She needed support in her search for strength and a new start. She needed my friendship now more than ever. So I took her hand and told her that I was there and that it was okay to cry — so she did.

— Daphna Renan —

Lessons in Friendship

"There's the people you've known forever. Who like… know you… in this way. That other people can't. Because they've seen you change. They've let you change." This is a quote from an episode of *My So-Called Life,* one of the many subtly profound quotes characteristic of the show. This one in particular refers to an aspect of a certain kind of friendship, a very special kind of friendship, that I have and cherish. Let me explain.

Throughout my experience on the show, there were many character concepts and story lines from *My So-Called Life* that touched me. In portraying Rayanne I was most deeply affected by the dynamic of her friendship with Angela.

Being Rayanne's friend was getting harder and harder for Angela. Rayanne was being knocked off, or was knocking herself off, the pedestal new friends have a tendency to put each other on. This awesome new friend, who lived life on the edge, actually fell over the side every once in a while, and fair or not, Angela was disappointed.

This happens. As Rayanne, I didn't have to go far to feel the frustration, the disappointment a situation like this causes because I've been there. I've been through the turn of events that sneak up on a friendship forcing it in another direction, the closeness suddenly gone and replaced by questions and doubts. This is that point many relationships come to where a decision has to be made: to stay in or bail out, to decide what it's worth.

I had a best friend from third grade through seventh grade. We were practically inseparable for those years. Then I changed.

After growing up with the same group of kids from age 5 to age 12, I hit junior high and a whole new world opened up to me. It seemed everyone was there, the boys from the Little League where I played ball, friends from the Pop Warner football teams I cheered for (and my brother played for), as well as a number of people from the summer drama workshop. Not to mention my big bro, who was a ninth grader, and all of his friends who adopted me as their own lil' sis. The "in" crowd welcomed me, figuring that I had to be cool to know so many people, and life was good. Always someone to pass notes to, always someone to gossip about, always someone else to call, always about something really important.

I was a different person with each new group of friends. I wanted to be everything to everyone, and I became so wrapped up in not only all of that, but so wrapped up in myself that I couldn't see what was really going on. I was just too busy to realize that I had gotten a little lost. My best friend started to distance herself from me. I don't think she liked what I was becoming. But I didn't see that then; I just felt her lose faith in me. It hurt so much, and I didn't understand. To keep from dealing with it I threw myself even further into my new life. It wasn't long before I made a few mistakes, some worse than others, and the "in" crowd got a peek at the real me. Or at least someone other than who they thought I was, and they were disappointed. That's when it got ugly.

These so-called friends (no pun intended) turned fast. In a melodrama of gossip and rumors, I was banished. I had been part of this "in" crowd until they found out I really wasn't cool enough to be there.

The time had come to step back and take a look around. This was one of the hardest times in my life. I felt alone and was very disappointed in myself. My first step was to go back to my old best friend. I tried so hard to show her that I was sorry for messing up, that I still loved her and missed her incredibly... that I needed her. In return, I received blank stares and emotionless responses. So I tried harder. Still, barely a trace of that sisterhood she once shared with me. It took me a long time to realize that I had lost her, that she had changed, too. And our best-friendship was gone.

At school, I found myself wandering around at nutrition and lunch, no longer floating from group to group being the social butterfly. It was then, when I thought I had nowhere else to go, that I rediscovered the "kindergarten group." This group had a base of five or six of us who had actually gone to kindergarten together, along with a few additions welcomed in throughout elementary school. We had all grown up in the same community, shared the same schools, classes, birthday parties, and all the ups and downs of our pre-pubescent lives.

The group was even bigger now. They had all made new friends, but instead of choosing one over the other, as I had done, they simply included them. At my lowest, I had gone so far as to not invite them to my bat mitzvah. I can still hear my mom asking, "What about Susie and Greg and the rest of the 'kindergarten group'?" as she shook her head at my invite list. "*Mom*, I don't hang out with them anymore," I'd said. "They don't even know my new friends... besides, if I invite one, I have to invite them all." I received invitations to every one of their birthday parties and bar or bat mitzvahs that year.

I tried to inconspicuously make my way back into this circle of friends, not expecting it to be easy. I assumed I was going to get what I deserved which was for them to be cold and exclude me as I had done to them. I had to take that chance.

I was completely caught off guard by how little effort was needed to feel welcomed again. There was absolutely no resentment, only comfort and an unexpected sense of belonging. It was incredible, as though there were no time lapse. We just picked up right where we left off. Over the next months I realized the more I hung out with them, the less insecure I became. I was a new person with them... one I liked.

But, there was something that I didn't get, something about it being too easy. I mean, weren't they hurt when I had so obviously chosen these other friends over them? Didn't they lose faith in me, or resent the fact that I had taken their friendship for granted? I just didn't feel I could truly fit in again until these issues were dealt with. I needed answers.

They came a few months later at a camp-out I organized just for the kindergarten group (we joked that it was a makeup for not inviting them to the bat mitzvah). When the sun went down we huddled up around the campfire. All night we laughed, roasted marshmallows (and old teachers), counted shooting stars and talked. I finally felt safe enough to bring up my questions. I stumbled through them and waited. After a moment, only awkward for me, one of them said, "Yeah, maybe it hurt a little, but..." he shrugged, "I don't know, I guess... we just understood." And that was that. They just understood.

They saw me change. They gave me room, freedom to screw up, to grow and learn my own lessons, my own way, in my own time. Through the years, we've *all* had our phases, our ups and downs, and I expect we'll continue because that's the way it goes. We know we will be each other's constant from now on. We will all continue to grow separately together, all the while providing the unconditional love, understanding and support only friends like these are capable of.

"There's the people you've known forever. Who like... know you... in this way. That other people can't. Because they've seen you change. They've let you change."

I might never have understood the true magnitude of this seemingly simple concept without having experienced those defining years. From the kindergarten group, the best friend and the cool crowd, I had learned two things: the type of friends I wanted, and the type of friend I wanted to be.

— A. J. Langer —

Editor's note: A. J. Langer is an actor who played the character Rayanne on the television show *My So-Called Life*.

Heaven Sent

You will suffer and you will hurt.
You will have joy and you will have peace.
~Alison Cheek

Making the transition from middle school to high school is always a tough one. Luckily, I had my five best friends, Kylie, Lanie, Laura, Mindy and Angela, to help me through it. We experienced our most important moments together and shared everything, the good and the bad. Their friendship completed me. With their help, I went from being a shy little girl to a confident and excited young woman. Life without them was unimaginable, or so I thought.

The unexpected all began on a beautiful spring day during my sophomore year. Life was perfect. It was a Friday and the weekend was upon us. After my friends and I made our plans, I said goodbye to each of them and gave them all a great big hug. As always, I told them that I loved them and we went on our own ways.

Laura and I decided to go to the mall and do some shopping before we went out that night. As we returned to her house, I noticed something very odd: both of her parents were home and waiting outside. I knew right away how peculiar this was, since even Laura seemed surprised to see her father home so early. As we approached the door, Laura's father quietly uttered, "Reality is going to hit right now." My stomach sank and my heart began to pound quickly. *What was he about to tell us?*

Once I found out, I no longer wanted to know what he was trying to say. Seeking comfort, I looked into the eyes of Laura's mother but saw her eyes fill up with nothing but tears. As she tried to speak, she choked on her words. But slowly the words came. The five words that would forever destroy my life were, "There has been an accident."

Images of the people I loved raced through my mind as my heart began to beat faster. My first instinct was to retreat to denial. Nothing was wrong, nothing had happened and no one was hurt. This would all go away and things would be back to normal in the morning. Unfortunately, I couldn't run away from the truth. I sat on the edge of my seat in shock as I was told the news.

My best friends had been in the accident. Lanie and Mindy had walked away. Kylie, however, was in bad shape. I soon realized that no one was telling me what had happened to Angela. As I prepared to ask, I took a deep breath and swallowed hard. Deep down inside, I already knew what I didn't want to hear. I tried to ignore my instincts. After all, Angela couldn't be dead. She was only fifteen!

Then the news came and there was nowhere I could run to escape. Angela was dead. After hearing the news, all I could do was laugh. This had to be some kind of sick joke. My inner refusal to accept what I had been told prevented me from crying. I had no tears. I was in shock, utter shock. From the moment the accident had happened, each of our lives had been changed forever.

As I arrived at the hospital, the first person I saw was Lanie. Even though it truly was Lanie, this wasn't *my* Lanie. The Lanie I knew was full of spunk. As I looked into her eyes, I thought I was looking into the eyes of a stranger. For the first time in our lives, she was out of my reach. I was devastated to see her in so much pain. She couldn't even speak to me.

As if that weren't hard enough, I was then told that before I could see Kylie, there were certain conditions that I had to agree to. I was to remain calm and tell her that everything was going to be okay. The hardest part, though, was being told that I couldn't cry, because this would upset her. I quickly agreed. I just wanted to see her.

I walked into the emergency room to find Kylie hooked up to many machines. She was screaming and crying. It was beyond difficult to pretend that all was well when all I could see was the hell that she was going through. My heart stopped. She was in agony and I could do nothing but watch. As I told her that I loved her, I felt my eyes well up with tears, so I turned and ran away.

Once I was outside of Kylie's room, I tried to regain my composure. However, I panicked once again when I found out that Angela's father was on his way over to the hospital to check on the other girls. My only instinct was to run, and that is exactly what I did. I ran as fast as I could to the other side of the hospital. I was not running away from him, but from the truth. I just couldn't bear facing him. I knew if I did, I would have to face the truth that Angela was gone forever. I wasn't ready for that truth. Somewhere deep down, I was still hoping that this was really an awful nightmare that I was going to wake up from any minute. Unfortunately, it wasn't.

That night all of my friends gathered at Laura's house. We consoled each other and reminisced about the times we had shared with Angela, times that we would have no more. At this point, I was still not allowing myself to grieve. If I did, it would mean that I believed it was true. I knew it was true but I could not accept it, so I didn't.

Later that week was the viewing. The once-vibrant young woman lay lifeless and cold. That was not my Angela; I did not know or recognize that person. What followed was the funeral. That was where the spirit of the Angela that I knew actually was.

It was a beautiful sight to see the community come together to express their love for her. The microphone was open to all of those who wanted to share their personal memories or their love for Angela. Seeing all the people that were there to remember her made me realize that Angela not only touched my life but the lives of everyone she came into contact with. She was my sunshine, and now without her my days were darker. How does a person live without the love, warmth and security of her best friend?

I didn't think my life could get any worse, but I was wrong. Without notice, I was told that my parents were getting a divorce. As soon as I heard the news, I automatically wanted to call Angela. After all, she was the one I always ran to when I needed someone to talk to or cheer me up. But she was gone.

All my friends were still hurting from the devastation of losing Angela, so I didn't think that I could burden them with my new crisis. I ended up feeling completely lost and abandoned. I bottled up all my thoughts, questions and frustrations inside of me. I thought that meant that I was strong. It took me some time before I realized that there was someone that would always be there for me no matter what happened: God. He always had a way of coming into my life with open arms when I had nowhere left to run. I soon learned that God has a mysterious way of working. This time, he placed a situation in my life path that enabled me to grow as an individual.

Unexpectedly, Brenda Hampton, the creator, writer and executive producer of *7th Heaven*, came to me and asked if I would be willing to do an episode about "dealing with the death of a young friend." Up until this point, I had not let myself grieve over the loss of Angela. Simply put, I had been acting. I had put up this perfect façade that I was totally happy. When Brenda asked me if I was willing to do this episode, I suddenly realized that I needed to let out my emotions and fears if I ever wanted to get over my pain. As a result, I agreed to what Brenda proposed, and she developed "Nothing Endures but Change."

At first, I wasn't prepared for the emotional tidal wave that would be released. Filming that episode was both emotionally and physically exhausting. Emotions that I had ignored for so long were now being unleashed, and I did not know how I was going to deal with them. Luckily, this time around I felt comfortable enough to turn to my friends and family for the love, advice and security that only they could offer. I came to the realization that it was okay to hurt. Once the tears came, they didn't stop until weeks after. That was when I realized that even though Angela wasn't physically with us any longer, her spirit had never left my side.

One day, after visiting Angela's grave at the cemetery, I was listening to the radio. I noticed that the songs playing were those that I always associated with Angela and our friendship. Five of "our" songs played back to back. As I came over a hill, I saw a beautiful rainbow. I immediately got chills all over my body. I knew that this was a sign and it instantly caused me to smile. To all of my friends and me, rainbows had symbolized our friendship with Angela. There she was, as beautiful as ever, just reminding me that she was still by my side and had never truly left me. I cried, but this time out of happiness and joy. I knew then that I have an angel watching over me, now and forever, and her name is Angela.

— Beverley Mitchell —

Editor's note: Beverley Mitchell is an actor and country music singer. She portrayed Lucy Camden on the television series *7th Heaven*. This story was originally published in *Chicken Soup for the Preteen Soul*, but we moved it to this new anniversary edition of *Chicken Soup for the Teenage Soul* based on the age of the writer when this story occurred.

Chapter 3

Family

The family—that dear octopus from whose tentacles we never quite escape nor, in our inmost hearts, ever quite wish to.
~Dodie Smith

The Pool Party

If you're having fun, that's when the
best memories are built.
~Simone Biles

My mom and I woke up early the day of Hannah's pool party to do my hair. It needed to look "right," not only for the social event, but also for church the next day.

I was about to withstand seventeen minutes of the creamy chemical to relax my hair. My mom worked quickly to make sure my strands were smoothed out and evenly saturated. The noxious odor of the relaxer permeated the entire kitchen.

Mom then carefully set my hair with big hard plastic rollers so that it would come out straight. She set me under an old beautician's dryer that she bought at a yard sale. The neck of the dryer could not be lowered, so I sat on a couple of phone books. Those old-fashioned dryers had one setting: High. I sat sweating under there for an hour and twenty minutes. By the time my mom lifted the hood, my back was moist and stuck to the chair.

She took the rollers out slowly, quietly praying for a "miracle." She gently combed out the parts, smoothed out the roller lines, and sat back to admire her work with a smile.

Thanks to my mom, I felt ready for the pool party.

"Don't get your hair wet. I don't know what that chlorine will do."

"Okay."

"Keeana, I'm serious now. Don't get it wet."

"Okay!"

My dad drove me to Hannah's house, and we chatted cheerfully during the quick trip. He let me wear his T-shirt over my bathing suit because I didn't have a cover up.

When we got there, I surprisingly found the rest of the kids already in the pool. Hannah was fully soaked and immersed in a water game.

I sat comfortably at the shallow end of the pool's edge, an obedient observer. My shirt remained dry as I baked in the sun. The water lapped quietly against the side of the pool. It seemed angelically harmless. I dipped my right foot in and felt a jolt of joy.

I looked longingly at Hannah, who seemed to be having so much fun in the pool. I wished I knew how to swim like that.

"Keeana, why don't you come in?" she asked.

"Oh, um, I don't know how to swim that well."

"We'll teach you! You can't sit at the edge of the pool the whole time. Come down here!"

"Well, I don't want my hair to get wet."

"I have a swimming cap. Your hair will be fine. Trust me!"

Problem solved! The cap would protect my hair. And how much damage could chlorine really do to relaxed hair anyway?

Getting the cap on was a team effort. I wondered if my curls would get flattened by the tight rubber. My mom wouldn't like that. But it was time to have fun!

I took off my dad's T-shirt and jumped in. I splashed. I laughed. I felt included in the crowd. I had a blast.

My dad came to pick me up four hours later. My heart had begun to pound sometime before he arrived because, in all my splashing, the devilishly sneaky water had seeped under the cap. I knew when it had happened: the cannonball. When I felt it, my heart skipped a beat, but I calmed down when I concluded, nay, declared, that it was my day — a great day to be reckless.

"Wow… It looks like Keeana had fun," Dad said slowly as he raised an eyebrow in my direction.

"Yes, your daughter is a delight! She picked up quite a few pointers in a short amount of time. You know, George, your daughter should really learn how to swim!"

"Yes... Thanks... Bye now."

Hannah gave me a quick hug and waved as my dad and I got into the car.

The entire car ride was silent. I knew I was in trouble. My chlorine-soaked hair was limp and plastered to my head. Worst of all, it was air drying into straw.

When my mom saw me, she gasped. "George! What about church tomorrow?"

"I know, Tina... but she did have fun at least."

"FUN? You call ruining one's hair fun?"

I spent the rest of the evening under my mom's wrath, under the faucet, under her exasperated hands, and under that blasted old-fashioned hair dryer again.

That night, as I tossed and turned trying to find a comfortable spot on my head full of rollers, I relived that cannonball. It was worth it.

— Keeana Saxon —

She Didn't Give Up on Me

She never once gave up. My mom is my hero.
~Kimberly Anne Brand

I lay on the floor, furiously kicking my legs and screaming until my throat felt raw — all because my foster mother had asked me to put my toys away.

"I hate you," I shrieked. I was six years old and didn't understand why I felt so angry all the time.

I'd been living in foster care since I was two. My real mom couldn't give my five sisters and me the care we needed. Since we didn't have a dad or anyone else to care for us, we were put in different foster homes. I felt lonely and confused. I didn't know how to tell people that I hurt inside. Throwing a tantrum was the only way I knew to express my feelings.

Because I acted up, eventually my current foster mom sent me back to the adoption agency, just as the mom before had. I thought I was the most unlovable girl in the world.

Then I met Kate McCann. I was seven by that time and living with my third foster family when she came to visit. When my foster mother told me that Kate was single and wanted to adopt a child, I didn't think she'd choose me. I couldn't imagine anyone would want me to live with them forever.

That day, Kate took me to a pumpkin farm. We had fun, but I didn't think I'd see her again.

A few days later, a social worker came to the house to say that Kate wanted to adopt me. Then she asked me if I'd mind living with one parent instead of two.

"All I want is someone who loves me," I said.

Kate visited the next day. She explained that it would take a year for the adoption to be finalized, but I could move in with her soon. I was excited but afraid, too. Kate and I were total strangers. I wondered if she'd change her mind once she got to know me.

Kate sensed my fear. "I know you've been hurt," she said, hugging me. "I know you're scared. But I promise I'll never send you away. We're a family now."

To my surprise, her eyes were filled with tears.

Suddenly I realized that she was as lonely as I was!

"Okay... Mom," I said.

The following week I met my new grandparents, aunt, uncle and cousins. It felt funny — but good — to be with strangers who hugged me as though they already loved me.

When I moved in with Mom, I had my own room for the first time. It had wallpaper and a matching bedspread, an antique dresser and a big closet. I had only a few clothes I'd brought with me in a brown paper bag. "Don't worry," Mom said. "I'll buy you lots of pretty new things."

I went to sleep that night feeling safe. I prayed I wouldn't have to leave.

Mom did lots of nice things for me. She took me to church. She let me have pets and gave me horseback riding and piano lessons. Every day, she told me she loved me. But love wasn't enough to heal the hurt inside me. I kept waiting for her to change her mind. I thought, "If I act bad enough, she'll leave me like the others."

So I tried to hurt her before she could hurt me. I picked fights over little things and threw tantrums when I didn't get my way. I slammed doors. If Mom tried to stop me, I'd hit her. But she never lost patience. She'd hug me and say she loved me anyway. When I got mad, she made me jump on a trampoline.

Because I was failing in school when I came to live with her, Mom was very strict about my homework. One day when I was watching TV, she came in and turned it off. "You can watch it after you finish your homework," she said. I blew up. I picked up my books and threw them across the room. "I hate you and I don't want to live here anymore!" I screamed.

I waited for her to tell me to start packing. When she didn't, I asked, "Aren't you going to send me back?"

"I don't like the way you're behaving," she said, "but I'll never send you back. We're a family, and families don't give up on each other."

Then it hit me. This mom was different; she wasn't going to get rid of me. She really did love me. And I realized I loved her, too. I cried and hugged her.

When Mom formally adopted me, our whole family celebrated at a restaurant. It felt good belonging to someone. But I was still scared. Could a mom really love me forever? My tantrums didn't disappear immediately, but as months passed, they happened less often.

Today I'm 16. I have a 3.4 grade point average, a horse named Dagger's Point, four cats, a dog, six doves and a bullfrog that lives in our backyard pond. And I have a dream: I want to be a veterinarian.

Mom and I like to do things together, like shopping and horseback riding. We smile when people say how much we look alike. They don't believe she's not my real mom.

I'm happier now than I ever imagined I could be. When I'm older, I'd like to get married and have kids, but if that doesn't work out, I'll adopt like Mom did. I'll pick a scared and lonely kid and then never, ever give up on her. I'm so glad Mom didn't give up on me.

— Sharon Whitley —
Excerpted from *Woman's World* magazine

Unconditional Mom

My mother had a great deal of trouble with me,
but I think she enjoyed it.
~Mark Twain

I was a rotten teenager. Not your average spoiled, know-it-all, not-going-to-clean-my-room, getting-an-attitude-because-I'm-15 teenager. No, I was a manipulative, lying, acid-tongued monster, who realized early on that I could make things go my way with just a few minor adjustments. The writers for today's hottest soap opera could not have created a worse "villainess." A few nasty comments here, a lie or two there, maybe an evil glare for a finishing touch, and things would be grand. Or so I thought.

For the most part, and on the outside, I was a good kid. A giggly, pug-nose tomboy who liked to play sports and who thrived on competition (a nice way of saying: somewhat pushy and demanding). Which is probably why most people allowed me to squeak by using what I now call "bulldozer behavior tactics," with no regard for anyone I felt to be of value. For a while, anyway.

Since I was perceptive enough to get some people to bend my way, it amazes me how long it took to realize how I was hurting so many others. Not only did I succeed in pushing away many of my closest friends by trying to control them; I also managed to sabotage, time and time again, the most precious relationship in my life: my relationship with my mother.

Even today, almost 10 years since the birth of the new me, my former behavior astonishes me each time I reach into my memories.

Hurtful comments that cut and stung the people I cared most about. Acts of confusion and anger that seemed to rule my every move — all to make sure that things went my way.

My mother, who gave birth to me at age 38 against her doctor's wishes, would cry to me, "I waited so long for you, please don't push me away. I want to help you!"

I would reply with my best face of stone, "I didn't ask for you! I never wanted you to care about me! Leave me alone and forget I ever lived!"

My mother began to believe I really meant it. My actions proved nothing less.

I was mean and manipulative, trying to get my way at any cost. Like many young girls in high school, the boys whom I knew were off limits were always the first ones I had to date. Sneaking out of the house at all hours of the night just to prove I could do it. Juggling complex lies that were always on the verge of blowing up in my face. Finding any way to draw attention to myself while simultaneously trying to be invisible.

Ironically, I wish I could say I had been heavy into drugs during that period of my life, swallowing mind-altering pills and smoking things that changed my personality, thus accounting for the terrible, razor-sharp words that came flying from my mouth. However, that was not the case. My only addiction was hatred; my only high was inflicting pain.

But then I asked myself why. Why the need to hurt? And why the people I cared about the most? Why the need for all the lies? Why the attacks on my mother? I would drive myself mad with all the why's until one day, it all exploded in a suicidal rage.

Lying awake the following night at the "resort" (my pet name for the hospital), after an unsuccessful, gutless attempt to jump from a vehicle moving at 80 miles per hour, one thing stood out more than my Keds with no shoelaces. I didn't want to die.

And I did not want to inflict any more pain on people to cover up what I was truly trying to hide myself: self-hatred. Self-hatred unleashed on everyone else.

I saw my mother's pained face for the first time in years — warm, tired brown eyes filled with nothing but thanks for her daughter's new lease on life and love for the child she waited 38 years to bear.

My first encounter with unconditional love. What a powerful feeling.

Despite all the lies I had told her, she still loved me. I cried on her lap for hours one afternoon and asked why she still loved me after all the horrible things I did to her. She just looked down at me, brushed the hair out of my face and said frankly, "I don't know."

A kind of smile penetrated her tears as the lines in her tested face told me all that I needed to know. I was her daughter, but more important, she was my mother. Not every rotten child is so lucky. Not every mother can be pushed to the limits I explored time and time again, and venture back with feelings of love.

Unconditional love is the most precious gift we can give. Being forgiven for the past is the most precious gift we can receive. I dare not say we could experience this pure love twice in one lifetime.

I was one of the lucky ones. I know that. I want to extend the gift my mother gave me to all the "rotten teenagers" in the world who are confused.

It's okay to feel pain, to need help, to feel love — just feel it without hiding. Come out from under the protective covers, from behind the rigid walls and the suffocating personas, and take a breath of life.

— Sarah J. Vogt —

The Birthday

A s I sat in the chair by the window and felt the warm June sunshine on my arm, I had to remind myself where I was. It was hard to believe that behind the nicely finished oak cabinets hid various medical equipment, and that in a moment's notice the ceiling tiles could be removed to reveal surgical lights. Except for the few instruments and the IV cart next to the bed, it barely looked like a hospital room. While looking at the carefully selected wallpaper and furnishings, I remembered back to that day, not so long before, when this adventure first began.

It was a crisp October day. Our field hockey team had just won a 2-1 victory over Saratoga. I dropped, exhausted but excited, into the passenger side of our car. While leaving the school my mother mentioned that she had gone to the doctor that day. "For what?" I asked, becoming nervous as I ran through all the ailments my mother could possibly have.

"Well…" She hesitated and my worry increased. "I'm pregnant."

"You're what?" I exclaimed.

"Pregnant," she repeated.

I was speechless to say the least. I sat in the car and all I could think was that these things do not happen to your parents when you are a sophomore in high school. Then the realization that I was going to have to share my mother hit me. The mother who had been all my own for 16 years. I was overcome with resentment and confusion over a tiny person nesting inside my mom. I had never wanted my mother to have another child after she remarried. This was a selfish feeling, but when it came to my mom, I was reluctant to share the smallest bit of her.

When I saw the shock and joy in my stepfather's eyes when he was told of the impending arrival of his first child, I could not help but feel excited. I could hardly wait to tell everyone and my joy showed on the outside. On the inside, though, I was trying to deal with my fear and anger.

My parents involved me in all the preparations, from decorating the nursery to picking out names to going to Lamaze classes and deciding that I could be present for the baby's birth. But despite all the excitement and happiness this pregnancy brought, it was hard to hear my friends and relatives constantly talk about the new baby. I feared that I would be pushed back into the woodwork when the baby came. Sometimes when I was alone, all the resentment for what this child was going to take from me would overcome the joy.

Sitting in the delivery room that June 17th, knowing that the baby would soon be here, I began to feel all my insecurities surface. What was my life going to be like? Would it be one endless baby-sitting job? What would I have to give up? Most important, would I lose my mother? The time to ponder and worry was rapidly melting away. The baby was coming.

It was the most incredible experience of my life, being in the delivery room that day, for birth is truly a miracle. When the doctor announced that it was a girl, I cried. I had a baby sister.

All my fears and insecurities have passed now, with the help of a warm and understanding family. I cannot explain how special it is to have a tiny person who waits with me every morning until my ride to school comes and then, as Mom holds her in the window, waves her little hand good-bye. It is so wonderful to come home and not even have a chance to take off my coat before she is tugging at me to come play with her.

I realize now that there is plenty of love in my home for Emma. My resentment for what I thought she would take away had been erased with the realization that she took away nothing and instead brought so much to my life. I never thought I could love a baby this much, and I would not trade the joy I get from being her big sister for anything.

— Melissa Esposito —

The Home Run

On June 18th, I went to my little brother's baseball game as I always did. Cory was 12 years old at the time and had been playing baseball for a couple of years. When I saw that he was warming up to be next at bat, I decided to head over to the dugout to give him a few pointers. But when I got there, I simply said, "I love you."

In return, he asked, "Does this mean you want me to hit a home run?"

I smiled and said, "Do your best."

As he walked up to the plate, there was a certain aura about him. He looked so confident and so sure about what he was going to do. One swing was all he took and, wouldn't you know, he hit his first home run! He ran around those bases with such pride — his eyes sparkled and his face was lit up. But what touched my heart the most was when he walked back over to the dugout. He looked over at me with the biggest smile I've ever seen and said, "I love you too, Ter."

I don't remember if his team won or lost that game. On that special summer day in June, it simply didn't matter.

— Terri Vandermark —

My Big Brother

First say to yourself what you would be;
and then do what you have to do.
~Epictetus

I never thought that the absence of smelly socks and loud music would make my heart ache. But my brother is off at college, and at age 14, I miss him terribly. We share a rare kind of closeness for siblings, but then, my brother is a rare kind of guy. Of course he's smart and kind, plus my friends say he is gorgeous and all that. But it's more how he handles things, how he treats his friends and his family, how he cares about people that makes me so proud. That's the stuff that I aspire to be. If it's okay with you, I would like to show you what I mean...

He applied to 14 colleges. He was accepted to all but one, the one he wanted, Brown University. So he opted for his second choice, and off he went to a fine though uneventful first year. When he came home for summer vacation, he informed us that he had come up with a plan. He was going to do whatever it took to get into Brown. Would we support him?

His plan was to move to Rhode Island near Brown, find a job, and do whatever he could to become known in the area. He'd work his heart out, he said, and do the very best at everything. Someone, he was sure, would notice. This was a big deal for my parents because it meant agreeing to a year without college, a scary thing for them. But they trusted him and encouraged him to do whatever he thought it would take to achieve his dream.

It wasn't long before he was hired to produce the plays at — yes, you guessed it — Brown. Now was his chance to shine, and shine he did. No task was too big or too small. He put every bit of himself into the job. He met teachers and administrators, talked to everyone about his dream and never hesitated to tell them what he was after.

And sure enough, at the end of the year, when he reapplied to Brown, he was accepted.

We were all really happy, but for me the happiness went very deep. I had learned an important lesson — a lesson no one could have taught me with words, a lesson I had to see with my own eyes. If I work hard for what I want, if I keep trying after I've been turned away, my dreams also can come true. This is a gift I still hold in my heart. Because of my brother, I trust life.

Recently, I flew to Rhode Island all by myself to visit him, and I had a blast hanging out for a week in an apartment without parents. The night before I left, we were talking about all kinds of stuff like boyfriends, girlfriends, peer pressure and school. At one point, my brother looked me right in the eye and said he loved me. He told me to remember to never do anything that I feel isn't right, no matter what, and never to forget that I can always trust my heart.

I cried all the way home, knowing that my brother and I will always be close, and realizing how lucky I am to have him. Something was different: I didn't feel like a little girl anymore. Part of me had grown up on this trip, and for the first time I thought about the important job that I had waiting for me at home. You see, I have a 10-year-old little sister. It looks as though I've got my work cut out for me. But you know, I had a great teacher.

— Lisa Gumenick —

A Brother's Voice

Most people have an inspiration in their life. Maybe it's a talk with someone you respect or an experience. Whatever the inspiration, it tends to make you look at life from a different perspective. My inspiration came from my sister Vicki, a kind and caring person. She didn't care about accolades or being written about in newspapers. All she wanted was to share her love with the people she cared about, her family and friends.

The summer before my junior year of college, I received a phone call from my father saying that Vicki was rushed to the hospital. She had collapsed and the right side of her body was paralyzed. The preliminary indications were that she suffered a stroke. However, test results confirmed it was much more serious. There was a malignant brain tumor causing her paralysis. Her doctors didn't give her more than three months to live. I remember wondering how could this happen? The day before Vicki was perfectly fine. Now, her life was coming to an end at such a young age.

After overcoming the initial shock and feeling of emptiness, I decided that Vicki needed hope and encouragement. She needed someone to make her believe that she would overcome this obstacle. I became Vicki's coach. Every day we would visualize the tumor shrinking and everything that we talked about was positive. I even posted a sign on her hospital room door that read, "If you have any negative thoughts, leave them at the door." I was determined to help Vicki beat the tumor. She and I made a deal that was called 50-50. I would do 50% of the fighting and Vicki would do the other 50%.

The month of August arrived and it was time to begin my junior year of college 3,000 miles away. I was unsure whether I should leave or stay with Vicki. I made the mistake of telling her that I might not leave for school. She became angry and said not to worry because she would be fine. There was Vicki lying ill in a hospital bed telling me not to worry. I realized that if I stayed it might send a message that she was dying and I didn't want her believing that. Vicki needed to believe that she could win against the tumor.

Leaving that night, feeling it might be the last time I would ever see Vicki alive, was the most difficult thing I have ever done. While at school, I never stopped fighting my 50% for her. Every night before falling asleep I would talk to Vicki, hoping that there was some way she could hear me. I would say, "Vicki I'm fighting for you and I will never quit. As long as you never quit fighting we will beat this."

A few months had passed and she was still holding on. I was talking with an elderly friend and she asked about Vicki's situation. I told her that she was getting worse but that she wasn't quitting. My friend asked a question that really made me think. She said, "Do you think the reason she hasn't let go is because she doesn't want to let you down?"

Maybe she was right? Maybe I was selfish for encouraging Vicki to keep fighting? That night before falling asleep, I said to her, "Vicki, I understand that you're in a lot of pain and that you might like to let go. If you do, then I want you to. We didn't lose, because you never quit fighting. If you want to go on to a better place then I understand. We will be together again. I love you and I'll always be with you wherever you are."

Early the next morning, my mother called to tell me that Vicki had passed away.

— James Malinchak —

I Love You, Dad

If God can work through me,
he can work through anyone.
~St. Francis of Assisi

I met a man who came to Tampa for his father's funeral.

Father and son hadn't seen each other in years. In fact, according to the son, his father had left when he was a boy, and they had had little contact until about a year ago, when his father had sent him a birthday card with a note saying he'd like to see his son again.

After discussing a trip to Florida with his wife and children and consulting his busy schedule at his office, the son tentatively set a date to visit his father two months later. He would drive his family down when school was out for vacation. He scribbled a note and with mixed emotions, dropped it in the mail.

He heard back immediately. Written on lined paper torn from a spiral notebook, such as a schoolboy would use, were words of excitement penned in a barely legible scrawl. Misspelled words, poor grammar and incorrect punctuation bounced off the page. The man was embarrassed for his father. He thought twice about the upcoming visit.

It just so happened that the man's daughter made the cheerleading squad at her school and had to go to a camp conducted for cheering techniques. Coincidentally, it started the week after school was out. The trip to Florida would have to be postponed.

His father said he understood, but the son didn't hear from him again for some time. A note here or there, an occasional call. They didn't say much — muttered sentences, comments about "your mother," a couple of clouded stories about the man's childhood — but it was enough to put together a few of the missing pieces.

In November the son received a call from his father's neighbor. His father had been taken to the hospital with heart problems. The son spoke with the charge nurse, who assured him his father was doing well following a heart attack. The doctor could provide details.

His father said, "I'm fine. You don't have to make a trip out here. The doctor says there was minor damage, and I can go home day after tomorrow."

He called his father every few days after that. They chatted and laughed and talked about getting together "soon." He sent money for Christmas. His father sent small gifts for his children and a pen and pencil set for his son. It was a cheap set, probably purchased at a discount pharmacy or variety-type store, and the kids tossed their tokens from Grandpa aside without much notice. But his wife received a precious music box made of crystal. Overwhelmed, she expressed her gratitude to the old man when they called him on Christmas Day. "It was my mother's," the old man explained. "I wanted you to have it."

The man's wife told her husband that they should have invited the old man for the holidays. As an excuse for not having done so, she added, "But it probably would be too cold for him here, anyway."

In February, the man decided to visit his father. As luck would have it, however, his boss's wife had to have an operation, and the man had to fill in and work a few extra hours. He called his father to tell him he'd probably get to Florida in March or April.

I met the man on Friday. He had finally come to Tampa. He was here to bury his father.

He was waiting when I arrived to open the door that morning. He sat in the chapel next to his father's body, which had been dressed in a handsome, new, navy blue pinstriped suit and laid out in a dark blue metal casket. "Going Home" was scripted inside the lid.

I offered the man a glass of water. He cried. I put my arm around his shoulder and he collapsed in my arms, sobbing. "I should have come sooner. He shouldn't have had to die alone." We sat together until late afternoon. He asked if I had something else to do that day.

I told him no.

I didn't choose the act, but I knew it was kind. No one else came to honor the life of the man's father, not even the neighbor he spoke of. It cost nothing but a few hours of my time. I told him I was a student, that I wanted to be a professional golfer, and that my parents owned the funeral home. He was an attorney and lived in Denver. He plays golf whenever he can. He told me about his father.

That night, I asked my dad to play golf with me the next day. And before I went to bed, I told him, "I love you, Dad."

— Nick Curry III, 19 —

I Am Home

Peace, like charity, begins at home.
~Franklin D. Roosevelt

You know how some people say that they never realized how much they loved their childhood until after they grew up? Well, I always knew that I was having a great childhood while it was happening. It wasn't until later on, when things weren't going so well, that I clung to the memories of that happiness and used them to find a way back home.

I grew up on a farm with a huge family. There was lots of love, lots of space and lots to do. From gardening to cutting hay, from working the horses to doing household chores, the word "bored" never found its way into my vocabulary— I loved it all and none of it seemed like work to me. Peer pressure was nonexistent, since the only "gang" I ran around with was the gang of animals on the ranch. My family and I were very close, and living so far out in the country kept us all at home most nights. After supper, my brothers and sisters and I would play games or tell stories, laughing and having fun until it was time to go to bed. Falling asleep was never a problem for me. I just listened to the sounds of chirping crickets and dreamed of another day on the farm. This was my life, and I knew I was lucky.

When I was 12, something tragic happened that would change my life forever. My father suffered a severe heart attack and underwent a triple bypass. He was diagnosed with hereditary heart disease, and it became a terrifying time for all of us. The doctors informed my dad that he would need to drastically change his lifestyle, which meant no more horse training, no more tractor driving… no more ranch life. Realizing that we couldn't keep up the place without him, we were forced to sell our home and move west, leaving behind family and friends and the only life that I knew.

The dry Arizona air was healing for my father, and I was adjusting to a new school, new friends and a new way of living. Suddenly I was going on dates, "cruising the mall" and dealing with the pressures of being a teenager. While things were different and strange, they were also exciting and fun. I learned that change, even when it is unexpected, can be a good thing. Little did I know that my life would be changing again, and in a very big way.

I was approached by a personal manager from Los Angeles who asked me if I had ever thought about acting. The idea had never crossed my mind, but now that it did, my interest was sparked. After giving it some thought and talking it over with my mom and dad, we decided that my mother and I would move to L.A. for a while and give it a shot. I had no idea what I was getting myself into!

Thank goodness my mother was right by my side from the very start. Together, we approached it like an adventure, and as my career grew, so did I. By the time that *Beverly Hills, 90210* had become successful, my mom and I both decided that it was time for her to return to Arizona and the rest of the family. The little girl from the farm was disappearing and being replaced by the grown-up woman in the big city.

I truly loved my job and my success was more than I could have ever dreamed of. And yet… something was missing. Slowly a dark void found its way into my heart and began to eat away at my happiness.

I tried to figure out what was missing. I tried working harder, then working less. I made new friends and lost touch with old ones. Nothing I did seemed to fill the void. I realized that I wasn't going to find the solution to the problem while going to clubs and endless parties, and living in the fast lane. I tried to remember when I was happiest, when the things in my life mattered most. I asked myself what was important to me. Finally, I had the answer. I knew what I had to do to be happy. Once again, my life was about to change.

I called my mom and dad and said, "I miss you too much. I need my parents back. I'm buying a place out here and I want you to move to California." My father wasn't too keen on the idea of being back in the rat race, but I assured him that this time, it would be nothing like that. So we began looking for a place outside of the city— a place complete with animals running all around and a garden full of vegetables just waiting to be picked for the supper table. A place that could be the family home where everyone could visit. A gathering place for the holidays. A haven, safe from the outside world. A place just like I remember growing up in.

Then one day we found it: the perfect ranch, nestled in a warm and sunny valley. My dream had become reality. The dark void that gnawed inside me began to fade, and a sense of balance and serenity returned to my soul. I was home.

—Jennie Garth—

Editor's note: Jennie Garth is an actor who played Kelly in the TV show *Beverly Hills, 90210*.

Loving Equally

We are taught you must blame your father, your sisters, your brothers, the school, the teachers — you can blame anyone, but never blame yourself. It's never your fault. But it's ALWAYS your fault, because if you wanted to change, you're the one who has got to change. It's as simple as that, isn't it?
~Katherine Hepburn

My parents had been married for eighteen years and dating since my mother was fourteen. Their marriage had been on the rocks for as long as I can remember. They had talked about divorcing many times but never went through with it for the sake of their only child, me.

One of their last fights that I can remember was very physical. My parents destroyed all of each other's belongings, and it soon came to the point where there was nothing left in the house that wasn't demolished. There were holes in the walls and pieces of everything covering the floor.

My father shoved my mother around and bruised her pretty badly, and I had to witness it all with my fourteen-year-old eyes.

Before I knew it, we were in court and I had to make the decision of whose hands to put my life into. I had to choose which parent I would live with every day. I felt like my heart was being cut out of my chest and my parents were tugging at each end of it. I loved both of my parents, and I knew one way or the other I was going to hurt one of them. After I thought for a while, I decided to live with my mom even though I knew my dad would be upset.

But it was much harder than I thought it would be. My mom was always talking about my dad and how terrible she thought he was. She still held a lot of anger inside of her heart, and she wanted to get back at my dad through me. I felt like she wanted me to love only her and to despise my father. Because I loved my dad, too, I was upset a lot and we started to argue all the time.

Nine months later, I went to live with my dad because my mother and I could no longer stand each other. I was blaming her for my feelings of confusion and anger. At first, it was better with my dad, but after only a week he started the same thing that my mother had been doing—only in reverse. My dad seemed to want me to have a lot of feelings of hatred towards my mother. I stuck it out at his house for a while. Then I began to see that he wasn't as interested in me as I thought that he would be. He never asked me when I would be home or who I was hanging out with. I had pretty much all the freedom I wanted. Without any curfews or rules, I began to feel like he didn't even care about me. I began partying too much, and my life was getting completely off track.

After I had a few fights with my dad and spent many nights alone, crying myself to sleep, I realized that I had to figure out what to do.

I recognized that there were ups and downs about living with both of them. They both had their faults and made mistakes. Neither of them wanted to admit their own mistakes, and they were both quick to point out the mistakes of the other. There was no way for me to decide who was right or who was wrong. I couldn't love one of them more than the other and leave the other one behind. I decided that I had to love both parents equally.

I could no longer let them influence me and take control of my feelings so easily. I began by asking them to please keep their feelings for each other to themselves. I think that they tried, but it didn't work. When that failed, I realized that I would have to do this myself. I'd just have to try and be strong and ignore what they said about each other. As soon as I made that decision, I felt more in control and my life began to change.

My mom and dad still say things out of anger about each other and they don't speak to one another. But do you know what? That's *their* problem. Not mine. I'm just doing the best I can to be fair to both of them. In my life, it has been a welcome change to not get caught up in their personal battles, but to focus on loving them instead.

—Nicole Peters, 15—

Editor's note: This story was originally published in *Chicken Soup for the Preteen Soul*, but we moved it to this new anniversary edition of *Chicken Soup for the Teenage Soul* based on the age of the contributor.

Together, We Can Do Anything

Sticking together as a family has always been important to my sisters, my mom and me — especially after my dad left us. I guess he didn't feel the same way about us as we did about him, and he went off to start a whole new family.

I didn't always want to talk to my mom about my feelings, because she had her own problems taking care of our ranch without my dad around. I was old enough to help out and we all pitched in, but it was still hard on her. I talked to my older sister, Alana, while we worked — and I talked to the Sisters B.

That's what we called our six cows. All of their names started with a B. They were definitely part of the family. I got my first calf when she was three days old. We bottle-fed her and named her Belle. She grew into a beautiful cow who gave birth to two other cows, Brandy and Betsey, and was grandmother to Bootsie. I gave Bootsie to my little sister, Adena. Then I got one other cow that I gave to my older sister, Alana. We named her Blue, and Blue had a calf named Bailey.

All six of the Sisters B hung out and stayed close to each other all of the time. It was clear to us that they loved each other. And we loved them, too. We showed them at local 4H shows and took really good care of them.

When my dad left, he moved down the street from us. We would see him every day, driving down the street in his truck or working in his yard. He never visited us and had a new family to keep him busy.

Finally, it was just too painful for all of us, especially my mom. We decided to sell our home and move.

We had to sell all the animals on our ranch, and we wanted to sell the Sisters B together. They were family, in more ways than one. We wanted them to go to someone who would love them like we did and be willing to keep them together. We put an ad in the paper.

We thought it was an answer to our hopes when a man called and told us he wanted to buy our cows for breeding. He told my mom that he could only pay eighteen hundred dollars for all of them, but that he had other cows, lots of pasture and a large barn.

That afternoon, my mom, my sisters and I went to his place. It looked really nice, and we were happy that we had found the right home for the Sisters B. He looked right at my sister, Adena, and told her that she could visit Bootsie anytime and that he would take special care of her. My mom told him once again that we would only sell the cows to him if he would not sell the cows separately or kill them for meat, and he promised us that he would not.

The next day it was my job to help put the Sisters B in the trailer for delivery to their new owner. They trusted us and wanted to please us so much that they went right into the trailer without even a fuss. My sisters both had tears on their faces and I could feel tears stinging my eyes, too. But I convinced myself that the Sisters B would be better off in their new home — and besides, they couldn't go with us when we moved.

A week later, while we were having our moving sale, one of our neighbors came up to my mom and told her that she had almost bought my "big red cow" before the cow went to auction. My mom said she had to be mistaken and asked who was selling the cow. When our neighbor told us who it was, I felt sick. We had trusted him, and just a week later he was selling Belle away from her baby and from the rest of her family. He had lied to us.

My mom piled us in the car and we drove to his house. When he answered the door, my mom told him what the neighbor had said and he shut the door right in our faces. My sisters were really crying now, and my mom was begging him to tell us where the Sisters B were, and to sell them back to us. Mom was crying too, but he wouldn't open the door.

I have never seen my mother so determined in my life. She told us she was going to find out where the cows were. She started calling a lot of auctions and finally found one that had a record of our cows and told us that the cows would be auctioned off the next morning at 8:00.

That night, I couldn't sleep. I kept thinking, *How could someone do something like this?* Finally, the sun started to come up and we were on our way. We arrived at the auction at 7:00 in the morning.

When we got there, we found the cows in a pen. They looked pretty bad. They had cuts all over them and looked thin, but we were just thankful that they were still alive. Belle saw us first and came right up to where we were standing. They were just as glad to see us as we were to see them. Just then a man came by who was there to buy stock, and he said it would cost us about three thousand dollars to buy our cows. I couldn't believe it! That's why we'd been deceived: the man who bought the cows from us had just wanted to make a profit.

I suggested to my mom and sisters that we get busy praying. We didn't know what else to do; we sure didn't have three thousand dollars to buy back our cows, and we didn't even know how to bid at an auction. We prayed really hard for God to show us the way.

Then Alana had an idea. She had brought some pictures of the Sisters B with her from our showing at the county fair. Every time someone arrived at the auction, she would hurry over to them, show our photos and share our story. The man who had bought the Sisters B from us was watching Alana, and when he realized that people were talking about him, and what he had done, he got all red in the face and left in a hurry. Most of the men that Alana talked to said that they wouldn't bid on our cows when they came out for auction, and that's when we got excited. Maybe we did have a chance, after all!

We waited until almost 11:00 before we saw the first of our cows. It was Brandy. Because we didn't understand the bidding process well, Alana didn't hold her number up fast enough and the men bidding on Brandy didn't see Alana. The price went up too high and we lost her. But then we understood how it worked.

Every time one of our cows would come into the ring, Alana would raise her number, and no one would bid on the cow. At one point the auctioneer stopped the whole auction and yelled that this had better stop, but everyone ignored him. Alana kept holding up her number, and the men resisted bidding on our cows. By 5:00, we had bought back all of the cows, except for Brandy, for twenty-two hundred dollars. Belle, her mother, kept mooing for her baby, and we were all sad to lose her. Mom used the eighteen hundred dollars we had from selling the cows, and we had to use our moving-sale money to make up the difference, but we had done it. We had them back!

Some friends of ours gave the Sisters B a new home. At first, we didn't get any money for them, but money wasn't as important to us as what could have happened to our cows. Recently, our friends sent us fifteen hundred dollars for the cows. After all we had sacrificed, it was a really nice surprise.

Family needs to love and protect family, and they were our family. Now when we go to visit them, they are always together — just like my mom, my sisters and me.

What happened to us was hard, but we survived and we learned a lot. Although there are dishonest people in the world, there are also many kind people who are willing to help you, even if they don't know you. But the best part is that we did it together. Together, we can do anything.

— Jarod Larson, 16 —

Editor's note: This story was originally published in *Chicken Soup for the Preteen Soul*, but we moved it to this new anniversary edition of *Chicken Soup for the Teenage Soul* based on the age of the writer.

Gains and Losses

The mind can have tremendous control of the body;
very few ailments can defeat focused energy
and a determined spirit.
~Katherine Lambert-Scronce

Most of us have experienced unforgettable moments in our lives. The moment that I will never forget happened in my family.

For the first fifteen years of my life, I was the only child in my family. I didn't have any siblings. Fortunately, I've always had my parents, who love and care about me a lot. They help solve any problem and they will do anything for me. What I'd never really thought about is that, someday, one of them could no longer be there for me.

One day, I found out that my mother was pregnant, which was big news in my family. Everyone was excited and happy, especially me. I imagined that I would have a baby brother, and I thought about playing and having fun with him. He would have a cute face and look at me with his naive eyes, begging me to play with him. I was expecting that day to come soon. I kept asking my mother questions about what my brother was going to look like, what he would eat and when he was going to be born.

Finally one morning, my mother went into labor and she and my father went to the hospital, while I went to school. Of course, I thought everything would be fine. After all, women have babies every day. Thus, I was hoping to see my baby brother as soon as I got to the hospital.

After school, when I went to the hospital, my brother had already been born. But my mother was still inside the operating room, while my father waited anxiously outside. After waiting for a long time, the doctor came out and told us that after my mother had given birth to my brother, they had trouble stopping the bleeding. He told us not to worry; my mother would be fine. Then, he went back into the operating room. Seconds later, lots of doctors and nurses rushed inside. My father and I were growing more anxious by the minute. Waiting was very painful for us, because we had finally realized that anything could happen and all we could do was wait.

At 7 p.m., my mother came out of surgery. She lay on the bed with an oxygen mask and an IV. Her skin was ghastly pale, and her eyes were closed.

"Mom, Mom…," I called to her, but she didn't react. The doctor told us that if my mother survived this night, she would be fine. Then the doctors sent my mother to the intensive-care unit.

Inside the room were many instruments for checking blood pressure, pulse rate and heart rate. Standing next to the bed, I tried to talk to my mother, whether she could hear me or not.

"You have to wake up, you have things that you have not done yet…. You have me, my father and your newborn son. You cannot just leave us… and you will be fine… trust me…."

I was scared to death. At that moment, I felt that I would lose my mother forever — that she was never going to come back.

Many thoughts flashed through my mind. *What would life be like if the unthinkable happened — life without my mother?* I could only imagine that my life would be full of darkness, sadness and hopelessness. I would lose my closest relative, my dearest friend, and I would never again have the chance to enjoy the love of my mother. Remember, during these fifteen years, my mother was always around, watching over me, no matter what. I could not imagine how I was possibly going to survive without her.

Of course, I told myself that it would not happen, that she might leave me after thirty, forty, fifty or more years, but definitely not now, not yet. It was too early. I wasn't ready to let her go.

After I slowly came back to reality, I noticed that a flood of tears was running down my cheeks.

My mother survived that night. You can imagine my great relief when she woke up the next morning. I was so excited. I gave her a big hug as I cried tears of happiness.

My mother told me that she had actually heard the words that I had said to her when she was unconscious. Three times she had almost stopped breathing, but she told herself to stay alive, for us, her family.

Later, many nurses said my mother was incredibly lucky to survive because she had lost a lot of blood. Of course, I gave them the most glorious smile, which said it all.

Today, my brother is almost two years old. On the day of his birthday, I always remember this unforgettable event in my life. I remember that I'm a really lucky person, with great parents and a wonderful little brother.

— Xiao Xi Zhang, 17 —

Editor's note: This story was originally published in *Chicken Soup for the Preteen Soul*, but we moved it to this new anniversary edition of *Chicken Soup for the Teenage Soul* based on the age of the writer.

Chapter
4

Love and Kindness

Kindness in words creates confidence. Kindness in thinking creates profoundness. Kindness in giving creates love.
~Author Unknown

Unlikely Connections in the Age of COVID-19

There are few things that are more beautifully infectious than true kindness. It spreads like a magnificent wildfire.
~Keith Wynn

I didn't have many friends before the pandemic began, so the closing down of schools and the cancelation of all social functions didn't exactly help me make more. Gone were my chances to say "hi" to people I was vaguely familiar with in the hallways, to spend lunchtimes talking about grades and stress with a friend, to tackle group projects with people I had never before spoken to.

But the fact that I didn't have a lot of deep friendships to begin with was exactly what softened the blow of isolation that many of my peers experienced more severely. Still, I craved some sort of antidote to my loneliness. At first, I browsed social media endlessly — learning about what people were reading, cooking, and doing. It seemed shallow and one-sided, though. Soon this mindless scrolling through platforms like VSCO, Instagram, and Facebook made me feel uneasy and restless.

It was Twitter that changed all that, however. There, I followed a well-known journalist who covered topics pertaining to culture in various magazines. She was my real-life, journalistic role model: I aspired to write just as prolifically as she did, and about subjects that were just as fascinating.

One day, this particular journalist/superhero posted an announcement about a pen-pal program she was starting. The rules were simple: should you want to participate, you had to sign up on a special website. After a period of time, she would match you to another of her followers and you could write a letter to your match's home address.

When I read her post, I imagined myself sitting down in my living room, in front of a well stoked fire, and writing on smooth, fancy stationery. I'd use a rollerball pen and adorn my pages with cutesy stickers. Maybe I'd even throw a teabag or two in the envelope to my dear pen-pal, before sealing it with a flourish and wishing it a fast journey.

This vision seemed magical, cozy, and somehow perfect in our pandemic-ravaged world. Of course I signed up.

My match was Kelly from California. Writing to a person who I knew absolutely nothing about was daunting, but I asked lots of introductory questions about her and her life. I wrote a little about myself, as well, and even added a small photo of my mom and me on a recent vacation.

A couple of weeks later, I received not only Kelly's letter but also Emma's (from New York), Meghan's (from California), and Isabella's (from Florida). How heartwarming it was to read through everything these women had to say to me, in their equal parts unique and adorable handwriting.

I had schoolwork to do, but I chose to procrastinate by writing immediate answers to all of their questions. My letters to each of these pen-pals could span four or five pages. I wasn't ashamed of pouring out my soul and writing of my dreams, goals, frustrations, and best memories.

It was cathartic, really. By writing to my new friends, I could start making sense of what was happening to me personally and to the whole world collectively. By hearing about others' struggles and doubts, I could also gain perspective on my own.

Being "initiated" into this club of people who still preferred handwritten letters over instant messaging had other benefits, as well. I found inspiration from other "pen-palers" who posted pictures on

Twitter of their letters: such gorgeous and precious artifacts these were. I also learned about proper letter-writing etiquette and just how many stamps you needed to affix based on envelope weight!

Maybe the journalist had started a letter-writing revolution of sorts. I mean, when else have more than 7,000 individuals worldwide participated in a carefully curated exchange of physical letters? I was honored to be a part of something so special.

Soon enough, I got to know Kelly and Meghan and Emma and Isabella better. Kelly had recently moved and was tasked with the tiresome but ultimately rewarding job of decorating her apartment. Emma lived in Manhattan and so witnessed all the big-city atrocities of COVID-19 at its peak. Meghan was married, had a view of a pond from her office window, and loved to take cooking classes. Isabella was my age and was also interested in journalism; she had started her own magazine and interviewed many inspiring creatives.

Learning all of this was a gradual process akin to watching a TV show — better than that even! The time between asking a question and getting a response took much longer than simply wondering what would happen to a character on screen and watching the next episode. It left room for much anticipation and excitement. These weren't characters, after all: they were real, accomplished, and compassionate individuals!

I finally did buy the letter-writing supplies I dreamed about. It felt so good to drop some goodies into an envelope and surprise my pals, especially if the gifts were exactly what I knew they liked or wanted. I'd finish each cozy letter-writing session with a smudged right hand, a heart full of glee, and a renewed hope in the power of human connection.

Around the start of December, the pen-pal program got a little upgrade. The journalist on Twitter made another announcement: this time, she was opening a Secret Santa exchange. It would work exactly like her previous initiative, except that, instead of letters, we would be matched with a person and send them a gift. In return, each participant would receive their own token of appreciation from a thoughtful stranger.

As soon as I got my match, I sent her a nice box of chocolates, hoping and praying that she was free of related allergies and actually liked sweets. Would this be a sufficient gift? I pondered. Being a seventeen-year-old college student, I didn't have much of an income. It's the thought that counts, I reassured myself. Besides, chocolates were an indulgent miracle perfect for wintry weather.

As the days went by, I forgot that I too would receive some sort of Secret Santa gift from a random match.

One Sunday, when I felt particularly melancholy, a beautiful and bountiful package found its way to my doorstep. I opened it anxiously and found a gift set inside containing a tumbler, three flower-adorned notebooks, a pen (which I would use, no doubt, for writing more letters!), and a carrier bag. The perfect pick-me-up. The most unexpected and wonderful gift.

My Secret Santa hadn't put a return address in her gift message, so there was really no way I could thank her directly.

Maybe that is the beauty of receiving letters and gifts from strangers through snail mail: there is no opportunity for a follow-up, in-person interaction (forced or otherwise). So everything that you send out can be genuine — stripped down to precisely what you want to convey through words or a present.

In the absence of a way to contact this stranger named Terra and thank her for her kindness, I simply extended my deepest internal gratitude to her, hoping it would stretch all the way from Virginia to Newton, Massachusetts and land safely in her heart.

— Stacia Datskovska —

Tigress

Be kind, for everyone you meet
is fighting a hard battle.
~Ian Maclaren

'm not sure how Jesse got to my clinic. He didn't look old enough to drive, although his body had begun to broaden and he moved with the grace of young manhood. His face was direct and open.

When I walked into the waiting room, Jesse was lovingly petting his cat through the open door of the carrier on his lap. With a schoolboy's faith in me, he had brought his sick cat in for me to mend.

The cat was a tiny thing, exquisitely formed, with a delicate skull and beautiful markings. She looked like she was about 15 years old, give or take a year. I could see how her spots and stripes and her fierce, bright face had evoked the image of a tiger in a child's mind, and Tigress she had become.

Age had dimmed the bright green fire of her eyes and there was a dullness there now, but she was still elegant and self-possessed. She greeted me with a friendly rub against my hand.

I began to ask questions to determine what had brought these two to see me. Unlike most adults, the young man answered simply and directly. Tigress had had a normal appetite until recently, when she'd begun to vomit a couple of times a day. Now she was not eating at all and was withdrawn and sullen. She had also lost a pound, which is a lot when you weigh only six.

Stroking Tigress, I told her how beautiful she was while I examined her eyes and mouth, listened to her heart and lungs, and felt her stomach. And then I found it: a tubular mass in mid-abdomen. Tigress politely tried to slip away. She did not like the mass being handled.

I looked at the fresh-faced teen and back at the cat he had probably had all his life. I was going to have to tell him that his beloved companion had a tumor. Even if it were surgically removed, she probably would survive less than a year, and might need weekly chemotherapy to last that long.

It would all be very difficult and expensive. So I was going to have to tell him that his cat was likely to die. And there he was, all alone.

It seemed he was about to learn one of life's toughest lessons: that death is something that happens to every living thing. It is an omnipresent part of life. How death is first experienced can be life-forming, and it seemed that I was going to be the one to guide him through his first. I did not want to make any mistakes. It had to be done perfectly, or he might end up emotionally scarred.

It would have been easy to shirk this task and summon a parent. But when I looked at his face, I could not do it. He knew something was wrong. I could not just ignore him. So I talked to Jesse as Tigress's rightful owner and told him as gently as I could what I had found, and what it meant.

As I spoke, Jesse jerked convulsively away from me, probably so I could not see his face, but I had seen it begin to twist as he turned. I sat down and turned to Tigress, to give Jesse some privacy, and stroked her beautiful old face while I discussed the alternatives with him: I could do a biopsy of the mass, let her fade away at home, or give her an injection and put her to sleep.

Jesse listened carefully and nodded. He said he didn't think she was very comfortable anymore, and he didn't want her to suffer. He was trying very hard. The pair of them broke my heart. I offered to call a parent to explain what was going on.

Jesse gave me his father's number. I went over everything again with the father while Jesse listened and petted his cat. Then I let the father speak to his son. Jesse paced and gestured and his voice broke a few times, but when he hung up, he turned to me with dry eyes and said they had decided to put her to sleep.

No arguing, no denial, no hysteria, just acceptance of the inevitable. I could see, though, how much it was costing him. I asked if he wanted to take her home overnight to say good-bye. But he said no. He just wanted to be alone with her for a few minutes.

I left them and went to sign out the barbiturate I would use to ease her into a painless sleep. I could not control the tears streaming down my face, or the grief I felt welling up inside for Jesse, who had to become a man so quickly and so alone.

I waited outside the exam room. In a few minutes he came out and said that he was ready. I asked if he wanted to stay with her. He looked surprised, but I explained that it was often easier to observe how peaceful it was than forever to wonder how it actually happened.

Immediately seeing the logic of that, Jesse held her head and reassured her while I administered the injection. She drifted off to sleep, her head cradled in his hand.

The animal looked quiet and at rest. The owner now bore all the suffering. This was the finest gift you could give, I said, to assume another's pain so that a loved one might rest.

He nodded. He understood.

Something was missing, though. I did not feel I had completed my task. It came to me suddenly that though I had asked him to become a man instantly, and he had done so with grace and strength, he was still a young man.

I held out my arms and asked him if he needed a hug. He did indeed, and in truth, so did I.

— Judith S. Johnessee —

Bright Heart

The greatest gift is a portion of thyself.
~Ralph Waldo Emerson

L ast year around Halloween, I was invited to participate in a carnival for Tuesday's Child, an organization that helps children with the AIDS virus. I was asked to attend because I'm on a television show; I went because I care. I don't think that most of the kids recognized me as a celebrity. They just thought of me as a big kid who came to play with them for the day. I think I liked it better that way.

At the carnival they had all kinds of booths. I was drawn to one in particular because of all the children that had gathered there. At this booth, anyone who wanted to could paint a square. Later that square was going to be sewn together with the others, to make a quilt. The quilt would be presented to a man who had dedicated much of his life to this organization and would soon be retiring.

They gave everyone fabric paints in bright, beautiful colors and asked the kids to paint something that would make the quilt beautiful. As I looked around at all the squares, I saw pink hearts and bright blue clouds, beautiful orange sunrises and green and purple flowers. The pictures were all bright, positive and uplifting. All except for one.

The boy sitting next to me was painting a heart, but it was dark, empty, lifeless. It lacked the bright, vibrant colors that his fellow artists had used.

At first I thought maybe he took the only paint that was left and it just happened to be dark. But when I asked him about it, he said his heart was that color because his own heart felt dark. I asked him why and he told me that he was very sick. Not only was he very sick, but his mom was very sick also. He said that his sickness was not ever going to get better and neither was his mom's. He looked straight into my eyes and said, "There is nothing anyone can do that will help."

I told him I was sorry that he was sick and I could certainly understand why he was so sad. I could even understand why he had made his heart a dark color. But... I told him that it isn't true that there is nothing anyone can do to help. Other people may not be able to make him or his mom better... but we can do things like give bear hugs, which in my experience can really help when you are feeling sad. I told him that if he would like, I would be happy to give him one so he could see what I meant. He instantly crawled into my lap and I thought my own heart would burst with the love I felt for this sweet little boy.

He sat there for a long time and when he had had enough, he jumped down to finish his coloring. I asked him if he felt any better and he said that he did, but he was still sick and nothing would change that. I told him I understood. I walked away feeling sad, but recommitted to this cause. I would do whatever I could to help.

As the day was coming to an end and I was getting ready to head home, I felt a tug on my jacket. I turned around and standing there with a smile on his face was the little boy. He said, "My heart is changing colors. It is getting brighter... I think those bear hugs really do work."

On my way home I felt my own heart and realized it, too, had changed to a brighter color.

— Jennifer Love Hewitt —

Editor's note: Jennifer Love Hewitt is an actor who played Sarah on the TV show *Party of Five*.

The Secret of Happiness

If you would be loved, love and be lovable.
~Benjamin Franklin

There is a wonderful fable about a young orphan girl who had no family and no one to love her. One day, feeling exceptionally sad and lonely, she was walking through a meadow when she noticed a small butterfly caught unmercifully in a thorn bush. The more the butterfly struggled to free itself, the deeper the thorns cut into its fragile body. The young orphan girl carefully released the butterfly from its captivity. Instead of flying away, the little butterfly changed into a beautiful fairy. The young girl rubbed her eyes in disbelief.

"For your wonderful kindness," the good fairy said to the girl, "I will grant you any wish you would like."

The little girl thought for a moment and then replied, "I want to be happy!"

The fairy said, "Very well," and leaned toward her and whispered in her ear. Then the good fairy vanished.

As the little girl grew up, there was no one in the land as happy as she. Everyone asked her the secret of her happiness. She would only smile and answer, "The secret of my happiness is that I listened to a good fairy when I was a little girl."

When she was very old and on her deathbed the neighbors all rallied around her, afraid that her fabulous secret of happiness would die with her. "Tell us, please," they begged. "Tell us what the good fairy said."

The lovely old woman simply smiled and said, "She told me that everyone, no matter how secure they seemed, no matter how old or young, how rich or poor, had need of me."

— The Speaker's Sourcebook —

Mrs. Link

I was 18, about to start college, and broke. To make some money, I plodded down a quiet street of older homes, selling books door-to-door. As I approached one gate, a tall, handsome woman in her eighties came to the gate in her bathrobe. "There you are, darling! I've been waiting for you! God told me you'd be coming today." Mrs. Link needed help around her yard and house, and, apparently, I was the one for the job. Who was I to argue with God?

The next day I worked for six hours, harder than I had ever worked before. Mrs. Link showed me how to plant bulbs, what flowers and weeds to pull up, and where to haul the wilted plants. I finished off the day by mowing the lawn with a mower that looked like an antique. When I had finished, Mrs. Link complimented me on my work and looked under the mower at the blade. "Looks like you hit a stone. I'll get the file." I soon learned why everything Mrs. Link owned looked like an antique, but worked like brand-new. For six hours of work she gave me a check for three dollars. It was 1978. God's funny sometimes, isn't he?

The next week I cleaned Mrs. Link's house. She showed me exactly how to vacuum her antique Persian rug with her antique-looking vacuum. As I dusted her beautiful treasures, she told me where she had acquired them while she traveled the world. For lunch she sautéed fresh vegetables from her garden. We shared a delicious meal and a lovely day.

Some weeks I got to be a chauffeur. The last gift to Mrs. Link from Mr. Link was a glorious new car. By the time I met Mrs. Link, the car was 30 years old, but still glorious. Mrs. Link was never able to have children, but her sister, nieces and nephews lived nearby. Her neighbors also were fond of her, and she was active in civic affairs.

A year and a half passed since I met Mrs. Link. School, work and church were taking up more of my time, and I saw Mrs. Link less and less. I found another girl to help her around the house.

Valentine's Day was coming, and being very undemonstrative and very broke, I was compiling a very short list of my valentines. Mom glanced at my list and said, "You need to get Mrs. Link a valentine."

I incredulously asked, "Why? Mrs. Link has a lot of family, friends and neighbors. She's active in the community. I don't even spend a lot of time with her anymore. Why would Mrs. Link want a valentine from me?"

Mom was unimpressed. "Get Mrs. Link a valentine," she insisted.

On Valentine's Day I self-consciously presented Mrs. Link a small bouquet, which she graciously accepted.

A couple of months later, I visited Mrs. Link again. Centered on her mantel, in her living room full of beautiful things, stood my wilted and faded Valentine's Day bouquet — the only valentine Mrs. Link received that year.

— Susan Daniels Adams —

A Mason-Dixon Memory

Dondre Green glanced uneasily at the civic leaders and sports figures filling the hotel ballroom in Cleveland. They had come from across the nation to attend a fundraiser for the National Minority College Golf Scholarship Foundation. I was the banquet's featured entertainer. Dondre, an 18-year-old high-school senior from Monroe, Louisiana, was the evening's honored guest.

"Nervous?" I asked the handsome young man in his starched white shirt and rented tuxedo.

"A little," he whispered, grinning.

One month earlier, Dondre had been just one more Black student attending a predominantly white Southern school. Although most of his friends and classmates were white, Dondre's race had never been an issue. Then, on April 17, 1991, Dondre's black skin provoked an incident that made nationwide news.

"Ladies and gentlemen," the emcee said, "our special guest, Dondre Green."

As the audience stood applauding, Dondre walked to the microphone and began his story. "I love golf," he said quietly. "For the past two years, I've been a member of the St. Frederick High School golf team. And though I was the only Black member, I've always felt at home playing at mostly white country clubs across Louisiana."

The audience leaned forward; even the waiters and busboys stopped to listen. As I listened, a memory buried in my heart since childhood began fighting its way to life.

"Our team had driven from Monroe," Dondre continued. "When we arrived at the Caldwell Parish Country Club in Columbia, we walked to the putting green."

Dondre and his teammates were too absorbed to notice the conversation between a man and St. Frederick athletic director James Murphy. After disappearing into the clubhouse, Murphy returned to his players.

"I want to see the seniors," he said. "On the double!" His face seemed strained as he gathered the four students, including Dondre.

"I don't know how to tell you this," he said, "but the Caldwell Parish Country Club is reserved for whites only." Murphy paused and looked at Dondre. His teammates glanced at each other in disbelief. "I want you seniors to decide what our response should be," Murphy continued. "If we leave, we forfeit this tournament. If we stay, Dondre can't play."

As I listened, my own childhood memory from 32 years ago broke free.

In 1959, I was 13 years old, a poor Black kid living with my mother and stepfather in a small black ghetto on Long Island, New York. My mother worked nights in a hospital, and my stepfather drove a coal truck. Needless to say, our standard of living was somewhat short of the American dream.

Nevertheless, when my eighth-grade teacher announced a graduation trip to Washington, D.C., it never crossed my mind that I would be left behind. Besides a complete tour of the nation's capital, we would visit Glen Echo Amusement Park in Maryland. In my imagination, Glen Echo was Disneyland, Knott's Berry Farm and Magic Mountain rolled into one.

My heart beating wildly, I raced home to deliver the mimeographed letter describing the journey. But when my mother saw how much the trip would cost, she just shook her head. We couldn't afford it.

After feeling sad for 10 seconds, I decided to try to fund the trip myself. For the next eight weeks, I sold candy bars door-to-door, delivered newspapers and mowed lawns. Three days before the deadline, I'd made just barely enough. I was going!

The day of the trip, trembling with excitement, I climbed onto the train. I was the only nonwhite in our section.

Our hotel was not far from the White House. My roommate was Frank Miller, the son of a businessman. Leaning together out of our window and dropping water balloons on tourists quickly cemented our new friendship.

Every morning, almost a hundred of us loaded noisily onto our bus for another adventure. We sang our school fight song dozens of times — en route to Arlington National Cemetery, and even on an afternoon cruise down the Potomac River.

We visited the Lincoln Memorial twice, once in daylight, the second time at dusk. My classmates and I fell silent as we walked in the shadows of those 36 marble columns, one for every state in the Union that Lincoln labored to preserve. I stood next to Frank at the base of the 19-foot seated statue. Spotlights made the white Georgian marble seem to glow. Together, we read those famous words from Lincoln's speech at Gettysburg, remembering the most bloody battle in the War between the States: "…we here highly resolve that these dead shall not have died in vain — that this nation, under God, shall have a new birth of freedom…"

As Frank motioned me into place to take my picture, I took one last look at Lincoln's face. He seemed alive and so terribly sad.

The next morning, I understood a little better why he wasn't smiling. "Clifton," a chaperone said, "could I see you for a moment?"

The other guys at my table, especially Frank, turned pale. We had been joking about the previous night's direct water balloon hit on a lady and her poodle. It was a stupid, dangerous act, but luckily nobody got hurt. We were celebrating our escape from punishment when the chaperone asked to see me.

"Clifton," she began, "do you know about the Mason-Dixon line?"

"No," I said, wondering what this had to do with drenching ladies.

"Before the Civil War," she explained, "the Mason-Dixon line was originally the boundary between Maryland and Pennsylvania — the dividing line between the slave and free states." Having escaped one disaster, I could feel another brewing. I noticed that her eyes were damp and her hands were shaking.

"Today," she continued, "the Mason-Dixon line is a kind of invisible border between the North and the South. When you cross that invisible line out of Washington, D.C. into Maryland, things change."

There was an ominous drift to this conversation, but I wasn't following it. Why did she look and sound so nervous?

"Glen Echo Amusement Park is in Maryland," she said at last, "and the management doesn't allow Negroes inside." She stared at me in silence.

I was still grinning and nodding when the meaning finally sank in.

"You mean I can't go to the park," I stuttered, "because I'm a Negro?"

She nodded slowly. "I'm sorry, Clifton," she said, taking my hand. "You'll have to stay in the hotel tonight. Why don't you and I watch a movie on television?"

I walked to the elevators feeling confusion, disbelief, anger and a deep sadness. "What happened, Clifton?" Frank said when I got back to the room. "Did the lady tell on us?"

Without saying a word, I walked over to my bed, lay down and began to cry. Frank was stunned to silence. Junior-high boys didn't cry, at least not in front of each other.

It wasn't just missing the class adventure that made me feel so sad. For the first time in my life, I was learning what it felt like to be a "nigger."

Of course there was discrimination in the North, but the color of my skin had never officially kept me out of a coffee shop, a church — or an amusement park.

"Clifton," Frank whispered, "what is the matter?"

"They won't let me go to Glen Echo Park tonight," I sobbed.

"Because of the water balloon?" he asked.

"No," I answered, "because I'm a Negro."

"Well, that's a relief!" Frank said, and then he laughed, obviously relieved to have escaped punishment for our caper with the balloons. "I thought it was serious."

Wiping away the tears with my sleeve, I stared at him. "It is serious. They don't let Negroes into the park. I can't go with you!" I shouted. "That's pretty damn serious to me."

I was about to wipe the silly grin off Frank's face with a blow to his jaw when I heard him say, "Then I won't go either."

For an instant we just froze. Then Frank grinned. I will never forget that moment. Frank was just a kid. He wanted to go to that amusement park as much as I did, but there was something even more important than the class night out. Still, he didn't explain or expand.

The next thing I knew, the room was filled with kids listening to Frank. "They don't allow Negroes in the park," he said, "so I'm staying with Clifton."

"Me too," a second boy said.

"Those jerks," a third muttered. "I'm with you, Clifton." My heart began to race. Suddenly, I was not alone. A pint-sized revolution had been born. The "water balloon brigade," 11 white boys from Long Island, had made its decision: "We won't go." And as I sat on my bed in the center of it all, I felt grateful. But, above all, I was filled with pride.

Dondre Green's story brought that childhood memory back to life. His golfing teammates, like my childhood friends, had an important decision to make: standing by their friend when it would cost them dearly. But when it came time to decide, no one hesitated. "Let's get out of here," one of them whispered.

"They just turned and walked toward the van," Dondre told us. "They didn't debate it. And the younger players joined us without looking back."

Dondre was astounded by the response of his friends — and the people of Louisiana. The whole state was outraged and tried to make it right. The Louisiana House of Representatives proclaimed a Dondre Green Day and passed legislation permitting lawsuits for damages, attorneys' fees and court costs against any private facility that invites a team, then bars any member because of race.

As Dondre concluded, his eyes glistened with tears. "I love my coach and my teammates for sticking by me," he said. "It goes to show that there are always good people who will not give in to bigotry. The kind of love they showed me that day will conquer hatred every time."

My friends, too, had shown that kind of love. As we sat in the hotel, a chaperone came in waving an envelope. "Boys!" he shouted. "I've just bought 13 tickets to the Senators-Tigers game. Anybody want to go?"

The room erupted in cheers. Not one of us had ever been to a professional baseball game in a real baseball park.

On the way to the stadium, we grew silent as our driver paused before the Lincoln Memorial. For one long moment, I stared through the marble pillars at Mr. Lincoln, bathed in that warm, yellow light. There was still no smile and no sign of hope in his sad and tired eyes.

"…We here highly resolve… that this nation, under God, shall have a new birth of freedom…" In his words and in his life, Lincoln had made it clear that freedom is not free. Every time the color of a person's skin keeps him out of an amusement park or off a country club fairway, the war for freedom begins again. Sometimes the battle is fought with fists and guns, but more often the most effective weapon is a simple act of love and courage.

Whenever I hear those words from Lincoln's speech at Gettysburg, I remember my 11 white friends, and I feel hope once again. I like to imagine that when we paused that night at the foot of his great monument, Mr. Lincoln smiled at last. As Dondre said, "The kind of love they showed me that day will conquer hatred every time."

— Clifton Davis, actor —

A Gift for Two

*You never know what happiness a simple act
of kindness will bring about.*
~Bree Abel

It was a beautiful day for sightseeing around downtown Portland. We were a bunch of counselors on our day off, away from the campers, just out for some fun. The weather was perfect for a picnic, so when lunch time came, we set our sights on a small park in town. Since we all had different cravings, we decided to split up, get what each of us wanted, and meet back on the grass in a few minutes.

When my friend Robby headed for a hot dog stand, I decided to keep her company. We watched the vendor put together the perfect hot dog, just the way Robby wanted it. But when she took out her money to pay him, the man surprised us.

"It looks a little on the cool side," he said, "so never mind paying me. This will be my freebie of the day."

We said our thanks, joined our friends in the park, and dug into our food. But as we talked and ate, I was distracted by a man sitting alone nearby, looking at us. I could tell that he hadn't showered for days. Another homeless person, I thought, like all the others you see in cities. I didn't pay much more attention than that.

We finished eating and decided to head off for more sightseeing. But when Robby and I went to the garbage can to throw away my lunch bag, I heard a strong voice ask, "There isn't any food in that bag, is there?"

It was the man who had been watching us. I didn't know what

to say. "No, I ate it already."

"Oh," was his only answer, with no shame in his voice at all. He was obviously hungry, couldn't bear to see anything thrown away, and was used to asking this question.

I felt bad for the man, but I didn't know what I could do. That's when Robby said, "I'll be right back. Please wait for me a minute," and ran off. I watched curiously as she went across to the hot dog stand. Then I realized what she was doing. She bought a hot dog, crossed back to the trash can, and gave the hungry man the food.

When she came back to us, Robby said simply, "I was just passing on the kindness that someone gave to me."

That day I learned how generosity can go farther than the person you give to. By giving, you teach others how to give also.

— Andrea Hensley —

Like People First

The more we know the better we forgive.
Whoever feels deeply, feels for all who live.
~Madame de Staël

Craig, a close friend of mine in graduate school, brought energy and life into any room he entered. He focused his entire attention on you while you were talking, and you felt incredibly important. People loved him.

One sunny autumn day, Craig and I were sitting in our usual study area. I was staring out the window when I noticed one of my professors crossing the parking lot.

"I don't want to run into him," I said.

"Why not?" Craig asked.

I explained that the previous spring semester, the professor and I had parted on bad terms. I had taken offense at some suggestion he had made and had, in turn, given offense in my answer. "Besides," I added, "the guy just doesn't like me."

Craig looked down at the passing figure. "Maybe you've got it wrong," he said. "Maybe you're the one who's turning away — and you're just doing that because you're afraid. He probably thinks you don't like him, so he's not friendly. People like people who like them. If you show an interest in him, he'll be interested in you. Go talk to him."

Craig's words smarted. I walked tentatively down the stairs into the parking lot. I greeted my professor warmly and asked how his summer had been. He looked at me, genuinely surprised. We walked off together talking, and I could imagine Craig watching from the window, smiling broadly.

Craig had explained to me a simple concept, so simple I couldn't believe I'd never known it. Like most young people, I felt unsure of myself and came to all my encounters fearing that others would judge me — when, in fact, they were worrying about how I would judge *them*. From that day on, instead of seeing judgment in the eyes of others, I recognized the need people have to make a connection and to share something about themselves. I discovered a world of people I never would have known otherwise.

Once, for example, on a train going across Canada, I began talking to a man everyone was avoiding because he was weaving and slurring his speech as if drunk. It turned out that he was recovering from a stroke. He had been an engineer on the same line we were riding, and long into the night he revealed to me the history beneath every mile of track: Pile O'Bones Creek, named for the thousands of buffalo skeletons left there by Indian hunters; the legend of Big Jack, a Swedish track-layer who could lift 500-pound steel rails; a conductor named McDonald who kept a rabbit as his traveling companion.

As the morning sun began to tint the horizon, he grabbed my hand and looked into my eyes. "Thanks for listening. Most people wouldn't bother." He didn't have to thank me. The pleasure had been all mine.

On a noisy street corner in Oakland, California, a family who stopped me for directions turned out to be visiting from Australia's isolated northwest coast. I asked them about their life back home. Soon, over coffee, they regaled me with stories of huge saltwater crocodiles "with backs as wide as car hoods."

Each encounter became an adventure, each person a lesson in life. The wealthy, the poor, the powerful and the lonely; all were as full of dreams and doubts as I. And each had a unique story to tell, if only I were willing to hear.

An old, stubble-bearded hobo told me how he'd fed his family during the Depression by firing his shotgun into a pond and gathering up the stunned fish that floated to the surface. A traffic patrolman confided how he'd learned his hand gestures by watching bullfighters and symphony conductors. And a young beautician shared the joy of watching residents in a nursing home smile after receiving a new hairstyle.

How often we allow such opportunities to pass us by. The girl who everyone thinks is homely, the boy with the odd clothes — those people have stories to tell, as surely as you do. And like you, they dream that someone is willing to hear.

This is what Craig knew. Like people first, ask questions later. See if the light you shine on others isn't reflected back on you a hundredfold.

— Kent Nerburn —

Lilacs Bloom Every Spring

When it comes down to it, we all just want to be loved.
~Jamie Yellin, age 14

Today (here is my cue to sigh) is one of my bad days. Everything feels out of my reach, but I'm especially dreading my psychology class next hour. As a silly final project for the year, we are to bring a photo of ourselves that represents a truly happy time in our childhood.

The trouble was not in selecting a photo — I knew right away the one to bring. Framed on my desk is a picture of Grandma Sherrie, now dead, and myself, when I was eight years old. She had taken me on a lengthy bus ride to a lilac festival in the spring. We spent the afternoon sniffing, eyes closed, bent over lilac blossoms. The picture was taken by a really funny old man, who told us hilarious stories as he walked us to the bus stop late in the afternoon. We never saw him again, but looking back I wonder if he was smitten with Grandma Sherrie.

Looking at the picture, as I wait for my lunch period to end, I know my grandma's beauty isn't there in the photo — short, straight, silver hair, and large, slightly protuberant brown eyes. The nose is too big and the forehead is too high. She is short and a little squat. Beside her, clutching her hand, I am a smaller, younger replica. We even had the same narrow, skinny feet and unbelievably long toes. Had. Now it's just my ridiculous feet to laugh at, except that I haven't found anyone with whom it's quite as funny as it was with her. When she died two years ago, I lost some of my reality.

So this is the only picture I could bring. I can't miss an opportunity to bring her back a little bit, to celebrate her imprint on life. Even though I know that few, if any, will appreciate the gift I foolishly, eagerly share.

I sit down at my desk, feeling relief at arriving safely. Somehow the halls are where I feel the most isolated. Surrounded by people, I am more aware than ever of how far away I am from them. I have no one to walk with, or shriek gossip to. I see these same people every day, brush against them sometimes. But I don't know them any more than a stranger on the street. We don't even make eye contact.

As people trickle in, I sit with the picture in my lap, framed by my hands. *Why didn't I bring another? Why was I so sure my words could explain?*

The teacher steps to the front of the room. I don't like her any more than she likes me. She prefers students who stay after class to talk about boyfriends and complain about curfews. I stay after to show her articles about new treatments for autism. I'd like her to like me, even though I can't respect her.

She asks for volunteers to begin the presentations. She smiles expectantly at me in the front row. (Where else would I be?) I rise to my feet, the ultimate volunteer-to go-firster. A voice from behind.

"I bet she brought a picture of her first set of encyclopedias." *Nope, sorry, that one's framed over the fireplace.*

Eyes, all these eyes looking at me with that blank stare reserved for observation without attention or thought.

"This is a photograph of my Grandma Sherrie and me when I was eight years old. She took me to a lilac festival. It was an annual event." *Event?* I should have said something else. "They had all sorts of lilacs, rare and common varieties, pinks and purples and whites. It was wonderful." *Boring.*

I looked down at the photo. The woman and the girl, holding hands framed by a tall hedge dotted with sprays of purple lilac blooms. The pair seems ready to march off and conquer the world, just the two of them in their sensible walking shoes.

"When I look at this picture, I can almost smell the lilacs. Especially now, in the spring. It was a perfect outing, and after we went home, my grandma made me spaghetti, and let me put chocolate sprinkles on my ice cream…" Getting a little off topic here. I'm losing the audience I never had.

"But it was a perfect day, um, like I said. It's hard to remember another day like that as I got older. My grandma got sick when I was nine…" suddenly, there are tears on my cheeks. "…and she never got better." Time to run, escape, at least sit down.

I thud into my chair, clutching the picture. No applause. The teacher abruptly, too cheerfully, calls on someone else. The class is soon over, after 10 or 12 years pass. I escape to the whirling chaos in the hallway.

Talk about a bad day.

But, like they say, there is always tomorrow. Which to me it seems to imply there's no use in getting through today, because you'll just have to do it again in less than 24 hours.

But here I am, tomorrow, at the door to my psych class, feeling like I just left. Only today, I'm late, having dropped a folder that spewed its contents with abandon. Everyone is looking at me. The day before I had broken two big rules. I not only displayed excessive emotion but admitted that I really cared about something as inconsequential as a grandmother. Well, I'm invisible one day and the next the object of public scorn. Both unenviable life situations. I move to my desk. There is a paper shopping bag on the seat of the chair. Expecting a smelly gym uniform and tennis shoes, I look inside without thinking.

Oh. Oh. My God. I feel my outline melt.

The bag is full of lilac branches. I can smell them with my soul, can feel them with a part of me I thought had withered and died. *Am I still in my real life?* I look up. Everyone is still staring blankly. But it must be one of them, some sentimental rebel in disguise. Which one?

I move the bag and sit down. The teacher is annoyed.

"Shall we begin, folks? Your presentations yesterday will be counted…"

There is a piece of paper tucked among the blossoms. I open it to find two lines:

We will find our right to be.
Until then, lilacs bloom every spring.

— Reprinted with permission from *Blue Jeans Magazine* —

Paint Brush

I keep my paint brush with me
Wherever I may go,
In case I need to cover up
So the real me doesn't show.
I'm so afraid to show you me,
Afraid of what you'll do — that
You might laugh or say mean things.
I'm afraid I might lose you.

I'd like to remove all my paint coats
To show you the real, true me,
But I want you to try and understand,
I need you to accept what you see.
So if you'll be patient and close your eyes,
I'll strip off all my coats real slow.
Please understand how much it hurts
To let the real me show.

Now my coats are all stripped off.
I feel naked, bare and cold,
And if you still love me with all that you see,
You are my friend, pure as gold.

I need to save my paint brush, though,
And hold it in my hand,
I want to keep it handy
In case somebody doesn't understand.
So please protect me, my dear friend
And thanks for loving me true,
But please let me keep my paint brush with me
Until I love me, too.

—Bettie B. Youngs—

Learning

*School has taught me not only how to learn in the classroom,
but outside the classroom as well. Where do you think I learned
how to climb, swing and skip? Where do you think I learned
how to meet my best friend?*
~Jessie Braun, age 18

Lessons from Loss

You don't go around grieving all the time,
but the grief is still there and always will be.
~Nigella Lawson

I ran down the beach in a panic, the salty air burning my lungs as I called out again and again. The roar of the waves drowned out my words. I had to find… what did I have to find? I couldn't remember and my anxiety rose. Tears streamed down my face, and I sobbed as a deep sense of loss overcame me. I screamed but no sound came out.

I sat straight up in bed, drenched in sweat, my heart pounding. It took a moment before I got my bearings and calmed my breathing. That was the most vivid nightmare I had ever had in my life. I sat on the edge of my bed, the late morning sun shining through the crack in my curtains. I didn't know what to think about what I had just experienced, but I decided I would think about it later as I stood and made my way to the bathroom. It was April Fool's day and a Saturday, and while I was happy that I didn't have to deal with all the April Fool's jokes at school, I still had to contend with the pranks my friends and family liked to pull.

I got dressed and went outside to meet up with some of my friends. My sister intercepted me on the patio of our family's three-bedroom, bottom floor apartment. She looked upset, but I was on guard. It was April Fool's Day, after all.

"I have some bad news, Tabby," she said, her eyes brimming with unshed tears. My middle sister, Shanna, could have been an actress, that's how good she was at faking emotions to make someone believe that she was being serious. I waited for her to deliver the "bad news" and then spring the old "April Fool's" joke at me. "Dean was skateboarding across the highway this morning," she continued. "He went across in front of a car, thinking he could make it, but he got hit."

"What?" That had not been something I was expecting her to say. What kind of April Fool's joke was that? I suddenly got angry. "You don't joke about that kind of stuff, Shanna. It's not funny." I'd met Dean three years before when my family moved from Laurel to the Mississippi Gulf Coast, and over those three years my feelings went from friendship to first love pretty rapidly.

"It's not a joke, Tabby. He's in the hospital right now. They don't know if he's going to make it." My whole body went numb and I sat down on the ground unable to speak, and unable to believe what she just told me. It wasn't possible. Dean was thirteen; he was too young for this kind of thing to happen to him.

The next few days were a blur. I don't remember eating, sleeping or even moving. I could tell my family was worried about me because I hadn't cried yet. I'm not sure if that was due to being in shock or because I still didn't believe that he had been hurt. April 4th was a Tuesday and I had to go to school. I went through the motions in my classes but didn't listen to anything that was being taught. How could I pay attention to anything when someone I cared about that deeply was battling for his life?

I don't remember what class period I was in when the announcement came over the intercom and they called us for an assembly. The whole school gathered in the gym. My friends Maggie and Tori sat next to me to make sure I was okay. They knew what happened and knew how I felt about Dean, so they were just as worried as my family about my lack of emotion.

"...was hit by a car while crossing the highway Saturday, and succumbed to his injuries this morning," the principal said. Maggie's grip on my hand tightened, and I looked up at her. Tears were streaming down her face, but there were no tears in my eyes.

Maggie hugged me tight. "I'm so sorry, Tabby," she said. I didn't know how to react. The numbness settled deeper and bottled up my emotions. He couldn't be dead. I absolutely refused to believe it.

The funeral was scheduled for that Friday. Students who wanted to attend the funeral were given an excused absence that day, and I found myself sandwiched in the back seat of Shanna's friend Trish's car. We were heading to the funeral home for the viewing and then to the cemetery at the church next to the middle school I attended. Dean's parents said we could bring something to put in the casket to be buried with him, so in my lap, clenched tightly in my hands, was a notebook with a few poems I had written for Dean telling him how I truly felt about him. I remember thinking how stupid it was, that he would never be able to read them and would never know my true feelings, all because I'd been too scared of him rejecting me and losing our friendship to tell him while he was still alive.

We reached the funeral home and I sat numb throughout Dean's family and friends speaking about his life, and that, even though he was gone, he would live on in our hearts and in the lives of the people who were saved by his donated organs. The line was long to view the body, and it was a while before it was my turn. I approached the casket, looked down and thought, "It's not him. It doesn't look like him." And that was when the floodgates that had been holding back my grief burst wide open. Once the tears began to flow, they wouldn't stop.

I cried all the way back to the car, to the cemetery, all through the funeral, on the way back to the car and most of the way home with a bunch of Shanna's friends crammed into the car with us. As we were turning off the highway, the song "Another One Bites the Dust" by Queen came on the radio. The whole situation, with all of us crammed into the car and that song coming on the radio just after the funeral was so ridiculous that we all burst out laughing.

It was a sign from Dean, we all thought. He was telling us not to be sad that he was gone, but rather to celebrate the life he did have. He always did like to laugh and to make people laugh, and his smile and laugh were so contagious that you couldn't help but join in.

I still think about Dean all these years later and I've never stopped loving him. Sometimes I wonder what things would have been like for him had he lived. Would I have ever told him how I felt? Would we have dated, gotten married, had a family? And then I remember that ridiculous ride home after the funeral and realize that he wouldn't want me to live my life always thinking of the "what if's." The fact of the matter is, he would want me to LIVE. So, when something happens that is out of my control, and my life seems like it's going askew, I remember Dean and the lessons losing him taught me.

— T.C. Zimmerman —

Time to Think

We cannot lead anyone farther
than we have been ourselves.
~John C. Maxwell

It was the last day of the month-long summer camp. All the camp leaders and volunteers were preparing for the grand wrap-up event that evening. Some were setting up chairs and tables outside; some were preparing water balloons for games we would play later; and some were cutting fruits and veggies for snacks.

The pastor came to me, handed me a small broom and a dustpan, and asked me to sweep the gym. Alone. While the others were chatting and laughing outside. While the gym was dusty and stuffy after weeks of camp and crafts.

I didn't have a choice. I was sixteen, and the pastor was my elder. I was a staff member at camp, and this pastor was my employer. I put on as cheerful a face as I could and began to sweep the floor of the gymnasium.

Every time I made a decent pile of dust and scraps to push into the dustpan, I had a nice little part of the gym cleared. But I would look up and see the rest of the gym and realize how big the job was. The whole situation felt so unfair.

I wasn't really happy then. I'm not proud of it, but I was angry as well. I could hear the sounds of people talking, laughing, and generally having a great time outside. There was silence in the gym, except for my *sweep, sweep, sweep.*

During a break between sweeps, I looked up. The same pastor

who told me to sweep the gym was quietly and matter-of-factly moving the speakers and cleaning the stage at the front of the gym. I noticed he worked alone as well. He didn't seem particularly excited about what he was doing, but I noted the calmness and joy in his eyes as he went about his work, doing what had to be done because he was there and he was able to do it.

I watched him surreptitiously for the next ten minutes. My broom and I were making slow but sure progress across the gym. Slowly, my unhappiness and resentment left my heart, and in its place grew an appreciation for what I saw in the pastor, and why he had asked me to complete this job.

First, being a leader doesn't mean getting to do all the fun things, all the time. It means sacrifice. It means hard work. To be a good leader, it means doing things one doesn't really enjoy with a cheerful, genuine smile. I realized *that* wasn't the way I had led my teams throughout the summer.

Second, taking the time to think is crucial to being a good leader — or being "good" at anything, really. Without time for reflection, you might get lost in the hustle and bustle of everything. You might overlook what's more important, such as connecting with others on a personal level, building character, and actually making a difference in the lives of other people. I saw that I had thrust myself headlong into camp and had not slowed down to think and improve on what I was saying or doing as a leader.

Third, no matter how simple or complex a task may be, no matter how long you have to work on it, you have to stick to the task. It didn't seem like I could clean the whole gym with a small broom. But I did, one sweep at a time.

I passed the pastor on my way to the garbage bin beside the doorway of the gym. He looked up and smiled at me — and I smiled back. I was tired; it was a tired smile; but it was a real smile.

"Thanks, Odelia." He nodded at the front door leading to where the other teens were, as if acknowledging the small sacrifice I had made.

I forgot what I said in return. Probably "You're welcome."

But what I should have said — and what I want to say to him

now is this:

"Thank you for teaching me — and showing me — what being a good leader looks like. Thank you for forcing me to do something I would rather not do — and getting me to think through things I would have otherwise overlooked. Thank you for the opportunity to sweep the floor of the gym, because now whenever I feel discouraged or resentful, I remember that half hour, and am reminded that doing the hard, right thing matters, no matter how I feel about it."

— Odelia Chan —

Powerless to Powerful

Sometimes you have to stop to think, regroup and regather yourself and realize how lucky you are to still be living and to still be breathing and still be able to even have a chance.
~Ciara Princess Wilson

It had never occurred to me that a virus like COVID-19 would take over my life. I remember hearing the news headlines: "Deadly virus spreads to New York." "Be prepared for lockdown." "We have reached a record of 100 cases a day." But it didn't seem real, until I found myself sitting in my apartment for more than three months, hearing my parents fight, missing my friends, and feeling so trapped. It sucked feeling so powerless.

I didn't understand why I sat in my room each day and cried. Was it because I was so bored or because I hated having to do school from my room? I didn't understand how the pandemic could affect a person's wellbeing so much. I felt all alone and I felt like I was the only one going through this. The only one who was so sick of it all and who just wanted it to come to an end.

I would sit on my couch each day and listen to the news, trying to become more educated about this virus, but that only made it worse. It only made me feel more scared and less hopeful. The numbers of cases, the numbers of deaths, and the restrictions just made me feel like I was a baseball getting hit with a bat over and over again. Powerless. Nothing felt like it was getting better. I would wake up at the same time each day, do my schoolwork from my room, walk outside, and eat dinner. My life felt like it was on repeat. I felt detached and lost in the world. I was sick of going on walks with my mom. I was sick of sitting on the same green rusty bench by the water near my house, seeing the same things each time. All I could think about was what was left behind. My "old" life.

I had become so accustomed to going to school every day, being around so many people, and having a real schedule. Now, because of COVID, this was all gone. I would look forward to seeing my friends each day and although I hated getting up at six in the morning, it was part of my routine. I realized that when I wasn't around people five days a week, I felt lonely and isolated. I missed going to school and being surrounded by my friends. I missed having track each afternoon. And I missed coming home and hearing about everyone's day. Being around people kept me happy, and I loved going to school.

It seemed so out of the ordinary that I had to sit at home and be educated by my teachers through a computer screen. I hated having so little structure in my life. I just wanted to be back at school, laughing with my friends. It felt like I had lost something so important to me and I would never be able to get it back.

Online school wasn't the only thing that was making life more difficult for me. It seemed that this pandemic was bringing most of my friends' families closer together, but it didn't feel the same for mine. I was sick of being stuck in a small two-bedroom apartment for hours on end with my family. My older brother got on my nerves and I was sick of hearing my mom tell me to do something productive with myself. When we had dinner, we had fights and arguments. Why was my family starting to drift apart? I just didn't get it.

I was bored all the time and felt trapped in my house. Maybe that was why I was constantly in a bad mood and constantly getting into fights with my family. I finally decided to listen to what my parents were telling me and find hobbies that were outside my comfort zone. I started watching hip-hop tutorials on YouTube and I learned many different dance combinations. I found that this was something that I really enjoyed and it took my mind off everything that was going on. With my new love for dance, I decided to take private lessons on

Zoom once a week. I now take lessons in person and it has come to be one of my new favorite hobbies and something that I have excelled at.

While I enjoyed dancing, I also found that it made me feel more confident and powerful. Dance gave me a creative outlet and it helped me become less stressed during these tough times. This greatly improved my relationship with my family, and it was then that my brother and I actually began to bond. We figured out how to communicate with each other and how to work together to solve our arguments. Dinners were much more enjoyable, and I finally felt like things were starting to improve.

As the pandemic started to get better and stores began opening, I was much happier. I was able to see my friends again and I didn't have to sit in my house all day long.

This pandemic ended up helping me reach outside of my comfort zone and improve as a person. It taught me that there is always a silver lining in every bad situation and that things always get better. Most importantly, it simply taught me what this quote states: "When you can't control what's happening, challenge yourself to control the way you respond. That's where your power is." And for me, that was exactly where my power was during this pandemic.

— Alexis Farber —

Journey with Pride

*Be yourself. You're okay. And it really doesn't matter
what other people think.*
~Taylor Schilling

'm Jett and I am nonbinary, my pronouns are they/them/his, and
I am pansexual. I am a sophomore in high school now, but ever
since I was a kid, I felt different.

I grew up watching a lot of movies, shows, and YouTube. Most
of the girls in my grade wanted to be a vet or a model, while I wanted
to be a director or a YouTuber. I always found myself identifying with
characters who were awesome but didn't fit in.

My parents sent me to a film camp each summer where I met a
lot of different kinds of kids. The other campers were fun and creative
kids who valued our differences as a creative element to be celebrated,
not like the kids at school, who were more focused on fitting in socially.
At film camp I was able to script, shoot, edit and direct films, which
only made me want to be in the film industry more. Being at the camp
also made me feel appreciated for being unique.

By seventh grade I started questioning my sexuality and gender
identity. I found all genders to be attractive, but I didn't really know if
I was having feelings or if I was just admiring wonderful people, like
school friends said. I wasn't given much room to think about my sexuality
while school was in session, being surrounded by conventional and
traditional thinking (not to mention a busy middle school schedule).

Then in eighth grade I met new friends who helped me understand
gender as a spectrum (and not binary) and what the different letters in

the LGBTQ community meant. They helped me understand that there's not just one way to be gay. I'm glad I met some other kids to help me understand this better, it is very hard for kids who are surrounded by conventional relationships to know that love is love no matter who you are. And adults have a tough time thinking about gender as anything but binary, even if they are supportive. I felt alone in my thoughts until I met the kids at film camp and my new friends in eighth grade.

But like everything else, what seems simple one day can feel complicated the next. I had a better understanding about LGBTQ+ but not necessarily an understanding of myself and my place in that community. At the end of eighth grade, I came out as pansexual after first coming out as bisexual and realizing that something was off. My freshman year of high school I was genderfluid and my pronouns were she/they. But there was a whole month where I felt more and more uncomfortable with female pronouns, so I went with them/them and that stuck for a while.

I still didn't feel complete, like I was missing something. I didn't mind because I was on the right path, and besides I was fifteen, so I didn't want to rush myself on this journey.

A few months ago, I made some friends online who share my interest in video games and movies. They were very accepting and allowed me the freedom in our friendship to figure out the best pronouns for me. I started questioning my identity again. I felt more comfortable with male terms like son, king, and boy. With my newfound confusion I tried new pronouns, but none fit — I'm not exactly a boy, while also not completely female. Using they/them/his pronouns seemed most fitting to who I am.

I'm sixteen and very young so I know I don't need to have everything figured out; I'm still experimenting with pronouns and producing video. I have found kids at school who are wonderful friends; some are members of the LGBTQ+ community and some are cis and straight and inclusive. I've even been dating! "J" is trans male and is a great boyfriend who understands my journey.

I am not sure what my self-exploration would have been like without the understanding and loving people who have supported me through it all. It's also helpful to have the creative outlet of storytelling through film, and many of my cosplay videos allow me to explore gender even more. My personality and style haven't changed from my younger self, but my journey sure did broaden my mind, help me be proud of my uniqueness, and see much more deeply into the people who support and care about me because of my uniqueness.

It may be that the most important point here is that regardless of gender spectrum, fluidity, and the confusing use of different pronouns, the constant for me has been the consistent strength of people who support me on this journey. While I figure it all out, they value me for what makes me special.

—JS—

I Am Good Enough

*You can no longer hide it. You have to find someone in
your life that you trust will face it with you, help and
support you, and see you through it.*
~Callie Bowld

My first diet was in second grade, and I remember the day
clearly. I had overheard a family friend urge my mom to
take me for regular, brisk walks in the neighborhood. Her
message was clear: I was chubby and needed to lose weight.
I felt embarrassed and internalized her words to mean that I was not
good enough.

That marked the beginning of my issues with food. As a seven-
year-old, I didn't know anything about dieting. I thought if I ate celery
and carrot sticks all day the weight would miraculously disappear.
On that beautiful, sunny, spring day I ate more celery sticks than I
could count and stepped on the scale after finishing each one. I was
confused why the number on the scale never dropped. Wasn't I dieting the right way? I gave up and ate an Oreo. That evening I looked
out my bedroom window at the starry sky and prayed to God to be
skinny, to lose weight.

As the years passed, I was made fun of for developing breasts at an
early age and told I'd "get a waist" and "lose weight" once I hit puberty.
I waited and kept praying to be skinny. As part of an annual health
assessment in elementary school, the teachers weighed their students,
individually, in the hallway. My fifth-grade teacher chose to weigh us
in groups of three. My group consisted of two rail-thin girls and me.

I volunteered to go last, hoping they'd head back to class after being weighed. No luck. They each weighed approximately eighty pounds and then hovered around the scale as I stepped on it; humiliation set in as my teacher called out, "105 pounds." They called me "pregnant" for the rest of the school year.

As a shy kid entering sixth grade, I was on the fringe of popularity, teetering between the cool kids and the not-so-cool kids. Little Gridiron Cheerleading increased my confidence, and I made some friends. However, I quickly learned that I wasn't quite cool enough since I was never invited to the best parties. It hurt being excluded but I pretended not to care, building walls around myself.

Things changed in eighth grade. I was on the cheerleading squad with a busy social calendar. There were parties every weekend and the biggest challenge was deciding which one to attend! I was thirteen and life was good. That spring, I joined the track team and lost weight. Feeling proud, I ran more often and ate less to keep off the weight. Friends commented on my weight loss, but I brushed it off saying it was track season.

That fall, I entered high school and joined a competitive dance team, student council, and other social groups. High school was a brand-new ballgame. The stress of competitions, contests, and try-outs was a consistent, heavy burden, and I slowly began gaining back the weight I had lost. The pressure to be smart enough, thin enough, well-liked enough, and good enough was too much for me to handle on my own.

That shy second-grade kid re-emerged, and I recalled how lonely she had been on the inside and how lonely she felt now as a freshman in high school. I wasn't going to become anorexic. I loved food too much to give it up. After all, I had grown up in an Italian family where food was always around and solved all problems. Still, I wanted so badly to look good in tight, form-fitting dance uniforms and prom dresses.

Feeling self-conscious, I'd quickly change into dance uniforms before practices and performances as the locker room overflowed with fellow dancers walking around in size 32A bras and tiny panties. Then I started changing in a bathroom stall after one of the other girls called me a "heifer." That stung, but I considered the source. So, I turned to my best friend and enemy at the time: food. I began binging and purging in ninth grade, comforting myself from the days' struggles by eating whatever was in the fridge or pantry; I was battling bulimia every day. A "good" day was skipping breakfast, having a Diet Coke and piece of candy for lunch, and binging and purging at night.

My sister caught on over the months. There were various signs of my illness even though I covered my tracks well. She noticed changes in my behavior like taking more trips to the bathroom and withdrawing from the world by retreating to my bedroom at night. I hit rock bottom the night my parents discovered my "secret." One evening after dinner my mom asked me if I was bulimic. I emphatically responded, "No!" My sister had ratted me out, and I stormed upstairs to my comfort zone, the bathroom. I had lost all control and felt ashamed. My family followed me upstairs, pleading with me to open the door.

The secret I had kept to myself for so many months was finally exposed. The walls I had built around me were gone. The next day, I went to a family physician for a physical exam, a nutritionist, and a psychologist who specialized in eating disorders. The thing is, I wasn't ready to change. As much as I was abusing my body, mind, and spirit, I was terrified of "getting better" and continued battling the exhaustion, swollen glands, and rollercoaster of emotions.

Looking back, I realize hitting rock bottom that evening was my first step to recovery. I am grateful for having a supportive family. Healing from an eating disorder is a life-long process and, although I no longer binge and purge, there isn't a magic cure to recovery. In time, I found diversions that had nothing to do with soothing myself with food. I eventually took a leap of faith that was terrifying and seemingly impossible by ending all diets forever. Although relapse is not unusual, I eventually maintained a relapse-free, healthy lifestyle. Food is now my friend, though I still cringe when I see a scale and avoid stepping on it. It takes time, support, and space to talk about my struggles. But it feels liberating beating the disease every day!

Those suffering from bulimia and anorexia have commonalities: anxiety, feelings of isolation, and a yearning to be good enough. However, anorexia is easier to spot than bulimia. On the outside, I looked and acted normal through breakups, dance tryouts and performances, student council races, and homecoming contests. Nobody knew I was at war with myself.

When I look at pictures of my happy-go-lucky and free-spirited self as a four-year-old, my heart hurts for my second grade, fifth grade, and teenage self. I have come full circle and boy does it feel good to have that happy and spirited spark back that I had missed for so long. So, every time I meet a shy little girl or teen or college student, I make a point to tell her that she is good enough.

— Katie Greenan —

Egg Lessons

We should be careful to get out of an experience only the wisdom that is in it.
~Mark Twain

Robby Rogers… my first love. What a great guy, too. He was kind, honest and smart. In fact, the more I think about him, the more reasons I find for loving him as much as I did. We had been going out for a whole year. As you know, in high school that's a very long time.

I don't remember why I was not at Nancy's party that Saturday night, but Robby and I had agreed we would see each other afterward. He would come over around 10:30. Robby always showed up when he said he would, so at 11:00 I started feeling sick. I knew something wasn't right.

On Sunday morning he woke me with a phone call. "We need to talk. Can I come over?"

I wanted to say, "No, you cannot come over here and tell me something is wrong." Instead, I said, "Sure," and hung up with a knot in my stomach.

I had been right. "I got together with Sue Roth last night," Robby informed me, "and we're going out now." He followed with the usual, "I'm so confused. I would never do anything to hurt you, Kim. I'll always love you."

I must have turned white because I felt the blood leave my face. This wasn't what I expected; my reaction surprised me. I felt such anger that I was unable to complete a sentence. I was so hurt that everything but the pain in my heart seemed to be moving in slow motion.

"Come on, Kim, don't be like this. We can be friends, can't we?"

Those are the cruelest words to utter to someone you're dumping. I had loved him deeply, shared every little weakness and vulnerability with him — not to mention the four hours a day I had spent with him for the last year (not counting the phone time). I wanted to hit him really hard, over and over, until he felt as horrible as I did. Instead, I asked him to leave. I think I said something sarcastic like, "I hear Sue calling you."

As I sat on my bed and cried for hours, I hurt so bad that nothing could make it stop. I even tried eating an entire gallon of ice cream. I played all of our favorite songs again and again, torturing myself with memories of good times and kind words. After making myself ill with shameless self-indulgence, I made a decision.

I would turn to revenge.

My thinking went like this: Sue Roth is — was — one of my closest friends. Good friends do not throw themselves at your boyfriend when you're not around. Obviously, she should pay.

That weekend, I bought a few dozen eggs and headed for Sue's house with a couple of friends. I started out just venting a little anger, but it got worse. So when someone found an open basement window, we threw the remaining eggs inside. But that's not the worst part. The Roths were out of town for three days!

As I lay in my bed that night, I started to think about what we had done. *This is bad, Kim... this is really bad.*

Soon it was all over school. Robby and Sue were going out *and* someone had egged her house while she was out of town, *and* it was so bad that her parents had to hire a professional to get rid of the smell.

As soon as I got home from school, my mom was waiting to talk. "Kim, my phone has been ringing all day, and I don't know what to say. Please — you have to tell me. Did you do it?"

"No, Mom, I didn't." It felt really bad to lie to my mom.

My mother was furious when she got on the phone to call Mrs. Roth. "This is Ellen. I want you to stop accusing my daughter of throwing eggs at your house." She was yelling at Sue's mother now, her voice getting louder and louder. "Kim would *never* do such a thing, and I want you to stop telling people that she did!" She was really going now. "And what's more, *I want you to apologize to me and to my daughter!*"

I felt good about the way my mom was sticking up for me, but awful about the reality. The feelings were all sort of twisted inside of me, and I knew that I had to tell her the truth. I signaled for my mom to get off the phone.

She hung up, reached for the table and sat down. She knew. I cried and told her how sorry I was. Then she cried, too. I would have preferred anger, but she'd used all of that up on Mrs. Roth.

I called Mrs. Roth and told her I'd give her every penny of my baby-sitting savings to help pay for the damages. She accepted but told me not to come over until she was ready to forgive me.

Mom and I stayed up late that night, talking and crying. She told me about the time her boyfriend left her for her sister. I asked her if she'd egged her own house, and she actually laughed. She told me that although I'd done a terrible thing, it made her furious to think about the things Mrs. Roth had said on the phone. "After all," Mom said, "what about the fact that her daughter steals boyfriends?"

Then she told me how hard it is sometimes being a parent because you want to yell at everyone who causes your child pain, but you can't. You have to stand back and watch while your children learn hard lessons on their own.

I told my mom how incredible it had felt to hear her defend me like that. And at the end of the night, I told her how special it was to spend this kind of time with her. She gave me a hug and said, "Good. We can spend next Saturday night together, and the one after that. I did tell you, didn't I, that you're grounded for two weeks?"

— Kimberly Kirberger —

The Cost of Gratefulness

I was about 13. My father frequently took me on short outings on Saturdays. Sometimes we went to a park, or to a marina to look at boats. My favorites were trips to junk stores, where we could admire old electronic stuff. Once in a while we would buy something just to take it apart.

On the way home from these trips, Dad frequently stopped at the Dairy Queen for ice cream cones. Not every single time; just often enough. I couldn't expect it, but I could hope and pray from the time we started heading home to that critical corner where we would either go straight for the ice cream or turn and go home empty-handed. That corner meant either mouth-watering excitement or disappointment.

A few times my father teased me by going home the long way. "I'm just going this way for variety," he would say, as we drove by the Dairy Queen without stopping. It was a game, and I was well fed, so we're not talking torture here.

On the best days, he would ask, in a tone that made it sound novel and spontaneous, "Would you like an ice cream cone?" and I would say, "That sounds great, Dad!" I'd always have chocolate and he'd have vanilla. He would hand me the money and I would run in to buy the usual. We'd eat them in the car. I loved my dad and I loved ice cream — so that was heaven.

On one fateful day, we were heading home, and I was hoping and praying for the beautiful sound of his offer. It came. "Would you like an ice cream cone today?"

"That sounds great, Dad!"

But then he said, "It sounds good to me too, Son. How would

you like to treat today?"

My mind reeled. I could afford it. I got an allowance, plus some extra for odd jobs. But saving money was important. Dad told me that. And when it was my money, ice cream just wasn't a good use of it.

Why didn't it occur to me that this was a golden opportunity to give something back to my very generous father? Why didn't I think that he had bought me 50 ice cream cones, and I had never bought him one?

In a fit of selfish, miserly ingratitude, I said the awful words that have rung in my ears ever since. "Well, in that case, I guess I'll pass."

My father just said, "Okay, Son."

But as we turned to head home, I realized how wrong I was and begged him to turn back. "I'll pay," I pleaded.

But he just said, "That's okay, we don't really need one," and wouldn't hear my pleading. We drove home.

I felt awful for my selfishness and ungratefulness. He didn't rub it in, or even act disappointed. But I don't think he could have done anything to make a deeper impression on me.

I learned that generosity goes two ways and gratefulness sometimes costs a little more than "thank you." On that day gratefulness would have cost so little, and it would have been the best ice cream I'd ever had.

I'll tell you one more thing. We went on another trip the next week, and as we approached the crucial corner, I said, "Dad, would you like an ice cream cone today? My treat."

— Randal Jones —

Mrs. Virginia DeView, Where Are You?

There are high spots in all of our lives,
and most of them come about through
encouragement from someone else.
~George Matthew Adams

We were sitting in her classroom, giggling, jabbing each other and talking about the latest information of the day, like the peculiar purple-colored mascara Cindy was wearing. Mrs. Virginia DeView cleared her throat and asked us to hush.

"Now," she said smiling, "we are going to discover our professions." The class seemed to gasp in unison. Our professions? We stared at each other. We were only 13 and 14 years old. This teacher was nuts.

That was pretty much how the kids looked at Virginia DeView, her hair swirled back in a bun and her large, buck teeth gaping out of her mouth. Because of her physical appearance, she was always an easy target for snickers and cruel jokes among students.

She also made her students angry because she was demanding. Most of us just overlooked her brilliance.

"Yes; you will all be searching for your future professions," she said with a glow on her face — as though this was the best thing she did in her classroom every year. "You will have to do a research paper on your upcoming career. Each of you will have to interview someone in your field, plus give an oral report."

All of us went home confused. Who knows what they want to

do at 13? I had narrowed it down, however. I liked art, singing and writing. But I was terrible in art, and when I sang my sisters screamed: "Oh, please shut up." The only thing left was writing.

Every day in her class, Virginia DeView monitored us. Where were we? Who had picked their careers? Finally, most of us had selected something; I picked print journalism. This meant I had to go interview a true-blue newspaper reporter in the flesh, and I was terrified.

I sat down in front of him barely able to speak. He looked at me and said: "Did you bring a pencil or pen?"

I shook my head.

"How about some paper?"

I shook my head again.

Finally, I think he realized I was terrified, and I got my first big tip as a journalist. "Never, never go anywhere without a pen and paper. You never know what you'll run into."

For the next 90 minutes, he filled me with stories of robberies, crime sprees and fires. He would never forget the tragic fire where four family members were killed in the blaze. He could still smell their burning flesh, he said, and he would never forget that horrid story.

A few days later, I gave my oral report totally from memory, I had been so mesmerized. I got an A on the entire project.

As we neared the end of the school year, some very resentful students decided to get Virginia DeView back for the hard work she put us through. As she rounded a corner, they shoved a pie into her face as hard as they could. She was slightly injured physically, but it was emotionally that she was really hurt. She didn't return to school for days. When I heard the story, I felt a deep, ugly pit in my stomach. I felt shame for myself and my fellow students who had nothing better to do than pick on a woman because of how she looked, rather than appreciate her amazing teaching skills.

Years later, I forgot all about Virginia DeView and the careers we selected. I was in college scouting around for a new career. My father wanted me in business, which seemed to be sound advice at the time, except that I had no sense of business skills whatsoever. Then I remembered Virginia DeView and my desire at 13 to be a journalist.

I called my parents.

"I'm changing my major," I announced.

There was a stunned silence on the end of the phone.

"What to?" my father finally asked.

"Journalism."

I could tell in their voices that my parents were very unhappy, but they didn't stop me. They just reminded me how competitive the field was and how all my life I had shied away from competition.

This was true. But journalism did something to me; it was in my blood. It gave me the freedom to go up to total strangers and ask what was going on. It trained me to ask questions and get answers in both my professional and personal life. It gave me confidence.

For the past 12 years, I've had the most incredible and satisfying reporting career, covering stories from murders to airplane crashes and finally settling in on my forte. I loved to write about the tender and tragic moments of people's lives because somehow I felt it helped them in some way.

When I went to pick up my phone one day, an incredible wave of memories hit me and I realized that had it not been for Virginia DeView, I would not be sitting at that desk.

She'll probably never know that without her help, I would not have become a journalist and a writer. I suspect I would have been floundering in the business world somewhere, with great unhappiness shadowing me each day. I wonder now how many other students in her class benefited from that career project.

I get asked all the time: "How did you pick journalism?"

"Well, you see, there was this teacher…" I always start out. I just wish I could thank her.

I believe that when people reflect back over their school days, there will be this faded image of a single teacher—their very own Virginia DeView. Perhaps you can thank her before it's too late.

— Diana L. Chapman —

The Eternal Gifts

In the darkest hour the soul is replenished and
given strength to continue and endure.
~Heart Warrior Chosa

"Is that true, or did you just put it on the bulletin board because it sounds catchy?"

"Is what true?" I asked without looking up from my desk.

"That sign you made that says, 'Whatever the mind can conceive and believe, it can achieve.' I looked up into the face of Paul, one of my favorite people, but most definitely not one of my best students. "Well, Paul," I said, "the man who wrote those words, Napoleon Hill, did so after years of research into the lives of great men and women. He discovered that concept, stated in many different ways, was the one thing they all had in common. Jules Verne put it another way when he said, 'Anything one man can imagine, other men can make real.'"

"You mean if I get an idea and really believe in it, I can do it?" he asked with an intensity that captured my total attention.

"From what I have seen and read, Paul, that's not a theory, but a law that has been proved throughout history."

Paul dug his hands into the hip pockets of his Levi's and walked in a slow circle around the room. Then he turned and faced me with a new energy. "Mr. Schlatter," he said. "I've been a below-average student my whole life, and I know it's going to cost me later in life. What if I conceived of myself as a good student and really believed it... that even *I* could achieve it?"

"Yes, Paul, but know this: If you really believe it, you'll act on it.

I believe there is a power within you that will do great things to help you once you make the commitment."

"What do you mean, commitment?" he asked.

"Well, there's a story about a preacher who drove out to the farm of a member of his congregation. Admiring the beauty of the place, he said, 'Clem, you and the Lord have certainly created a thing of beauty here.'"

"'Thank you, preacher,' said Clem, 'but you should have seen it when the Lord had it all to himself.'

"In essence, Paul, God will give us the firewood, but we have to light the match."

A suspenseful silence followed. "All right," Paul said, "I'll do it. By the end of the semester, I'll be a B student."

It was already the fifth week of the term and in my class, Paul was averaging a D.

"It's a tall mountain, Paul, but I also believe you can achieve what you just conceived." We both laughed and he left my room to go to lunch.

For the next 12 weeks, Paul gave me one of the most inspirational experiences a teacher can have. He developed a keen curiosity as he asked intelligent questions. His new sense of discipline could be seen in a neater appearance and a fresh sense of direction in his walk. Very slowly, his average started to rise, he earned a commendation for improvement and you could see his self-esteem start to grow. For the first time in his life, other students started to ask him for his help. A charm and charismatic friendliness developed.

Finally came the victory. On a Friday evening, I sat down to grade a major test on the Constitution. I looked at Paul's paper for a long time before I picked up my red pen and started to grade it. I never had to use that pen. It was a perfect paper, his first A+. Immediately, I averaged his score into the rest of his grades and there it was, an A/B average. He had climbed his mountain with four weeks to spare. I called my colleagues to share the news.

That Saturday morning, I drove to school for a rehearsal of *Follow the Dream,* the play I was directing. I entered the parking lot with a light heart to be greeted by Kathy, the best actress in the play and one of Paul's best friends. Tears were streaming down her face. As soon as I got out of my car, she ran over to me and almost fell against me in a torment of sobs. Then she told me what had happened.

Paul was at a friend's house and they were looking at the collection of "unloaded" guns in the den. Being boys, they started to play cops and robbers. One boy had pointed an "unloaded" gun at Paul's head and pulled the trigger. Paul fell with a bullet lodged in his brain.

Monday, a student aide came in with a "check-out" notice for Paul. There was a box next to "book" to see if I had his test, and next to the box marked "grade" was written "unnecessary."

"That's what you say," I thought to myself, as I marked a big red B in the box. I turned my back to the class so they could not see the tears. Paul had earned that grade and it was here, but Paul was gone. Those new clothes he had bought with his paper route money were still in his closet, but Paul was gone. His friends, his commendation, his football award were still here, but Paul was gone. Why?

One good thing about total, complete grief is that it humbles a person to such an extent that there is no resistance to the voice of that loving, unleashed power that never leaves us.

"Build thee more stately mansions, oh, my soul." As the words of that old poem spoke to my heart, I realized that Paul did not leave everything behind. The tears started to dry and a smile came to my face as I pictured Paul still conceiving, still believing and still achieving, armed with his newly developed curiosity, discipline, sense of direction and self-esteem — those invisible mansions of the soul that we are here to cultivate.

He had left us with a great deal of wealth. Outside the church on the day of the funeral, I gathered my drama students around and announced that rehearsals would start the next day. In remembrance of Paul and all he had left us, it was time once again to follow the dream.

— Jack Schlatter —

Challenge Days

Shared joy is double joy. Shared sorrow is half sorrow.
~Swedish Proverb

My name is Tony. I always looked out for myself because I thought no one else would, and I thought it would always be that way. That changed the day I got out of class for something called Challenge Day.

The people running it had big hopes of helping us join together and making us leaders. I just wanted to get out of class. I figured that after signing in I would sneak out.

In the school gym, I found myself sitting in a big circle, face to face with a hundred students that no one could have paid me to spend the day with. I was keeping up my front, my cool, but I was kind of nervous. I'm used to either sitting hidden in the back of a classroom waiting for a break, or skipping school and hanging with the guys. I wasn't used to not knowing what was going to happen.

I made fun of how a bunch of kids were dressed and of a girl who was fat. Some of the girls had worn pajamas and brought stuffed animals. Pretty stupid, I thought.

The day started with each of us standing up and saying our names into a microphone "loud and proud." A bunch of kids were really shy, but since I rap sometimes, I acted really cool when it was my turn. No one knew there was a lump in my throat. You see, I'm from a tough neighborhood, and showing your weakness only makes you a target. I was a target when I was real young, both for my brothers and for the people who called themselves my friends. We sure didn't know how to be friends, though. Fighting and putting each other down were a normal way of life.

Anyway, we started playing these games I thought were really childish. I hung back a little with my buddies, acting cool and not wanting to play like a little kid. After a couple of games, though, it didn't seem like anyone else was hanging back, and they were all having a good time. I thought, "Why not me?" I have to admit that I was playing a little rough, but it beat sitting on the edge.

What happened next was almost unbelievable. Carl, one of the only guys who is more feared and respected than me at school, was helping one of the leaders demonstrate how to give hugs. Everyone was laughing at first, but it was getting harder and harder to put anyone down that day. The leaders kept teaching us to open our hearts and minds, to share our true feelings and to give put-ups instead of put-downs. It wasn't what I was used to.

Then we did an exercise called "the power shuffle." Before the game started, the leaders talked about oppression. "Yeah," I thought, "like they really know what it's like to be oppressed. Here I am, a young Latino growing up in a white society. I get harassed and pushed around every day by store owners, teachers and all these adults who think I'm a gangster just because of the color of my skin. Yeah, I act hard, but what am I supposed to do when I have to watch my friends drop from drive-bys?"

The leaders said we had to be silent, to make it safe for everyone. They called out broad categories and asked us to cross over the line if we fit into the category. I was still snickering in my buddy's ear as the first few were called out.

But the leaders meant it about being quiet. One of the adults softly put his hand on me and said, "You'll want them to respect you; please respect them."

Category after category was called out. In silence, group after group, people crossed the line. Then a topic was called that I fit into, and I figured I would be the only one who experienced this kind of pain. "Cross the line if you've ever been hit, beaten or abused, in any way." I walked heavy in my shoes. Looking straight down as I walked,

I turned around, having a hard time not laughing to cover what was going on inside me.

But as I looked up, half the group was walking with me. We stood together in silence, looked into each other's eyes, and for the first time in my life, I felt like I wasn't alone.

One by one we dropped our masks. I saw that these people, whom I had judged before, were in reality very much like me. Like me, they, too, knew how it felt to be hurt.

I walked back across the line. My friend tried to joke with me but it didn't seem right any more. Another topic was called, one where all the women and girls crossed. I had never seen before how much men and boys disrespect and hurt women. I became more uncomfortable as I noticed tears appearing in many of my friends' eyes.

We crossed the line next for having lost someone close to us in gang violence. So many of us crossed that line. It just wasn't right! I started feeling really angry inside, and tears were coming to my eyes. The leaders kept saying, "When the tears are on the outside, the inside is healing," and, "It takes a strong man to cry."

I had to make the choice of whether or not to have the courage to show my tears. I was still scared of being called names, but the tears came out. I cried, and with my tears I proved that I was a strong man.

Before we left that day, each of us stood up and shared our experiences. I stood up, again not sure if I should fight the tears or not. The leader encouraged me to look out at the group and ask if it was okay for a man to cry. So I did.

Then each person stood up in front of their chairs to show they respected me for showing my tears. Amazed, I started talking. I said I was sorry to a few of those people I had judged and pushed around in the halls because I thought they had it so much better than me. With tears in their eyes, they came up to me, one by one, and gave me a hug. Now I know what it is really like to share love with someone. I hope I can do this with my dad someday.

Here was a day I thought I was cutting from school, but instead I found myself telling the people I hurt that I was sorry, and people were saying the same thing to me. It was like we were all one family and we never knew it until that day. It wasn't magic — we just looked at each other in a different light.

Now it is up to us. Do we look through these eyes for just one day, or do we have the courage to remember that most people are just like us, and help others learn that it is safe to be themselves?

— as told to Andrew Tertes by Tony —

Please Hear What I'm Not Saying

Don't be fooled by me.
Don't be fooled by the face I wear.
For I wear a mask, a thousand masks,
masks that I'm afraid to take off,
and none of them is me.
Pretending is an art that's second nature to me,
but don't be fooled.
For God's sake don't be fooled.
I give you the impression that I'm secure,
that confidence is my name and coolness is my game,
that the water's calm and I'm in command,
and that I need no one.
But don't believe me.
My surface may seem smooth but my surface
is my mask, ever-varying and ever-concealing.
Beneath lies no complacence.
Beneath lies confusion and fear and aloneness.
But I hide this. I don't want anybody to know it.

I panic at the thought of my weakness and fear being exposed.
That's why I frantically create a mask to hide behind,
a nonchalant sophisticated facade, to help me pretend,
to shield me from the glance that knows.
But such a glance is precisely my salvation.

My only hope, and I know it.
That is, if it's followed by acceptance,
if it's followed by love.
It's the only thing that can liberate me from myself,
from my own self-built prison walls,
from the barriers I so painstakingly erect.
It's the only thing that will assure me
of what I can't assure myself,
that I'm really worth something.
I don't like to hide.
I don't like to play superficial phony games.
I want to stop playing them.
I want to be genuine and spontaneous and me, but you've got to help me.
You've got to hold out your hand even when that's the last thing I seem to want.
Only you can wipe away from my eyes the bland stare of the breathing dead.
Only you can call me into aliveness.

Each time you're kind and gentle and encouraging, each time you try to understand because you really care, my heart begins to grow wings, very small wings, very feeble wings, but wings!
With your power to touch me into feeling you can breathe life into me.
I want you to know that.
Who am I, you may wonder.
I am someone you know very well.
For I am every man you meet, and I am every woman you meet.

— Charles C. Finn —

Editor's note: Charles "Charlie" Carroll Finn (born September 21, 1941) is an American poet notable for writing "Please Hear What I'm Not Saying" in September 1966.

I Am...

*The words "I am..." are potent words; be careful what
you hitch them to. The thing you're claiming has a way
of reaching back and claiming you.*
~A.L. Kitselman

I am an architect: I've built a solid foundation; and each year I go to that school I add another floor of wisdom and knowledge.

I am a sculptor: I've shaped my morals and philosophies according to the clay of right and wrong.

I am a painter: With each new idea I express, I paint a new hue in the world's multitude of colors.

I am a scientist: Each day that passes by, I gather new data, make important observations, and experiment with new concepts and ideas.

I am an astrologist: reading and analyzing the palms of life and each new person I encounter.

I am an astronaut: constantly exploring and broadening my horizons.

I am a doctor: I heal those who turn to me for consultation and advice, and I bring out the vitality in those who seem lifeless.

I am a lawyer: I'm not afraid to stand up for the inevitable and basic rights of myself and all others.

I am a police officer: I always watch out for others' welfare and I am always on the scene preventing fights and keeping the peace.

I am a teacher: By my example others learn the importance of determination, dedication and hard work.

I am a mathematician: making sure I conquer each one of my problems with correct solutions.

I am a detective: peering through my two lenses, searching for meaning and significance in the mysteries of life.

I am a jury member: judging others and their situations only after I've heard and understood the entire story.

I am a banker: Others share their trust and values with me and never lose interest.

I am a hockey player: watching out for and dodging those who try to block my goal.

I am a marathon runner: full of energy, always moving and ready for the next challenge.

I am a mountain climber: Slowly but surely I am making my way to the top.

I am a tight-rope walker: Carefully and stealthily I pace myself through every rough time, but I always make it safely to the end.

I am a millionaire: rich in love, sincerity and compassion, and I own a wealth of knowledge, wisdom, experience and insight that is priceless.

Most important, I am me.

— Amy Yerkes —

Editor's note: Have you ever noticed how often people ask you what you are going to be, what you do, or what you are planning to do when you grow up? For all of us who have suffered because what we do or who we're going to be doesn't cut it, the poem above is the true answer.

If I Knew

You know how you always hear people say, "If I knew then what I know now…?"

Have you ever wanted to say… yeah… well… go on…

So here we go…

I would listen more carefully to what my heart says.

I would enjoy more… worry less.

I would know that school would end soon enough…
and work would… well, never mind.

I wouldn't worry so much about what other people were thinking.

I would appreciate all my vitality and tight skin.

I would appreciate all my vitality and would play more, fret less.

I would know that my beauty/handsomeness is in my love of life.

I would know how much my parents love me and I would believe that they are doing the best they can.

I would enjoy the feeling of "being in love" and not worry so much about how it works out.

I would know that it probably won't… but that something better will come along.

I wouldn't be afraid of acting like a kid.

I would be braver.

I would look for the good qualities in everyone and enjoy them for those.

I would not hang out with people just because they're "popular."

I would take dance lessons.

I would enjoy my body just the way it is.

I would trust my girlfriends.

I would be a trustworthy girlfriend.

I wouldn't trust my boyfriends. (Just kidding.)
I would enjoy kissing. Really enjoy it.
I would be more appreciative and grateful, for sure.

— Kimberly Kirberger —

Life Is Short

For you and me, today is all we have;
tomorrow is a mirage that may never become a reality.
~Louis L'Amour

"Hey, man, I'm hungry," I said. "I'm going to go get something to eat."

My friend Gabe smiled and warmly responded, "Alright, but you're crazy. I can't stop. The weather's too good! Look for me here at the bottom of this lift when you're done. I'm gonna go take some more runs."

I released my bindings and began to walk in the direction of the smell of hot pizza. I shouted over my shoulder, "I'll catch up to you later."

I didn't think twice about those few little words at the time. My friend, Gabe Moura, and I had been snowboarding all morning. I was too hungry to take another run, so I decided to eat something at the lodge.

I remember the weather that day. It was one of those flawlessly sunny, crisp winter Sundays where it was just brisk enough to get your blood rushing but warm enough to wear a T-shirt. I had been riding in a T-shirt all day and despite the occasional patch of ice, the snow was great.

Earlier that morning, we had been tearing up the mountain. Huge aerials, blazing speed and unfading smiles were common for us. After a quick slice of pizza in the lodge, I would soon be back on the mountain with my friend. But taking a break from this snow-capped playground was just not something Gabe would do. He continued back to the crowded lift line with a sparkle in his eyes. I remember thinking, *That guy is never going to stop riding, not on a day like this at least.*

I finished my lunch and headed back out. The lifts were open and I didn't see Gabe anywhere, so I went on up. I figured he was having fun up there somewhere, and I was determined not to miss out just to wait around down at the bottom for him.

On the lift, I remember seeing a big crowd at a fork in the runs. I assumed it was just another minor collision and that somebody was just complaining about their back again. I rode for a few more hours with an intoxicating combination of adrenaline and excitement flowing through my veins. I recall seeing a crowd at the fork several more times and wondering what Gabe was up to.

The day flew by, and soon it was time to go back to the hotel. As I waited for my mom at the lodge, I saw the other kids Gabe and I had been riding with that day. Mona, one of Gabe's friends, was standing by the parking lot and she looked beat. I naturally figured it was from the insane day of riding we had all had.

As she was standing there with her shoulders drooped, I walked over to her. As I got closer, I saw that she had tears in her eyes. She told me that Gabe had been in an accident and was being flown by air-evac to Tucson. He was in a coma.

"WHAT!?!" My mind screamed, but my voice quivered. She explained that he had collided with a skier at full speed and the back of his head had landed on a patch of ice. The skier had gotten up, said a few words, then disappeared, leaving Gabe on the ground.

The car ride home to Tucson was undoubtedly one of the longest I recall. My mind played cruel games on me while my nerves wreaked havoc on my body. I remember crying uncontrollably and vomiting. That night I called the hospital but there had been no change. Gabe was still unconscious and the doctors had no prognosis.

The next day, my friends and I bought some get-well cards and headed for the hospital. Once there, we were herded into a large conference room with probably two hundred or so people. A chaplain took the podium and informed us that Gabe was brain-dead. They were taking him off life-support, and he would be officially dead within ten minutes.

My comical get-well card seemed so trivial now. My friend, who just yesterday had shared life with me on a beautiful mountaintop, was gone forever.

The ensuing weeks were filled with a funeral, candlelight vigils and mostly struggling to comprehend why. Why did someone so completely innocent, so full of life, die? How could this happen?

It's been about eight months since Gabe died, and I still don't know the answers to these questions. I know I never will. I do, however, know — more intimately now — that all those clichéd sports commercials are so true. Life is short. There is no method or reason to life if you just wander through day to day. You must find your passion and live it, but be safe. There is no reason to take chances with your life. If Gabe had been wearing a helmet he would probably be alive today. Life is fragile enough as it is. It comes and goes as fleetingly as a falling star.

I strive to make my life exceptional and extraordinary, but it is difficult. You can eat well and exercise daily for an hour at the gym, but unless you truly experience life, it is all for nothing. It is so much easier to become apathetic or lazy. I see people letting their lives revolve around the TV. I see people overcome by greed and the almighty dollar, working horrendous hours at jobs they despise.

But I know I must be different. I must strive to make a difference. Gabe is my inspiration. He made a difference, in life and now in death. While he was here, Gabe brightened people's days and made the world a richer, more loving place for his family and friends. His passion for life was something he spread to everyone, but an extraordinary person like Gabe couldn't stop there.

Just a few months prior to his accident, he told a family member, "If anything ever happens to me, I would want all of my organs to be donated."

The heart that so many girls fought for is now beating strongly inside of a sixty-two-year-old man, who is engaged to be married soon. Gabe's liver went to a thirty-three-year-old husband and father. One kidney went to a woman and the other to a man. Two people that could not see before, do, thanks to Gabe's eyes. Between thirty-five and fifty people received tissue from Gabe's body.

Gabe not only still lives in the memories of his family and friends, he lives on in the hearts and lives of fifty other people, who are now alive and healthy because of him. Gabe set an example for all of us. You never know how much time you are going to have to live your life, so pursue your passions and make the right choice now. Make your life matter.

— Scott Klinger, 16 —

Editor's note: This story was originally published in *Chicken Soup for the Preteen Soul*, but we moved it to this new anniversary edition of *Chicken Soup for the Teenage Soul* based on the age of the writer.

A Life Once Lived

*Every second brings a fresh beginning, every hour
holds a new promise, every night our dreams can bring
hope, and every day is what you choose to make it.*
~Jessica Heringer, age 15

When I was thirteen, I found myself at home alone after school every day while my parents worked until seven or eight o'clock each night. I was bored and I felt somewhat neglected. So, I started hanging around with other kids who were at home unsupervised after school.

One day, I was at my friend's house and she had some other friends over as well. There were no parents at her house and mine were in Nashville; we had total freedom! As we sat there doing nothing, one of the guys pulled some marijuana out of his coat pocket. In this crowd, I was the only one there that had never tried it, so, under pressure to be cool, I did.

As the weekend approached, everyone was talking about a party at my friend's house. I ended up partying with people I didn't even know and had my first experience of being drunk *and* high. I was now ruining my life, but as far as I knew, I was making more friends and hanging with a different crowd. The only thing that concerned me was partying on the weekends and looking for something to give me a better high.

One day, when I was in the eighth grade, my best friend and I were bored out of our minds. We thought that it would be really cool to go to my house where no one was home, find the keys to my dad's car and drive all over town showing off to our friends. When we ran a stop sign with a cop car right behind us, we were taken in for stealing my dad's car.

Things at school were equally as bad. I was suspended from school twice for fighting. The second time I was out for three days. I no longer cared about my grades and was literally failing school. I never looked at my parents' opinions as being important anymore. It seemed like I was always grounded, but I would sneak out of the house at night to see my friends. When my parents discovered that I was sneaking out, my dad no longer had any type of trust for me. I had put myself into a position of having no freedoms whatsoever. No matter what, I was never happy, and my parents and I argued constantly. My life was falling apart.

No longer was I the girl who was getting good grades, no longer did I have parents who trusted me, or friends that really even cared. I lost all that; it was gone.

So one night I sat with a bottle of prescription pills, sure these pills were going to get rid of all my pain. It was late at night so I thought, *No one's at home so who's going to stop me?* I stared at the pill bottle with a deep feeling of hate toward myself. I never thought that an emotion like this could take over my life.

I began sobbing and tears were rolling down my cheeks. I wondered if anyone was going to care. I told myself that they didn't care now, so why would they care when I'm gone?

Then I heard a car door shut, and I knew my parents had come home. I quickly took as many of the pills as I could with a couple drinks of water.

I sat on the couch with my dad, stepmom and one of their friends. They had no clue as to what was about to happen. We were watching my favorite TV show. Then, the weirdest thing happened. I laughed with my dad for the first time in what seemed like forever. Suddenly, I no longer wanted to die. I realized that I loved my family and that they really loved me. Now what was I to do? I ran to the bathroom and made myself vomit up all the pills.

I lay awake all night thinking. I realized that my priorities were all wrong and if I kept up this behavior and kept hanging around the same people, my life would never improve. I recognized that I was the one who made my life what it was, so I also had the power to change it.

The first thing that I did was stop taking drugs and hanging around that crowd. Within days, I noticed a huge improvement in my self-esteem. Then, right after the first of the year, I switched schools so that I could get away from my "friends" who only cared about partying all the time. It wasn't long before I had made new friends and my grades improved. (I now have a 4.0 grade average — straight A's!)

The new choices I've made totally beat waking up with hangovers and not caring about where my life was headed. I made cheerleading this year and I'm having so much fun. Drugs never made me feel this high.

I'll never know if I was going to die that night, but I do know one thing; I'm glad I didn't. I learned from my mistakes and found that ending life completely is not the way to go. It is *never* too late to change your direction. Every day, every hour is a new opportunity to begin again.

— Brandi Bacon, 15 —

Editor's note: This story was originally published in *Chicken Soup for the Preteen Soul*, but we moved it to this new anniversary edition of *Chicken Soup for the Teenage Soul* based on the subject matter.

Chapter 6

Tough Stuff

You gain strength, courage and confidence by every experience by which you really stop to look fear in the face. You are able to say to yourself, "I lived through this horror. I can take the next thing that comes along."
~Eleanor Roosevelt

One-Way Ticket

First you take a drink, then the drink takes a drink,
then the drink takes you.
~F. Scott Fitzgerald, The Great Gatsby

"Come on, just a few drinks before you leave tonight! We're on the way to pick you up," my friend insisted. I snapped my pink Razr phone shut, glanced at my suitcase neatly stuffed with jean shorts and floral tops, and thought, *One drink! I'll have just one drink before we leave for the airport.*

I zipped my suitcase and waited by the door until I saw my friend's black car pull into view. I hopped in the backseat and accepted the offer of a swig from a half-gallon of cheap vodka. Warmth crept throughout my body and I sighed with relief. My anxieties began to dissolve, and my mind calmed.

"I will only have one drink tonight." I whispered, knowing the truth. I was incapable of having just one drink.

My binge drinking began when I was thirteen. It was how I dealt with the emotional and physical strain my father's drug addiction had on my mother. Mom would lock herself in the bathroom and cry as she purged her food. I often saw burn or cut marks on her arms.

My father's alcoholism and his use of crack cocaine along with my mother's eating disorder and self-destruction were the familiar patterns I lived with throughout my teenage years. I always wondered why my father didn't love me enough to choose me over drugs, and why my mom didn't know that I needed her to protect me from it all.

Now, after years of drinking, I wondered if I was heading down the same path as my dad. Would I turn into him?

I only knew one way to escape the chaos and betrayal. I put on the mask of being the happy party girl. But my drinking was no party. I needed it. It was a constant comfort and shield. These were dark secrets I kept from everybody who knew me. I expertly masked the dysfunction in my household from my friends and teachers, or so I thought.

"I'll miss you both; see you soon!" I said to my friends, taking one more gulp from the bottle as we pulled up to the bus stop. My girlfriend greeted me at the bottom of the steps, eyes wide.

"Oh my gosh, are you drunk?"

I smirked. "Me? Drunk?"

Our laughter filled the air.

As I walked up the steps into the bus, my flip-flop got caught on the edge, and I tripped. I anxiously glanced up at my teacher taking attendance in the first seat.

She laughed, "Be careful, missy!"

"These silly shoes of mine. I'm okay!" I smiled back.

See, Brooke. You've got this! Nobody has a clue you're drunk, I thought as I stumbled to the back of the bus.

By the time I got to the airport I had passed out for so long I didn't remember any of the trip. My head pounded. I made my way to the front of the bus, but my body lost control and I tumbled on top of my teacher. I heard a muffled conversation between one of my girlfriends and my algebra teacher, "Brooke gets really car sick; she's not feeling well," my friend explained. Thick fog coated my mind. *How much did I drink? How long had I been passed out on the bus?*

I crouched down to steady myself and then it happened. My dinner and vodka spewed down the front of my pink spaghetti-strapped tank. The sound of vomiting drowned out the gasps and whispers from my classmates as they all watched, clutching their bags.

The smell of vodka lingered in the air.

"Brooke, I can smell alcohol. I am going to have to call your mother," my teacher said.

That was that—I would not be going on our senior trip to Florida.

Tears blurred my vision. My teacher guided me toward an airport bench. Her touch was gentle. I wanted to bury my head in her chest and weep. I wanted her to wrap her arms around me and tell me it would all be alright. She placed her hand on my shoulder. "Brooke, I'm going to have to leave you on this bench until your mother comes. I have to board the flight with the rest of the class."

I nodded, keeping my chin tucked to my chest. I tried to tell my mom over the phone how to find me, but my words were slurred. I had no idea where I was. At that moment, I realized that nobody was coming to help me. I had to help myself. I wiped the tears from my cheeks and for the first time since I sat on that bench I lifted my head. I locked eyes with a flight attendant passing by. She wore black tights, her arm extended behind her guiding her wheeled suitcase. I mouthed, "I need help." She came to my aid and spoke to my mother with compassion, describing my exact location. She waited with me until my mother rushed through the sliding airport doors to take me home.

The first day back from my out-of-school suspension I walked down the hallway, fixing my gaze on the white tiles outlined with blue and gold stripes. I avoided eye contact with every teacher and classmate I passed. I pretended I couldn't hear their giggles and whispers. It wasn't unusual for me to stumble into the school hallways with my hair tousled and my body smelling like alcohol. When people made comments like, "Does it really surprise you Brooke did that?" I tried to shrug them off.

The hallway narrowed as I walked to the principal's office. I could hear nothing but the sound of my heart beating.

"Brooke," Mr. McGee said, "You chose to represent our school in an unacceptable manner. Unfortunately, due to your actions, you will not be walking across the stage with your classmates for graduation." The edges of his office blurred. It was difficult to breathe. "Do not cry, do not cry," I repeated to myself.

My mouth was too dry to speak. I nodded to show I understood, pushed myself up from the wooden chair and walked out of his office. I sobbed the entire ride home.

I ached for a teacher or any adult to say, "Brooke, are you okay? Is everything okay at home? I am here for you."

Nobody did. I realized I needed to ask for help. I didn't need my dad to choose me or my mom to protect me. Just as the flight attendant showed me grace and compassion at the airport, I began to show myself the very same grace and compassion. The first step I took was confiding in a trusted teacher. The dysfunction I lived with was no longer a secret I had to mask. I might not have walked across the stage with the rest of my senior class, but I graduated and headed to college with confidence, knowing who I was and that I would never be my father.

— Brooke Wallace —

Holding the Door

*Look on every exit as being
an entrance somewhere else.*
~Tom Stoppard

As a young boy, I recall the countless times that I was told, "Now, Thomas, you always allow a lady to walk through the door first and be sure to hold the door for her. It's the gentlemanly thing to do." As a child, I always thought the situation silly. Wouldn't a perfectly capable human being want to open her own door?

And then I held the door at the cancer clinic. Mary Elizabeth Turner was still quite vibrant and capable at this point in her battle. It had become my duty as Mary's offspring to attend a couple of doctors' appointments a month with her. My sister and I shared the task.

I forget the day, not that it matters, but I remember it being sunny and bright. I pulled into the parking spot at the center in Hattiesburg, quickly jumped from the driver's seat, and met my mother on her side of the car. As we approached the entrance to the clinic, we noticed that the automatic doors were out of service. My mother laughingly told me, "Well, looks like you'll have to hold the door for your feeble mother." She often made such jokes to make herself feel better about facing death. During these moments, I would allow my childish naivety to take over and reassure myself that my mother was stronger than cancer.

As we approached the doors, I hopped in front of her. I dramatically opened the door, accompanying this task with a wave of my arm and a bow of my head.

"After you, your highness!" I exclaimed.

"Why, thank you, good sir!" she replied with a curtsy.

I smiled at her. She winked at me. I was thrilled by her seemingly endless ability to face every situation with happiness. As she walked through the door, she told me to wait for the woman coming up behind us. I turned my head to see the woman she was referring to, and it was as if I were shown the future.

I went pale. The woman was walking slowly and painfully, having problems grasping the handrail, which was an obvious sign of the joint deterioration brought on by radiation therapy. I attempted a quick move from my position of doorman but was halted by the woman.

"I've got it, son," she said with a raspy whisper. "Just please hold the door."

As the woman struggled toward me, I checked on my mother and saw her continue down the hallway and around the corner. I think I was looking for reassurance that the person walking toward me in need of someone to hold a door wouldn't one day be my mother.

After the woman made her way down the same hallway as my mother, I collapsed into a chair inside the door, crying before I even finished sitting down. I was a scared, sixteen-year-old.

I don't think I cried for more than a minute. I quickly gathered my faculties and wiped my eyes. I was afraid my mother would wonder where I gotten to and return to find her child crying.

Before this simple experience, endings in life were always happy for me. There was no outcome that ended any other way than my mother beating this disease — until I held that door. There were only going to be better days to come — until I held that door for that woman. My mind replaced the vibrant and capable woman who had just curtsied only moments prior with that other woman.

I shoved the thoughts to the back of my mind. I took the pain and buried it as deep as I could. I believe some of that pain will remain somewhere in my depths until I no longer roam this earth. None of that really mattered, however. My mother needed me. She didn't need a crying child that day. That day, she would be given chemotherapy, and she needed her smiling son. So, that's what I became. I picked up my broken beliefs from the floor, wiped my eyes, and went to find my mother. But I went to find my mother as a changed human being.

In the years to come, the cancer would become untreatable. My family would attend a meeting with a doctor that was meant to prepare us for the ultimate outcome — the same outcome my mind had envisioned as I watched the decrepit woman pass through that door. I would attend the funeral and distinctly remember being able to think about nothing but the simple experience I'd had at the cancer clinic that day. In my mind, there were two very distinct phases regarding my mother's illness. There was the time of unbridled optimism before I held that door, and there was the wiser, scarred view of the world after. At the time of my mother's passing, I was oddly thankful for the events that day at the clinic unfolding the way they did. They prepared me for everything that was coming.

— Thomas E. Turner —

American Pie

There is no magic cure, no making it all go away
forever. There are only small steps upward;
an easier day, an unexpected laugh, a mirror
that doesn't matter anymore.
~Laurie Halse Anderson

I'm lying, near catatonic across the rumpled duvet on my bed. I've kicked it near over the headboard in my haste to crawl away from dinner and the pleading eyes of my parents.

The plate glaring at me from my desk holds a smashed clump of salmon and plain new potatoes, even the peas and sweetcorn barely eaten. A few months ago, eating that for dinner wouldn't have kept me going for more than an hour. Between climbing, karate, ballet, netball and all the sports clubs I'd joined, I would've needed dessert, a snack and then some.

Now, that plate is the end of the world. My stomach aches with hunger but I refuse to reach for the plate.

I hear *Friends* or *How I Met Your Mother* or some other sitcom blasting from the TV downstairs. My brother and sister have turned it as loud as possible to drown out the shouting. It makes my heart break a little, but I still can't reach for the plate.

My mum knocks at the door. "I've got an idea, Emily… might cheer you up," she says, with a sad, desperate smile.

I don't reply.

"I was thinking about what you said on the way back from Dunelm yesterday and I thought we could take dinner on a drive."

Warehouse stores were all I saw of the outside world. I was commanded to bed rest and a grueling meal plan, not to dance a step or climb a hold or punch a bag until I gained back the weight I'd lost.

I take any chance to escape from the house, even if it means a ten-minute drive to Sainsburys. I nod, fighting dizziness when I stand from the bed and accept the sweater my mum hands me. She packs up dinner in a little plastic pot and I walk — not run, I'm definitely not allowed to run — through the rain to the car.

The car is warm, warmer than my bedroom where the radiator has stopped working. She leaves the radio on and we leave the house with no real plan.

I live in a tiny Suffolk village — the type of place where everybody knows everybody and the most exciting thing to happen in the last ten years was the school's fiftieth anniversary.

I love and hate it. I hate the size, but I love the rolling hills and woodlands that surround us. I hate the quiet, but I love the smell of chimney fires in the autumn and the peacefulness of the fields.

The redeeming feature, I suppose is Ickworth — a famous National Trust site with a mile-long drive to a grand but decaying manor house. I've missed Ickworth. I've missed walking the dog and running in the woods, cycling to the river or taking photos down at the lake.

Given the time of year, I especially missed walking down the drive to see the newly born lambs grazing on the greens that line the road.

I turn to Mum. "Can we go see the lambs?"

It's her turn to nod wordlessly.

Just as we're turning through the wrought iron gates, the radio picks up a station. I lean my head against the window and listen to the first chords of "American Pie." It's nostalgic. One of those songs everybody knows but doesn't listen to very often. It's not quite a happy song, but not quite sad either. It's the kind of song you can't help but smile at, the kind of song you can't help but sing.

I raise a bite of salmon, cold, but still nice, to my mouth.

I see my mum watch me take a mouthful from the corner of her eye, slumping against her seat in something between relief and exhaustion.

I take another bite, choking back tears as I feel it slide down my throat.

Then, I start to hum.

It's absurd. If this were a film the critics would say this scene is out of place, but ten seconds later we're singing at the top of our lungs.

The trees are blossoming in the first months of spring. The grass is greening up. The beautiful little lambs regard us with curiosity while their mothers usher them away from the car.

We're still singing. I can't remember the last time I raised my voice above a hoarse whisper, let alone the last time I sang. The loudest I've been since the diagnosis was screaming at my parents that I was fat and gross, and I didn't want to eat and that they couldn't make me.

This is so very different. This is happy.

I don't know all the lyrics, and when I fumble over the words we laugh and come back with the chorus even more enthusiastically. The rain comes down harder and we keep singing, tapping the dashboard, swaying to the music, out of tune, voices breaking on the high notes and completely out of sync with each other; the best thing I've ever heard.

We park the car at the bottom of the drive, singing the last notes, watching three lambs skip and leap around a fallen tree.

As the song ends, the feeling of it all starts to fade away.

I finish the meal.

It's one of the bravest things I've ever done.

— Emily Jones —

Revealing a Twelve-Year Secret

Truth is such a rare thing, it is delightful to tell it.
~Emily Dickinson

I've been told that thinking will not overcome fear, but action will. I didn't want to share my story due to my fear of being judged and humiliated, but I think of my teenage self and the traumatic experience she endured at a young age, and how much she needed hope. This is the story she needed to hear.

I'm a first-generation Asian American, who was raised on credit cards with interest rates that kept my family in poverty and I was placed in a difficult situation with impossible expectations. I started looking for jobs before my sixteenth birthday, but nobody wanted to hire a teenager without previous work history. Luckily, my summer internship brought me on part-time to work during the school year. By seventeen, I was working a second job at a restaurant as a junior, maintaining a 3.9 GPA.

The pressure and stress of having to financially support two alien immigrant parents and a younger sibling pushed me into a mild depression, and I began to entertain thoughts of suicide. My family was depending on me to pay the bills but also to get into a prestigious university and make a six-figure salary after graduation. My time was split between Advanced Placement classes, club meetings during lunch for the executive positions I held, competitive after-school sports, and finally rushing to work to end my day.

I typically started homework around 10 p.m. and woke up the next morning at my desk with drool running down my face, tardy as always to zero period. My weekends were messier, with work, internships, and community service. Summers were packed with national competitions, leadership camps, and conferences while getting ahead and taking classes at the junior college. I never took breaks or spent time with friends, and I rarely ate and slept properly. It eventually caught up to me by senior year and I failed one class. Next thing I knew, the university I was attending in the fall had rescinded my full-ride scholarship and acceptance.

On the first day of what would have been my freshman year at the university, I was told to my face that my appeal letter was rejected. I jumped back into my parents' car and explained (lied) that I didn't need to do orientation because I was a local. During the car ride home, I fought back salty tears. I believed my life was over. Twelve years later, I wish I could give eighteen-year-old me a big hug and hold her as we cry together, because my eyes still water when I think about that devastating car ride. I thought my future was over. I didn't know how to face my friends, teachers, and my parents. So, I didn't. I let them believe that I was still going to the university, and even now, they have no idea what actually transpired.

I made up elaborate stories; I really outdid myself! I became a master manipulator and convinced everyone that I was taking extra classes near home at the two-year college while I was commuting to the university. I even showed up on the university campus every once in a while to make my story believable to my old high school friends. I had learned that the lecture classes had over 300 students, so if anyone tried to find me, it wasn't worth the effort. I studied the course schedule and RateMyProfessor.com in order to speak the "university lingo" so if anyone asked me about the classes I was taking, I knew how to answer without skipping a beat. I even proudly wore school apparel as if I were a real student there.

In reality, I was back at the city college that I spent my summers at; and I was furious. I had done everything in my power to not end up there. I thought it was for students who weren't smart enough to get into a "real" university. In hindsight, it was the best thing that could have happened. The classes had about ten to twenty students and I received the individual attention that I had craved in high school. The professors and counselors invested in me and were happy to help me achieve my goal of transferring in a year, despite it sounding improbable. I made amazing friends who were just as eager as I was to transfer to an esteemed four-year university. They had goals even more ambitious than mine.

My new friends gave me a chance to redeem myself and I was inspired to take on a new laser-focused discipline unlike anything I had experienced before. They taught me to celebrate every win along the way, and to prioritize my health and self-care.

I managed to take on double the course units while maintaining my work and volunteering commitments, thanks to budgeting my time properly without overworking myself. I was able to reclaim my acceptance as a transfer within my first year — a feat that is considered impossible even today — with another full-ride and more merit-based grants and financial benefits than the previous year. And the best part: Two years later, I got to graduate a year before my high school friends did.

My fear is irrational, and I recognize that my teen years were over a decade ago. Sometimes, I wonder how my family and friends would react to the Olympic hoops that I jumped through to hide the truth. I don't know of anyone who has had a similar experience, but it is worth mentioning that I believe everyone in their teenage years has a secret they hope no one will discover.

My wish for all of us, whether our secrets are revealed or remain in the shadows, is to look back at those pivotal years with self-compassion, grace, and care. Above all, this is a reminder that the pain and the obstacles you face might be opportunities for a more beautiful future. You are always at the right place at the right time. You just don't know it yet.

— Gloria Ahn —

From Bullied to Blessings

I may not be there yet, but I'm closer
than I was yesterday.
~Author Unknown

When I was four years old, my parents noticed something strange about the way I was holding my head more to one side of my body than the other side. They also noticed that one of my shoulder blades was slightly higher than the other. They took me to the doctor, and the doctor told them that my neck and shoulder blades were fusing together. I was clueless about how severe my condition was, but I knew that my parents looked terrified.

I was diagnosed with Sprengel's deformity, or congenital high scapula. It is a rare congenital skeletal abnormality where a person has one shoulder blade that sits higher on the back than the other. The deformity is due to a failure in early fetal development where the shoulder fails to descend properly from the neck to its final position.

Shortly after the diagnosis, I was scheduled for surgery. Little did I know how much of a toll it would take on my life.

The bullying started in first grade. The kids told me I did not have a neck. By third grade the bullying got worse and I was noticing it more. Everyone thought it was so funny that I was fat and my neck was small, not knowing the challenges I had overcome. I was talked about and laughed at by almost everybody in the third grade.

The next few years in school were horrible for me. I would be teased for "not having a neck" almost every day. The emotional pain was becoming unbearable. I would come home from school and cry myself to sleep most nights. When I told my parents, they put me in karate to build my confidence and to be able to defend myself. Being in karate helped me cope with the pain and gave me the support I needed to partially feel at peace.

I started to take an interest in girls. I didn't have a lot of friends and was getting into trouble every now and again. I had the support of my family to get me through the storm, but not much support at school. Fifth grade was awful, with the constant bullying and harassment. I changed my image by dressing differently and letting my hair grow out. When I look back on it now, I was wishing to be invisible. I thought that if I blended in maybe all the pain and suffering would slowly fade away. However, the bullying intensified and after a while my sadness turned into anger. I said to myself enough is enough.

Although it was not easy, I am much better now than I was back then. My mom suggested counseling. My first reaction was I did not want to go, because I did not think I needed it. But, after a few sessions with my counselor, I realized that I had lots of things buried inside. My counselor is cool, and he has helped me a lot.

My parents also got me into roller skating. This helped me to release the stress I was under, and I have found it to be a highlight of my life. During seventh grade, I picked up skating more seriously, and the bullying declined to between one and three times a day, which compared to my earlier years was a blessing. At the start of eighth grade, I was cool with mostly everybody in the school, and I would say that the bullying was at a minimum. I started writing poetry to express my feelings, and I competed in several poetry slams at my school.

All the hardship and pain that I have endured would destroy a regular person, but I feel like my purpose on earth is to overcome every obstacle thrown in my direction. I have been through bullying. I have been through heartbreaks and breakups and more, but due to my relationship with God and the help of family and friends, I am still here.

My mother told me that my story should be told, because there may be a kid out there who has gone through or is going through the same problems. I agree. It's important to share that your experiences, even negative ones, can mold you and shape you into your full potential. My story is yet to end but if I can speak to a young boy or girl or even to an adult who was bullied and tell them things will be better one day if you believe it, then I will take my story all over the world. If I had one thing to say to a person being bullied, I would tell them, love yourself no matter what other people have to say, because if you don't, then they'll be right.

— Michael I. Mason —

Drowning in Lockdown

Happiness can be found even in the darkest of times,
if one only remembers to turn on the light.
~Albus Dumbledore,
Harry Potter and the Prisoner of Azkaban

In January 2020, my life wasn't just great; it was like living in the perfect movie. I was the youngest in my amazing group of best friends. They were all a year older, but you would never have known. I was only a sophomore but had managed to secure a spot on the varsity swim team. Then when February began, I had the best Sweet Sixteen a girl could ask for. Shortly after my birthday, my squad traveled for a week in Hawaii.

Little did we know we would return to chaos and a complete alteration of our way of life. It was March 13 and there was talk of school shutting down for two weeks. We were all excited, but on top of the news of the day, some punk students pulled the fire alarm and we found ourselves in the pouring rain on the wet, muddy field. About to be dismissed for what was only supposed to be a long spring break, my best friends, who I had seen practically every day, made promises to each other about how we would stay close during the lockdown.

Shortly into quarantine, I found myself taking up hobbies like learning French, catching up on TV shows, learning piano, and doing anything I could to keep myself busy. At the time, online school was a complete joke. It was all homework because the teachers didn't know how to teach online yet.

Looking back on March 13th, I felt like a fool for thinking two weeks would be a solution to a pandemic. Months went by and the new school year began. I couldn't wrap my head around the fact that I went from training in the pool for fifteen hours a week to zero. My desire to catch up on hobbies subsided, and the pain of missing my friends sunk in. I was in a battle for my mental and physical health. I felt like I was drowning.

I had already missed out on the high school experience pre-COVID because of swimming. Skipping parties, missing out on school events, all for this year-round training for the swim season that now couldn't even take place. Without swimming and my teammates, it felt like I had to find a whole new identity for myself.

It had just occurred to me that my best friends, who were now seniors, would leave me anyway when the next fall came. That made me anxious. Who would I eat lunch with at school? What would I do with my Saturday nights? And most of all, what were my own plans after high school?

Being by myself with these thoughts, I felt lonely, making November the darkest month for me. I couldn't describe the feeling of just lying on my bed, sulking in my twilight music, staring at the wall with tears streaming down my face. I dwelled on "what could have been." I could have been traveling to Europe. I could have been in the stands cheering for our football team. I could have been going to concerts and enjoying the simplicity of going to the cinema, seeing LA, going to camp, creating memories with my friends.

Alice in Wonderland became my life as I kept falling down a never-ending hole. Still, all the same, I felt ever so determined to climb out of this pit of darkness. With the holidays around the corner, things started to look up. Even though it couldn't have been warmer, I was adamant about finding the Christmas spirit. Granted, it was different this year but still, I still looked forward to the normal activities: Christmas eve dinner, opening gifts with my family on Christmas Day, no school for two whole weeks!

I made a New Year's resolution to become more devoted to my studies. As I did that, I found the college conversation became less stressful. I thought about all the possibilities for my future, the passions

I would pursue. I became more excited about the unknown.

As I allowed myself to embrace the future, everything started to align. We were getting a new President in a matter of weeks, the vaccination rolled out, I had my friends and family. My larger world and my unknown but exciting future became clearer.

—Lindsay Freiberger—

Anywhere Else

*It is very hard to explain to people who have never
known serious depression or anxiety the sheer
continuous intensity of it. There is no off switch.*
~Matt Haig

CAUTION: May cause nausea, vomiting, difficulty sleeping, dry mouth, heartburn, loss of appetite, weight changes, dizziness, excessive tiredness, headache, nervousness, uncontrollable shaking, changes in sex drive or ability, and excessive sweating. Those were the words that glared at me from the little red label stuck haphazardly on the orange pill container.

"It says to take one twenty-five milligram tablet every day," my mother's voice rang in my ears matter-of-factly. Quickly, her tone changed when she saw the anxiety in my eyes, the same anxiety she had faced just the day before when I finally confessed to her my true feelings about taking the medication. This time, she wanted to make sure there would be no more tears.

"Baby, I promise you'll be okay. It'll be just like glasses, remember? One moment, everything will be blurry and confusing, the next you'll have perfect twenty-twenty vision."

Her words comforted me, but still, the knot in my stomach twisted and turned. I felt as if I might experience some of the dreaded side effects right there in our kitchen that was usually too big, but that day was far too small. Yet, even through the doubt and panic-induced claustrophobia, I knew this was what needed to happen. I knew that at the end of the day, I would have to pop the lid off that pill container and swallow whatever concoction came out.

Throughout my entire life — even before I broke my sworn oath of silence and begged my mother for help at the age of thirteen — I experienced many symptoms of depression, of the smoke that clouded my senses and weighed me down each day, impenetrable and suffocating. It was my seventh birthday when I first smelled that smoke. That day, bright and early, my parents woke me with proud smiles and warm hugs of anticipatory celebration. They planned the whole day. First, breakfast. Then, we would pile ourselves into a blistering Toyota Sequoia, make a three-hour trip to Athens, and spend the day with my siblings: two twenty-something-year-olds who were probably a bit too excited for their little sister's birthday party. In theory, the whole day was perfect.

It should have been. But when I finally got home from our little family outing, I sat down at my mother's feet and realized I had not felt happy once that day. I hardly felt anything at all, except an ache that seemed to have settled throughout my small body. As I sat there, cold and unmoving, I had one thought: Why? I knew I was supposed to be happy; it was my birthday, and birthdays are always happy occasions. So, why did I feel like this? There was no reason to feel this way; nothing bad had happened. My family was perfectly functional despite their usual hectic habits. I got to be with my brother and sister who I always craved seeing. Even my birthday cake was delicious, although I only managed two bites. Everything was fine. But, somehow, it wasn't.

Apparently, my mother had taken notice of my thoughtful gaze and furrowed brow, and finally asked the question I would come to despise as I grew: "What's wrong?"

"I just feel… bad." It was the only answer I could come up with. I didn't know how to describe the aches, the void, the smoke that was beginning to choke me from the inside out. "I don't know what's wrong." And with that, I began to cry.

I don't think I ever stopped crying, honestly. Maybe my mother had calmed me and wiped the tears that had spilled over my cheeks, but still, the faucet persisted, whether I realized it or not. The damage it caused, though, was evident. The "bad" I had felt that day never truly went away. Of course, I had days where I didn't notice it as much, but it was always lurking there, ready to sink its teeth in at any moment.

When I was ten, I started noticing the marks left from the bad days, and at thirteen I finally decided to do something about it. "Mama, I can't take it anymore," My voice quivered as I ran my hand over my disheveled hair that I hadn't brushed in a week.

"What do you mean, baby?"

"I mean I can't keep living like this. I need something, anything. Therapy, pills, whatever anyone can give me. I just can't go on like…" I gestured to my grubby pajamas and the young girl inside them. "This."

Soon enough, my mother contacted our local counseling office and made my first appointment. After some odd weeks and question-naires, my therapist diagnosed me with moderate to severe clinical depression and suggested medication. I was relieved, yet frightened. This was all I knew. I didn't know who I was without my illness, and for some reason, the thought of change terrified me. But, despite the fear, I agreed.

I knew this is what I needed. So I closed my eyes, laid that perfect little blue pill on my tongue, took a sip of water, and swallowed. And I swallowed the next day. And the day after that. Somehow, in the series of collective days that have led to this one, I took pill after pill, each one easier than the last.

I never once suffered from nausea or vomiting; not a sleepless night was had. I did change, but for the better. I didn't forget who I was in the madness of it all, in the gulps of water between anxious days of waiting, hoping this new life wouldn't leave me dazed, confused, even wanting the sad comfort I left behind. No, I never forgot. If anything, the transition period between "non-medicated" to "medicated" was barely noticeable. One month passed, then another, and I didn't feel any change at all; no retrograde amnesia, no burst of newfound ecstasy. Everything was normal, but soon I began to realize: What was once my worst fear had become my greatest achievement.

People told me I acted happier, more myself. They no longer commented on my drooping eyes and uneaten birthday cake; they commented on my new posture. My new air of confidence and contentment. My new laugh.

I have changed, and I am grateful. I am here. I am here, surrounded not only by the love of others, but, most importantly, a love for myself. I am here, at sixteen, stronger than I once was and ready to admit it. I am here, still wanting, still fighting, still breathing. And, I can gladly say I wouldn't want to be anywhere else.

— Rylee Toole —

I'll Always Be with You

O n a quiet September night our 17-year-old son, Mike, got into his cherished yellow '68 Mustang, his heart broken after the sudden ending of his first romance. His girlfriend had told him she was going to get engaged to someone else. Sitting in the car he had so lovingly restored and treasured, Mike shot and killed himself. In the note he left, he wrote: "I wish I could have learned how to hate… Don't blame yourselves, Mom and Dad. I love you." His note ended "Love, Mike, 11:45 P.M." At 11:52 P.M. that night, we and Mike's older brother, Vic, pulled into the driveway alongside Mike's car — seven minutes too late!

It wasn't long before stories about Mike started coming in from all sides. We heard many of them for the first time. His oldest friend, Danny, told us about the time he was frightened to have his picture taken in kindergarten. "It's easy. Just go like this," Mike assured him as he grinned from ear to ear, displaying the bright smile that became his trademark. Years later, when a classmate became a single parent, Mike helped her care for her baby. One of Mike's friends was shot in a drive-by shooting but recovered, with Mike's support. When his high school band went to Florida to march in the Orange Bowl parade, Mike assisted a fellow band member who was blind.

A young mother phoned to tell the story of how Mike had helped her when her car broke down. She and her children were stranded on the roadside when Mike came by. He stopped, showed her his driver's license to assure her he wouldn't hurt her and her children, and got her car started. He followed them home to make sure they arrived safely.

One of Mike's friends revealed the truth about why Mike never got the new transmission we thought he planned to install in his Mustang in preparation for the local drag race. Mike canceled his order for the transmission and instead bought two transmissions from a salvage yard — so his friend could get his car running, too. Mike had told us the reason he didn't buy the brand-new transmission was that it just wasn't right for the way he wanted his car to perform.

Mike's niece was born with cerebral palsy. He learned how to replace her tracheotomy tube and how to perform CPR, should the need arise. He learned sign language with her (the tracheotomy tube made it impossible for her to speak), and they would "sing" together in sign language.

In the days following Mike's death, many teenagers came to comfort us and asked if they could do anything to help. Our response to their question was: "Don't ever do this. Don't commit suicide. Reach out to someone and ask for help!" Before Mike's memorial service, Mike's close friends met with us to share their grief, tell their stories about their friendship with him and discuss the tragedy of teen suicide. We talked about ways to prevent teen suicide. This was how the Yellow Ribbon Project came to life.

We decided to establish a foundation dedicated to eliminating suicide, a leading cause of death among teens. Within days after Mike's death, we began printing pocket-sized cards that read:

YELLOW RIBBON PROJECT
In loving memory of Michael Emme

THIS RIBBON CARD IS A LIFELINE! It carries the message that there are those who care and will help. If you are in need and don't know how to ask for help, take this card to a counselor, teacher, clergy, parent or friend and say:
"I NEED TO USE MY YELLOW RIBBON!"

Someone, remembering Mike's beloved yellow Mustang, had the idea of attaching yellow ribbons to the cards, which we did. At Mike's memorial service we set out a basket containing 500 of these yellow-ribbon cards.

By the end of the service, the basket was empty (and Mike's Mustang was covered with 100 yellow miniature roses, put there by his friends).

Mike's tragic death made us decide to help others, just as Mike did during his life. In the time since Mike's death, the Yellow Ribbon Project has touched — and saved — the lives of teens around the world. We receive many letters from teenagers about the Yellow Ribbon Project with comments such as:

"Your website has helped me recover from my depression."

"I've tried to commit suicide several times. This time I found the Yellow Ribbon card in my pocket and held onto it until a friend came by and I was able to give them the card. They recognized that I was suicidal and got me help."

"Thank you for being there to let those without hope know that there is always someone who cares."

Mike's final letter to us contained another important message. In that letter he told us, "I'll always be with you." Every time we speak to a group of teenagers or receive a letter from a teen or child who needs help, we know Mike's words are true.

— Dale and Dar Emme —

My Story

*The journey in between what you once were and who
you are now becoming is where the dance of life
really takes place.*
~Barbara De Angelis

I never thought about killing myself; it just became a condition. Kind of like catching a cold. One minute you are fine, and the next minute you are sick. Whenever people would talk about suicide, I would think to myself, "I would never do that." Why would someone want to do something so final, so stupid?

For me, I just wanted the pain to stop. And it got to the point where I was willing to do whatever it took to make that happen. It started with the usual stuff...

I am 16. I spend the summer with my mom and during the school year I live with my dad. I feel like an inconvenience to both of them. At my mom's I have no room. My mom isn't there for me when I need her because she always has something more important to do. At least, that is how it feels.

I was having trouble with my friends. The ones I had not lost already to "different lifestyles" were unable to help me. In their own words, my problems were "too much" for them. The intensity of my pain scared them, like it did me.

Oh, yeah... did I mention my boyfriend, John, had dumped me that day? My first boyfriend had left me, too. He said I had become impossible to love and now John was gone, too. And it wasn't that I would be without him that mattered... it was me. What was wrong with me? Why is it so hard to love me and why is it that when it gets hard, everyone bails? I was alone. All I had were the voices in my head telling me I blew it, I was too needy, I was never going to be loved once someone really got to know me. I felt that I wasn't even good enough to be loved by my own parents.

You know how, when you are really hurting, you feel like you can just call the person (the boyfriend, the friend) and tell him or her how much it hurts and they'll say, "Oh, I am so sorry; I didn't mean to hurt you; hang on, I will be right there"? Well, I called and I was crying, and I said it hurts too much, please come talk to me. He said he couldn't help me… and he hung up.

I went into my mom's bathroom and took a bottle of Tylenol PM, some tranquilizers and a couple pain pills I had left from an injury. Soon the pain would be over.

I will spare you the gruesome details of what followed. It was a whole new kind of pain. Physically, I puked until I couldn't move. Emotionally, I was more scared than I have ever been. I did not want to die. (Statistics show that immediately after "attempting" suicide, the person desperately wants to live… not die, which makes it even sadder to think about those who do succeed.) Luckily for me, I did not die. But I hurt my body (my stomach still aches). And I scared and hurt a lot of people. I scared myself, but I didn't die and I can't even begin to tell you how happy I am about that.

I cringe every time someone else finds out. I did not want to write this story, but I did want to help anyone else who might be thinking about it or who is in a lot of pain.

It has been a month since that night. I have laughed at least 500 times, many of those real "pee your pants" kind of laughing. I have a therapist who really cares about me, and we are making real progress in building up my confidence. She is also helping my mom and dad be "better parents." I have realized that they really do care and that they are doing the best that they can. I have a new friend who has gone through some hard stuff herself. My intense feelings do not scare her, and we know what it means to "be there" for someone you care about. I have worked things out with some of my old friends and we

are closer than ever. I have earned $500 and spent it all on myself...
without guilt (well, maybe a little). And I am starting to forgive myself.

Oh, yeah... I met a guy. He is really sweet and he knows "my
story." We have agreed to take things really slow.

These are only a few of the things I would have missed. Life
gets really hard sometimes and really painful. For me, I couldn't feel
everyone else's love because I had forgotten how to love myself. I'm
learning now — learning how to accept, forgive and love myself. And
I'm learning that things change. Pain *does* go away, and happiness is
the other side. Although the pain comes back, so does the happiness.
It is like waves in the ocean coming and going... coming and going...
breathing in and breathing out.

—Lia Gay, 16—

Just One Drink

There's a small cross by the side of Highway 128, near the town of Boonville. If this cross could talk, it would tell you this sad story: Seven years ago my brother, Michael, was at a friend's ranch. They decided to go out for dinner. Joe arrived and volunteered to drive — after just one drink.

Lightheartedly, the four friends traveled the winding road. They didn't know where it would end — nobody did. Suddenly, they swerved into the opposite lane, colliding with an oncoming car.

Back home we were watching *E.T.* in front of a warm fire. Then we went to bed. At 2:00 A.M. a police officer woke my mom with the devastating news. Michael had been killed.

In the morning, I found my mother and sister crying. I stood there bewildered. "What's wrong?" I asked, rubbing my sleepy eyes.

Mom took a deep breath. "Come here…"

Thus began a grueling journey through grief, where all roads lead to nowhere. It still hurts to remember that day.

The only thing that helps is telling my story, hoping you will remember it if you are tempted to get into a car with someone who has had a drink — even just one drink.

Joe chose the road to nowhere. He was convicted of manslaughter and served time. However, the real punishment is living with the consequences of his actions. He left us with an ache in our hearts that will never go away, a nightmare that will haunt him — and us — for the rest of our lives. And a small cross by the side of Highway 128.

— Chris Laddish, 13 —

The Premonition

Kyle, his mom Karen, and his sister Kari had been through their share of pain. When Kyle was twelve and Kari was nine, their father had walked out on the family in the middle of the night. They had little communication with him over the next few years and received no financial help.

To make ends meet, Karen and her children moved in with her mother in Dallas, Texas for a short period of time. Later, she was offered a job in Rock Hill, South Carolina, working for the gospel group The Happy Goodman Family. When the group moved their home base to Nashville, Karen, Kyle and Kari went along.

When Kyle entered his freshman year at Hillwood High School, Karen decided to settle down so that Kyle and Kari could both finish their remaining school years in one place. The family had finally arrived at a place where, for a moment, all the world was right.

Kyle grew into a handsome young man as well as a talented athlete. He excelled in football, and it became a big part of his life. When he put his uniform on, you could see his eyes light up. His coach and teammates called him "Hit Man" because he loved to hit people and wouldn't back down from anything. He was a good role model and poured his whole heart and soul into each game.

His senior year, Kyle made the most tackles on his team and was named Defensive Player of the Year. He was determined to play for Austin Peay State University where he would attend college the following autumn.

Kyle and his family had overcome so much. Finally things were going well. Kyle was happy and filled with dreams. In fact, he co-wrote a poem about it with his friend.

Dreams

A lost young petal
Wondering souls
I see the dream you seek
Follow me please, if you dare.
The dream is coming
For you and me.
I return by your side
With a heart in my hand.
It is like a bright fire dancing
To the slow music turning.
My heart as smooth as ivory
Has turned to a lonely, sulfur.
I retire my heart now to you,
Love me because I love you.

Still, a sense that he might fall hung over Kyle. He was at a crossroads; and though he couldn't see what lay ahead, he had a premonition of what would befall him.

One night Kyle told his mother, "I've got the crazy feeling something is going to happen to me, and they are going to dedicate the annual to me." Karen told him to never think like that, and Kyle laughed in his usual laidback way, saying, "Oh, Mom, it's just a crazy thought — nothing's gonna happen to me!"

Still the doubts troubled Kyle, as he wrote in this letter that was found tucked away in his room. It read:

> *This is to anyone. I'm writing because I need someone to talk to, someone to open myself to. I need to be held. Yes me. Even I am not made of brick. Although I'm strong, even strong things break down at times.*
>
> *Whoever reads, I don't want sympathy or talk, I just want someone to listen.*

I sit here laid back, tears are falling from my face. I'm so scared. I feel so alone, so lost, confused, sad... I realize I'm not going to have all the things I love forever.

Starting off... my friends. God, I've never felt this way. I look at their faces in my mind. What's going to happen? Will I see my friend Kenneth's face forever? I doubt it, even though our love for each other may stay, eventually we'll separate. The same with Marv, Chris, Brew. Brew's dad said he might move to Pensacola. I dread the thought of losing somebody so close, God...

And I'm going to college this year. God, I'm so scared, so afraid. I see Mom. God, I don't want to leave her. Sure I want to party, have a place of my own, but I'm so afraid of leaving because I love her and Kari so much.

My grandparents are going to die soon. I can't see living without... God...

Help...

Football. I'm so scared, I love the game so much. What if I don't make college or get a scholarship? It will be the bloody last time to put on a pair of pads, and that hurts... BAD.

And Mandy. I love her so much, but, God, I'm not even going to have that forever... I mean, sure, you never know... but the only thing that makes me happy and I can talk to might not be here either. And also talking to her about problems of hers. God, this sucks so bad... I love you Mandy.

Wherever you may go in the future, I will love all of you... Mom, Kari, Marvin, Chris, Kenneth, Alec, Rodrik, Brian, Travis, Brian, Paul, Bobby. Trey, Brew. Mandy. Luke...

I mean, you know, all I've really, really, really, really got is myself, and then eventually I'm gone.

Well, I'm going. I love everybody. Thanks for listening, piece of paper, or whoever reads it.

Love, Peace.
Your buddy, Love, Son, Brother, 4 ever
I love U All —

That spring, Kyle went to a party. The friend that had driven Kyle had to leave early, so Kyle caught a ride with a young man later that evening when he was ready to go home. The young man, whom Kyle did not know well, had been drinking. Perhaps Kyle didn't realize this when he climbed into the back seat, but it was a mistake that would cost him and his family dearly.

The car carrying Kyle and three other young people was traveling more than 100 miles an hour when the driver lost control in a curve. Police reports estimate that the vehicle slid sideways approximately 130 feet, then went airborne for 46 feet. The 1992 Mustang finally came to a stop when its rear end slammed into a tree. Kyle was thrown from the car through the back window.

Karen answered a knock on the door at 1:00 A.M. and experienced what she now calls "a mother's worst nightmare." She was told that Kyle had been in an accident and was at St. Thomas Hospital in critical condition.

On the way to the hospital, Karen kept thinking of all the hard times she, Kyle, and Kari had shared, and how they had always pulled together to make it through. She just knew in her heart that they would be able to again.

Karen's hopes were soon dashed. "We did all we could," said the doctor. Kyle had died.

Though Kyle's pain was over, the pain his mother and his sister would endure had just begun. On Karen's birthday a memorial service for Kyle was held in the Hillwood High gymnasium. With all the students, friends, and teachers present, Kyle's football coach, Jerry Link, presented Karen with Kyle's jersey, number 82, which they had retired in his honor. He also handed her Kyle's cap and gown, which had just come in for graduation. Karen spoke to the crowd.

She told Kyle's fellow students — among them many of his closest friends — that they must continue on, and that they must realize how precious life really is. She asked them not to take chances, and to live each day the best way possible.

Karen looked out into the faces of the young audience. Tears rolled down their cheeks as they remembered Kyle. They reflected upon his bright smile, his crazy sense of humor, his athletic ability — but most of all, the way he seemed to really care about everyone around him. She knew that they all realized, as she did, that it really was worth the pain just to have known him.

As the school year came to a close, Hillwood High School's yearbook was dedicated to Kyle, and his premonition from months before sadly came true. Karen was presented with a yearbook signed by many of his friends and fellow students.

— Bruce Burch —

Dead at 17

Agony claws my mind. I am a statistic. When I first got here, I felt very much alone. I was overwhelmed by grief, and I expected to find sympathy.

I found no sympathy. I saw only thousands of others whose bodies were as badly mangled as mine. I was given a number and placed in a category. The category was called "traffic fatalities."

The day I died was an ordinary school day. How I wish I had taken the bus! But I was too cool for the bus. I remember how I wheedled the car out of Mom. "Special favor," I pleaded. "All the kids drive." When the 2:50 P.M. bell rang, I threw my books in the locker. Free until tomorrow morning! I ran to the parking lot, excited at the thought of driving a car and being my own boss.

It doesn't matter how the accident happened, I was goofing off — going too fast, taking crazy chances. But I was enjoying my freedom and having fun. The last thing I remember was passing an old lady who seemed to be going awfully slow. I heard a crash and felt a terrific jolt. Glass and steel flew everywhere. My whole body seemed to be turning inside out. I heard myself scream.

Suddenly, I awakened. It was very quiet. A police officer was standing over me. I saw a doctor. My body was mangled. I was saturated with blood. Pieces of jagged glass were sticking out all over. Strange that I couldn't feel anything. Hey, don't pull that sheet over my head. I can't be dead. I'm only 17. I've got a date tonight. I'm supposed to have a wonderful life ahead of me. I haven't lived yet. I can't be dead!

Later I was placed in a drawer. My folks came to identify me. Why did they have to see me like this? Why did I have to look at Mom's eyes when she faced the most terrible ordeal of her life? Dad suddenly looked very old. He told the man in charge, "Yes — he is our son."

The funeral was weird. I saw all my relatives and friends walk toward the casket. They looked at me with the saddest eyes I've ever seen. Some of my buddies were crying. A few of the girls touched my hand and sobbed as they walked by.

Please — somebody — wake me up! Get me out of here. I can't bear to see Mom and Dad in such pain. My grandparents are so weak from grief they can barely walk. My brother and sister are like zombies. They move like robots. In a daze. Everybody. No one can believe this. I can't believe it, either.

Please don't bury me! I'm not dead! I have a lot of living to do! I want to laugh and run again. I want to sing and dance. Please don't put me in the ground! I promise if you give me just one more chance, God, I'll be the most careful driver in the whole world. All I want is one more chance. Please, God, I'm only 17.

—John Berrio—

"Gabby, You're Sooo Skinny"

I am a straight-A student. I am very involved in school activities and considered a "very together" teenager. Or at least, I was.

It all started innocently enough. I weighed about 125 pounds. I was not fat but felt I could stand to lose a few pounds. A friend of mine had gone on a health kick and was getting great results from it — she was losing weight, she felt better and her friends were telling her how great she looked. I wanted to feel that way, too.

I began exercising and eating healthy snacks instead of the usual Coke-and-chips marathon watching TV. Within a couple of weeks I had lost weight, I was feeling good, I cared more about what I wore and started feeling attractive in a way I had not experienced before. I would go to school and it seemed like everyone noticed. "Gabby, you look great," "Gabby, you look so beautiful," and "Gabby, you're so skinny." I don't think anything ever felt as good as those comments.

I was raised with the message that there is always room for improvement, so I figured if five pounds gets this much notice, just think what ten will do! If cutting back to 1,000 calories works, imagine 500! I figure that was the moment I took off down the road to anorexia.

My previous successes didn't feel as good to me as the success of this weight thing. I think it had something to do with the control I felt I had. I lost weight at a fast rate, and every time I lost a pound I was elated. It was a euphoria that, now in looking back, I realize I became addicted to. I lived for that feeling.

I remember the first time I went the whole day without eating. When I got into bed that night I felt this emptiness in my stomach. But I also felt thinness: a feeling I had come to connect with achievement and success. I remember thinking, *If I can go a whole day without eating, then why not two?*

There were many days I did just that. In fact, I could go three days without eating.

I don't remember exactly when it happened, but it was sudden and total: No one said nice things to me and no one was complimenting me. Instead of seeing the logical conclusion, which was that I was taking this too far, I started feeling that I was failing and needed to try harder. I needed to lose more weight; I would have to get serious now!

I had days where all I ate was an apple, and then I went to bed at night feeling like a failure, feeling fat. It got to the point that any food in my stomach felt like too much. It felt dirty and disgusting. I belittled myself for being so weak. My life was becoming a hell. I felt that if I could just control myself a little more, it would get better. The truth is, all happiness had long ago slipped away, and my whole being was devoted to the moments of success that I felt when I lost another pound.

A part of me knew this was probably wrong, but that part of me was out of reach. It was there, just not able to talk louder than my illness. I needed help, and yet there was no way I could ask for it. I could not even admit it to the people who tried so desperately to give it to me.

Teachers, school nurses, friends — they all suspected I had a problem. My concern was only to put them off and convince them I was fine. I wonder if they really believed me, or if they just knew they couldn't help until I was ready.

I remember one night my dad brought home steak and announced to me that I was going to eat it and he was going to watch me. He would not take no for an answer. I cried and begged him not to make me do this. This thing sitting on my plate had become my worst enemy. It was pure fat; one bite would ruin everything. I had to make him understand I could not eat this, and that if he really loved me, he would not make me. I was crying, begging him to let go of this crazy idea, but he wouldn't. He said he would sit there all night. I had no choice, NO CHOICE! But this was supposed to be my choice. The one thing I had control over. Those words pushed a button in me and I no longer cared about him or his feelings. All I felt were anger and hate. I hated him for making me do this, for making me feel my pain and face how distorted my reality had become. I hated him for making me eat that disgusting, evil food.

All my life I had done things for everyone else. The grades, the manners, the awards — everything for them, nothing for me. This eating thing, this losing weight had become *mine*. It represented me and *my* choices, and now my dad was trying to take that away from me, too!

As I lay in bed that night crying and feeling fat, I knew I needed help. I knew I was hurting people I loved.

After staying up all night, I came to the conclusion that it wasn't my dad I hated. I hated ME! I realized that I wasn't in control. For the first time in my life, I understood that this was *my* problem. I needed to take control of my life — not let the disease control it.

Things didn't change overnight. In fact, it was one long road to recovery. But slowly, with the help of friends and family, I began to heal. Now that I'm at my ideal weight, I have stopped weighing myself altogether. I no longer peruse fashion magazines, either — I may not be "in style," but I feel just right!

— Gabriella Tortes, 17, as told to Kimberly Kirberger —

Gold-Medal Winner

I spoke at a middle school and when the program was over the principal asked me if I would pay a visit to a special student. An illness had kept the boy home, but he had expressed an interest in meeting me, and the principal knew it would mean a great deal to him. I agreed.

During the nine-mile drive to his home, I found out some things about Matthew. He had muscular dystrophy. When he was born, the doctors told his parents that he would not live to see five, then they were told he would not make it to 10. He was 13 and from what I was told, a real fighter. He wanted to meet me because I was a gold-medal power lifter, and I knew about overcoming obstacles and going for your dreams.

I spent over an hour talking to Matthew. Never once did he complain or ask, "Why me?" He spoke about winning and succeeding and going for his dreams. Obviously, he knew what he was talking about. He didn't mention that his classmates had made fun of him because he was different; he just talked about his hopes for the future, and how one day he wanted to lift weights with me.

When we finished talking, I went into my briefcase and pulled out the first gold medal I won for power lifting and put it around his neck. I told him he was more of a winner and knew more about success and overcoming obstacles than I ever would. He looked at it for a moment, then took it off and handed it back to me. He said, "Rick, you are a champion. You earned that medal. Someday, when I get to the Olympics and win my gold medal, I will show it to you."

Last summer I received a letter from Matthew's parents telling me that Matthew had passed away. They wanted me to have a letter he had written to me a few days before.

Dear Rick,

My mom said I should send you a thank-you letter for the neat picture you sent me. I also wanted to let you know that the doctors tell me I don't have long to live anymore. It is getting very hard for me to breathe and I get tired very easy, but I still smile as much as I can. I know that I will never be as strong as you and I know we will never get to lift weights together.

I told you someday I was going to go to the Olympics and win a gold medal. I know now I will never get to do that. But I know I am a champion, and God knows that too. He knows I am not a quitter, and when I get to heaven, God will give me my gold medal, and when you get there, I will show it to you. Thanks for loving me.

Your Friend,
Matthew

— Rick Metzger —

Think Before You Act

I t was a cold evening, the night before Halloween, when something happened in my town that no one will ever forget. During lunchtime at school, some girls who were my brother's friends told him about a plan that they had to toilet paper a guy's house. They had already been playing pranks on this guy, and they were laughing about what his house would look like when they were through with it. My brother told me later that he knew what they were planning on doing was wrong, but he didn't say anything to the girls. Now, he wishes he would have.

That night my brother's six friends stayed overnight at one of the girl's houses. In the middle of the night, they sneaked out of the house. They piled into one of the girl's small blue car and set off to play their little prank. When they got to the guy's house, everything went as planned — until they got caught. The guy that they were playing the prank on came outside and saw them. Laughing, they all ran to the car and hopped in, hoping to get away. The guy got into his car and chased after them, trying to identify them. He was right on their tail, and it scared the girls really badly. They were not sure what he would do to them if he caught them, so they went faster.

Then, when they were turning on a blind curve in the road, they lost control of the car and hit a tree head-on. Three of the girls were ejected from the car and were killed instantly. The other three girls were seriously injured. One of the girls had just enough strength to get out of the car and go to a nearby house. The people who answered the door were afraid of her and didn't even believe that there had been an accident. They said, "Yeah, right, you really got into a wreck," and they would not call the police.

The three girls that died were all honor-roll students and were looking ahead to doing something great with their lives. But all of their dreams were shattered when they hit the tree on that cold night. Only one of my brother's friends was wearing a seat belt, and she was one of the survivors. Now whenever I get into a car, I think about the accident and put on my seat belt.

The guy that chased them went to court. All he got was a ticket for running a stop sign and for speeding. I often wonder if he feels anything at all about the death of the girls in that car that he chased. My brother feels bad that he didn't say anything to his friends that day when they told him what they were planning on doing. They still might have gone on their mission regardless of what he said, but he might have saved his friends' lives. We'll never know. So many people have suffered because of a stupid act that was never meant to go wrong.

The only good thing that came from this tragic event is that the mother of one of the deceased girls is setting up a teen center in town in memory of the girls that died. Now there will be a place for teens. Maybe that will keep some of them from getting into situations like this by providing a place to hang out and have fun, to talk to each other and hopefully give them a chance to help them think before they act.

— Lauren Wheeler, 12 —

Editor's note: This story was originally published in *Chicken Soup for the Preteen Soul*, but we moved it to this new anniversary edition of *Chicken Soup for the Teenage Soul* based on the subject matter.

Rediscovery

*Believing in our hearts that who we are is enough
is the key to a more satisfying and balanced life.*
~Ellen Sue Stern

Seven. The age of ballet lessons and Barbie dolls, of learning to add and subtract simple numbers; the time when the family dog is your closest companion. Seven. The age of innocence.

I was a typical-looking child. I had long, straight brown hair that fell past my shoulders. My almond-shaped hazel eyes were always full of adventure and curiosity. And I had a smile that could brighten a bleak winter day.

I was a happy child with a loving family, and many friends, who loved to perform skits on home videos. I was a leader in school, not a follower. My best trait was my personality. I had imagination. But what made me special was not seen from the outside: I had a special love for life.

At age twelve, my life had a huge breakdown. It was then that I developed obsessive compulsive disorder (OCD). OCD is a disorder that is the result of a chemical imbalance in the brain. People with OCD don't think the same way as people with chemically balanced brains. People with OCD do rituals. I started to wash my hands ten times an hour to avoid germs, and I constantly checked my kitchen oven to make sure that it was off. This way of life for me continued for four agonizing years, and by then, my OCD had led to depression. I was no longer the happy little girl I had been.

In the tenth grade I finally confessed to my mother that I was suffering from depression along with my OCD. I couldn't take the emotional pain anymore. I needed help if I wanted to continue living.

My mom took me to a doctor the same week. I started taking medicine that would hopefully cure my OCD and depression. Over the course of a few months, the medicine did help the OCD. I stopped doing rituals. I no longer took four showers a day to avoid germs. But one thing didn't change; I still was overwhelmed with depression. I still was constantly sad, and I started to believe that my life no longer mattered.

One autumn evening two years ago, I hit rock bottom. I thought that my life no longer had meaning, because I no longer brought joy to other people like I did when I was little. I decided suicide was the only solution to my depression problem, so I wrote a suicide note to all my friends and family. In the note I expressed that I was sorry for deciding to leave them, but that I thought it was for the best. As I was folding the note, my eyes fell on a photograph. It was a picture of an adorable little girl with natural blond highlights in her brown hair from spending so much time in the sun. She was wearing her red soccer uniform and held a biking helmet in her small hands. She had a carefree smile on her face that showed she was full of life.

It took me a few minutes to realize who the girl in the photo was. The photo had been taken one weekend at my uncle's house when I was seven years old. I almost couldn't believe that smiling child was me! I felt a chill go down my spine. It was like my younger self had sent me a message. Right then and there I knew I couldn't kill myself. Once I had been a strong little girl, and I had to become strong like that again.

I tore up my suicide note and vowed that I would not rely only on my medicine to help my depression. I would have to fight the depression with my mind, too. I could make myself happy again.

It has been two years since I "rediscovered" myself. I am OCD- and depression-free. I still take medicine to keep my disorder at bay, but the real reason I am healed is because I took action and refused to let depression ruin my life. I learned a lifelong lesson: Never give up. Life is good. Everyone has challenges in life, but everyone can survive. I am living proof of that. Also, it is important to keep smiling, because in the end, everything will work out.

Of course my life can still be a struggle, but I pull through with a smile on my face. I know I can't give up on life. I am here for a reason. Sometimes, I think it was strange that I had to look to who I was as a little girl in order to regain faith in myself at age eighteen. But I think everyone can look back on their early years and see that it was then that they knew how to live in peace and happiness.

I have plans for myself now. Once I graduate from high school this spring, I plan on going to college to major in journalism. I want to be a writer someday. And I am prepared for whatever challenges life may bring. I have a role model to look up to for strength, and who is guiding me through life. My hero is a seven-year-old girl, smiling back at me from a photo on my desk.

— Raegan Baker —

Editor's note: This story was originally published in *Chicken Soup for the Preteen Soul*, but we moved it to this new anniversary edition of *Chicken Soup for the Teenage Soul* based on the age of the writer.

April Morning

The date was April 19, 1995. I was getting ready for school like I usually did, and my mother, Diana, was getting ready for work. She worked at the federal building in Oklahoma City.

As I left for school, I told my mom goodbye. I told her that I loved her and that I would see her after school. Little did I know that I wouldn't be seeing her after school, and that my life would soon be changed.

Around 1:30, a call came over the intercom, asking for me to come to the office to be checked out from school. I thought, *Cool, it must be my mom.* She would always surprise me like that and take me somewhere.

When I got to the office, instead of my mom, it was my grandpa and my aunt. They were both crying and had confused and worried looks on their faces. I didn't have time to ask what was wrong. They grabbed me and we drove in a hurry to my house.

When I went in, my whole family was sitting around, crying and watching the news. I didn't see my mom there. I glanced at the TV and I saw the building where my mom worked. Most of the building had been blown up. People were coming out bleeding. I knew from that moment on, there was a chance my mom wouldn't be coming home. So I fell to my knees and began to pray. The only thing that was going through my mind was, *How could God let me down like this?*

We all stayed at my house and waited to see if maybe they would find her alive. Hours went by and nothing happened. During that time I saw my mom's friends coming out on stretchers. They were lifeless. I began to feel hatred toward whoever did this and cried even more. I felt useless. I couldn't do anything. But my family was there and they helped me.

Days went by with no answer. I was in shock. All I wanted was my mom to come home and tell me that everything would be okay, but that wish never came true.

One Wednesday morning, two and a half weeks after the bombing, the crying of my aunt and grandma woke me up. I got out of bed to see if they were okay. They told me that my mom had been found.

I was so happy I couldn't believe it. God had answered my prayers! I asked when she was coming home. They said she wouldn't be coming home. I was a little confused. Then they told me that she didn't survive the bomb. Mom worked on the seventh floor of the building. She was found on the second floor. I began to cry, and I thought, *How could God let this happen?*

My mother was the number one thing in my life, and now she is the number one thing in my heart. She did come home on the day of the bombing, not to our home but to her home in the sky. Now I feel that my mom is just waiting for the day when I come home. In the meantime, I will try to make her proud of me and always remember how special she was. Those thoughts and beliefs are what help me get through every day of my life.

— Justin Day, 15 —

Editor's note: This story was originally published in *Chicken Soup for the Preteen Soul*, but we moved it to this new anniversary edition of *Chicken Soup for the Teenage Soul* based on the age of the writer.

Getting Better

I was a nine-year-old girl beginning a journey to a whole new place. My mother and I were saying goodbye to our family, and were on our way to Kent, Washington, where we were going to live. My sisters, brother and dad were staying in Billings because my parents were divorced. My parents divorced when I was around two, and my dad remarried when I was four years old.

My mother and I were moving to Seattle because she had been offered a job as a special ed teacher. The only reason that I went with my mother was because she had told me so many bad things about my father, and I was too scared to live with him. I didn't even really want to leave because I wanted to stay with my sisters, but I didn't know what to do about my dad.

Let me tell you, it was incredibly scary to be all of a sudden moving to a whole new place where I didn't know anybody. My mother and I moved into an apartment. Just after we arrived and we were unloading our things, a somewhat nice-looking guy came walking down the stairs. He introduced himself as John and offered to help us unload our belongings. He seemed quite nice, so we said yes and just kept on unloading. We finally finished unloading so we began to unpack our things.

Pretty soon, my mother and John began to date, and after about three months, John would come over to our apartment all the time. To me it began to feel like they were married. He would stay until really late, and he loved to tuck me into bed. I was not sure how to deal with all of this because something about him scared me really badly. My mother and John decided to get married. I didn't get excited about it.

After the wedding, John started to come into my room more and more, and would stay for a long time. He began to touch me in very uncomfortable ways and I would get extremely scared. I didn't say anything, because I was too scared. Sometimes I would put my hands over my chest and roll over so that my back was facing him. During this particular time, my mother would usually be in her room watching TV, and I did not want to scream. I knew that if I did he would immediately stop and pretend to be innocent, and my mother would think that I was crazy.

A few months after the wedding, my mother and John found a new house. I was given the opportunity to live with my dad again, and based on what was going on with John, I decided to move back to Billings.

My family in Billings was extremely excited to have me back, but when I got home it was hard for me to get close to them. I found myself having a hard time showing any physical affection toward my dad and stepmom. John had confused me as to what was normal and what was appropriate. Any physical contact made me pull away.

My sister and I would go see my mother during every vacation. Sometimes neither of us wanted to, but we were expected to. I used to cry and beg my parents not to make me go. Every time I was there, John would touch me and I would get more scared about what was happening and whether or not anyone would believe me if I told.

At one point, I told my best friend Lindsey what was happening and she told me to tell my parents. I didn't think that they would believe me so I made her swear to keep quiet, and I didn't take her advice.

My dad and stepmom began to wonder if there was something going on that I just wasn't able to talk about. Then one day, my stepmom decided to have a school counselor come to the house to see if she could help me break through the awkward silence. Rather than tell a stranger what had been happening, I finally burst out and told my stepmom the truth.

At last, I had the courage to tell my family what John had been doing to me. My stepmom, Jean, pulled me close to her and we cried for a long time together.

Soon after that, we contacted an attorney who got in touch with the police in Washington. John was arrested, but it took nine months before we actually went to court. It was really hard on me to face my mother during the trial, but I got through it. All that I have to say is that it was one of the hardest times of my life.

John was found guilty and went to jail, but immediately he hired a new lawyer to appeal the case. Just before he was to be sentenced, he was granted a new trial. He decided to accept a plea bargain and was freed from jail after only five months. As unbelievable as it sounds, he was able to return to his job with the government and is living with my mother. As I suspected, she didn't believe me, even after a jury of twelve adults found John guilty. The family has not had any contact with her in nearly three years.

After the trial, I felt that the attorneys had taken such care with my case and treated me so wonderfully, I wanted to become a lawyer. I want to defend little kids, or anyone else, who is unfortunate enough to be in the same situation that I was.

I always have hope that one day my mom will see how much she has missed and get back in touch with us kids. There are days when it saddens me and I cry and get furious. I will always love my mother no matter what, and hopefully someday I will be able to accept the choices she has made and the person that she is.

I now live my life the best way that I possibly can. I know who I am inside, and that took a lot of counseling. I also don't think that I would be who I am right now if it weren't for my stepmom and dad and their intuition that something was terribly wrong in my life back then. I can't imagine what my future would have held. Now, it's better than it's ever been, and getting better.

— Tiffany Jacques, 15 —

Editor's note: This story was originally published in *Chicken Soup for the Preteen Soul*, but we moved it to this new anniversary edition of *Chicken Soup for the Teenage Soul* based on the subject matter.

Chapter
7

Making a Difference

Great opportunities to help others seldom come,
but small ones surround us every day.
~Sally Koch

Family Ties

Invisible threads are the strongest ties.
~Friedrich Nietzsche

During my senior year of high school, I took a course on World War II. It had been pretty simple — taking notes, watching documentaries, writing papers. So, when my teacher handed out an assignment asking us to research a member of our family who had served during the war, I was less than thrilled by the addition to my workload.

Of course, I knew who I would write about. My mom's father had flown B-17 bombers during the war, and there was no shortage of documents and photos around our house. I hadn't known him well since I was pretty young when he died, but I had heard plenty of stories over the years. One, particularly, stuck out: Before the war began, my grandfather had been married to a woman in Kansas named Esther. They had two children, and when he returned from his deployment, the marriage ended. He remarried and had five more kids, but he didn't mention his "first family" to them until they were adults, and, even then, he didn't say much.

This had always been fascinating to me. How could you fail to mention something so important? I quietly decided to learn as much as I could about my grandfather's first family.

I chatted with my mom and looked through some old letters to see if I could find out anything about my grandfather's first wife, whose name was Esther. As it turned out, a last name was all I needed! From that point forward, thanks to the magic of the Internet, things fell into place. Google led me to the Facebook account of a woman in California whose maiden name was the same as Esther's. One night, I mustered up my courage and sent her a message, then went to bed. I knew it was a stretch, so I quickly introduced myself and then spent about three paragraphs apologizing for any inconvenience, especially if we weren't actually related.

By this point in my senior year, I had already been accepted to a few colleges. I was on track to graduate with high honors. My high school life was pretty close to being tied up with a nice bow on top. I couldn't figure out why I had put so much energy into this small assignment. It wasn't going to make or break my college choice or help me cope with moving away from all my friends. It was just something that I felt like I had to do. Deep down, I was compelled to connect with this side of my family, even though I had no practical reason to ever reach out to them.

I woke up the next morning and got dressed for school. As I was walking out the door, I glanced down at my phone and saw a few messages. At first, I was scared to read them.

The first was a message from Esther and the second was from her twin sister! All my fears had been unfounded. They were thrilled to connect with their "East Coast" family, which they had only heard about in hushed conversations over the years. We talked a lot over the next few weeks. They spoke with my mom and her siblings, and I got to learn about my new cousins and second cousins.

It was the strangest thing that's ever happened to me. All my life, I had been living in Florida, going about my own business and never even stopping to consider that I had family on the other side of the country. While I was having my life, they were having theirs. Had it not been for that history-class assignment, we probably wouldn't have ever connected.

Life works in mysterious ways. Sometimes, you get a gut feeling that you have to do something. And you have to do it right now. The stars align and you learn more about yourself than you ever thought possible.

— Grace Hanna —

A Performance to Remember

The meaning of life is to find your gift.
The purpose of life is to give it away.
~Pablo Picasso

I love to play the piano and I greatly enjoy performing my music, so when the annual winter recital was canceled, I was disappointed. I had looked forward to it for a long time and had already prepared two of my best songs. My mom had a wonderful idea, however, to turn this disappointing letdown into something worthwhile. "You and your sister should perform your songs at Carriage House Senior Living," my mom suggested brightly. "I'm sure the seniors there would really appreciate the music and you could each play more than just two songs."

I immediately thought this was a great idea. One of the things I did not like about the recitals was that I was limited to playing just a couple of songs. Playing the piano at Carriage House seemed like a win-win situation because not only would I get to play more songs, but I would also have the chance to cheer up the residents at the home with some lively tunes.

My mom called Carriage House and made arrangements for my sister and me to perform. We were told we could play the piano during the Sunday dinner hour in two weeks. In the coming days, I worked especially hard to polish up fifteen pieces that I thought the crowd would enjoy, including many old classics. My sister and I decided that first I would play three songs and then she would, taking turns until the end of the hour.

When the much-anticipated day finally arrived, my family and I drove to Carriage House. Walking through the enormous double doors, we stepped into an entryway that overlooked the spacious grand dining room. Right at the entrance to the dining room stood the piano, a shiny black electric baby grand. The piano seemed as if it were just waiting to make some music to liven the place up a bit. The dining area was filled with circular tables set with gleaming silverware. At nearly every table several gray-haired women or men were seated enjoying an early dinner and the company that the crowded room provided. Despite the conversations going on at various tables though, isolation hung like a dark cloud in the room.

Almost immediately, we were greeted by an old woman with a walker who introduced herself as Phyllis. "You two must be the girls who came here to sing," she said smiling. When I told her that we had come to play the piano, she seemed just as pleased and told someone to go run and get a microphone. "I'll introduce you two to the audience," she informed us. She told us that she was always the one in charge of doing things like that. I asked her if I could introduce myself and she agreed I could. While we waited for the microphone, I pressed a key on the piano and was surprised to hear no sound. "It's not plugged in," Phyllis chuckled.

Soon a man returned with a microphone and plugged in the piano. Phyllis slowly made her way to the front of the crowd of diners and my sister and I stood next to the beaming woman as she announced to the room, "These two girls have come to sing and want to introduce themselves!" As she handed the microphone to me there was scattered applause.

"Hi, my name is Baylie," I said with a smile.

"Hi, I'm Chloe," my sister said shyly.

"We have come here to entertain you with some piano songs. We hope you enjoy our performance," I enthusiastically announced.

As I sat down on the hard bench and turned to my first song, I was a little bit nervous, but mainly I was excited to have the chance to share my songs with these people. Any nervousness melted away as I began the song and I actually started to enjoy myself as I played my next two pieces.

The dinner hour flew by with hardly a disruption. Several people stopped and paused by the piano before moving on to their tables. One woman got up and began to animatedly dance about the room. Some of the people swayed in their chairs to the beat of the music while others tapped theirs toes or snapped their fingers. I was amazed to see how just a little music brought big smiles to their faces. In no time at all, the dinner hour, which had stretched into an hour and a half, came to an end. I gathered my music, and my sister and I walked to the front of the room and curtsied as the crowd wholeheartedly applauded.

After performing at Carriage House, I realized that it was far better than a piano recital because almost everyone seemed to truly appreciate our music. Many of the people there do not have families that visit them that often, and tragically some do not even have families at all.

I realized that no matter how young you are, you still have the power to make a difference in the world and spread kindness to those desperately in need of it. It ended up being a blessing in disguise that the recital was canceled, because it led to us sharing the gift of music with those who needed it most.

— Baylie Jett Mills —

Miss Minnie and Me

Choose people who lift you up.
~Michelle Obama

They say it takes a village to raise a child, but what they don't tell you is that the village keeps on growing and changing as the child grows. Some people join the village, and others leave as time passes. As these changes occur in the village, the village itself gets stronger and bolder, making it something wonderful to behold.

As I have gotten older, my own village has grown — adding teachers, pastors, and even family members — but no one has touched my life in the way that Miss Minnie has. She, like myself, grew up in the church we attend regularly each Sunday. She, like myself, has a firm relationship with God. And she, like myself, has experienced hardships that have shaped her.

Yet, with all those similarities, I would have never guessed she would become part of my village. Every Sunday, I saw her in church — her small body bundled up in her huge winter coat as she perched at the end of her favorite wooden pew. When service began, I would walk past her, never really saying anything.

That all changed when my mom told me to speak to her one day. Saying hello that day turned into several hellos and how-are-you-doings, which grew into phone calls and eventually home visits. And it's the home visits that are my favorite part.

Each Sunday afternoon, I visit Miss Minnie. After knocking on her apartment door, I wait, knowing that it takes her a while to answer the door. When she opens the door, I step inside and take a look at the familiar surroundings: teddy bears and the Washington Team logos are everywhere. Her walls are filled with her accomplishments and photographs of loved ones. Her home is small and tidy, and there is a warmth about it that lifts my spirit each time I step inside.

Almost immediately, she tells me, "You can sit down."

Following her orders, I take my usual seat. I watch as she maneuvers her walker next to me before sitting down in her chair. Once she's comfortable, she looks at me.

"So, what's up, boo boo?" she asks. I smile at her and let whatever I need to say rattle off my tongue, letting our conversation begin. Sometimes I tell her the same thing as I did last week, but the simple fact that I'm once again in her presence fills me with so much joy.

Although Miss Minnie is small in stature, her voice is powerful and each time she speaks, it soothes my soul and gives me peace like a calmly flowing river. I watch her as she speaks, her brown face rich with wrinkles, and I am reminded of how much she has lived and how much more life I have to go.

Miss Minnie speaks without fear of the future, a quality that strengthens me as I navigate becoming an adult. Her wisdom is at the forefront of almost every conversation we have. And even when I'm getting fussed at (which happens more often than I'd like to admit), I know that I can take whatever she says with grace.

Somewhere in each of our conversations, Miss Minnie makes me laugh. And when I burst into a fit of giggles, she laughs too. As she laughs, her smile lights up the room, and it lets me know that everything in the world is just fine, even if it's only for a moment.

Eventually, my phone buzzes, and I know that my mother has summoned me home. Two hours have flown by, but it only feels like ten minutes. I look at Miss Minnie and say the words I hate to say every time: "Well, Miss Minnie, I have to get home." I stand, she looks up at me and nods, grabbing her walker to accompany me to the door.

"You know, God sent you to me," she says once we've reached the door. I touch the door handle and look down at her with a smile. "Yes ma'am, I do." She nods, knowing that I have heard her say that before. And yet each time she says it, I'm reminded of how important she is in my village. And even though we're generations apart, there is still something connecting and holding us together.

I promise to visit next week as usual and allow her to shut the door firmly behind me before I leave. On the way home, I smile to myself, knowing that God has surely put us together.

— Malaysia Barr —

Be Cool... Stay in School!

I n the eighth grade, I was student-body president of Erwin Middle
School in Asheville, North Carolina. I considered this quite an
honor since there were over 1,000 students in the school. At the
end of the year, I was asked to make a speech at the ceremony
where my class was promoted to high school. I knew this had to be
more than just the brief comments a student might normally give.
We're the class of 2000, so I wanted my speech to be as special as we
were.

I spent several nights lying in bed, thinking about what to say.
Many things crossed my mind, but none of them involved all my
classmates. Then one night, it hit me. Erwin High School has the
highest dropout rate of any high school in our county. What better
goal could we have than for every single one of us to graduate? What
if I could get my class to become the first class in the history of our
public school system to enter high school as freshmen and all graduate?
Wouldn't that be awesome?

The speech I gave on graduation day was only 12 minutes long,
but what it started is unbelievable. When I issued the challenge to my
classmates to become the first class in history to enter high school as
freshmen and all graduate, the entire audience, including the parents,
grandparents and teachers, erupted in applause. As I showed the per-
sonalized certificates and signs each student would get, I could tell
they were really enthused. At the end of my speech the whole audience
jumped to its feet with a standing ovation. It was all I could do to
keep my composure and not break down and cry. I'd had no idea my
challenge would bring this kind of response.

Throughout the summer, I worked on developing a program to carry our commitment into high school. I gave speeches to civic clubs and groups, and talked with several of my classmates. I told our high school principal that I wanted to start a "Dropout Patrol," made up of students who would be willing to help and support other students during bad times. I told him I wanted to design a special shirt to identify members of our class and would like to sell these to make money to publish a class directory. Then I told him I thought it would be good if we could have some type of party to celebrate if we made it through a whole semester without losing anyone.

"I'll go you one better than that," he told me. "I'll throw your class a party at the end of each grading period if you don't lose anyone." That was really exciting because a grading period was only six weeks: just 30 school days. The plan was beginning to come together.

Throughout the summer, word began to spread about our challenge. I appeared on local television and radio, the newspaper asked me to write a guest column and calls started coming in from everywhere. One day I received a call from CBS News in New York. One of their researchers had found my newspaper article and they were interested in featuring our class on their 48 Hours program. Ken Hamblin, the Black Avenger on national talk radio, featured us in his August 1996 publication, Ken Hamblin Talks with America. He invited me to appear on his show and tell the country about our commitment. All this was amazing, because I had told our class we could become the most famous class in America if we all made it to graduation. We were just beginning, and we were already drawing national attention.

As I write this story, our journey is just beginning. We have the first 12 weeks of school behind us. Our pledges are hanging in the school lobby across from the principal's office. Across from them is a large glass case where we mounted a piece of sheet metal with a huge hourglass painted on it. In the top of the hourglass there is a round magnetic dot for each day we have remaining in high school. We have appointed a committee of "Dropout Patrol" members to monitor the hourglass. Each day they move a dot from the top to the bottom. This lets us track our progress in a way the entire class can watch.

We began with 720 dots in the top, but now 60 of them have been moved to the bottom and we have earned our second party. It's fun to watch the dots move.

We are just starting a difficult four-year journey, but we have already made a significant impact. Last year, by the end of the second grading period, 13 kids had dropped out of the freshman class. So far this year, not a single person who signed the pledge has quit, and the "Dropout Patrol" has become the largest organized group in the school.

Businesses are seeing what a program run completely by kids can do, and they are throwing their support behind us. We have banks, car dealers, furniture stores, restaurants and more where we can get discounts for our entire family when we show our "Dropout Patrol" ID cards. Others are donating U.S. Savings Bonds and merchandise that we use to reward kids for supporting our program.

The Erwin High "Committed Class of 2000" would like to encourage your class to start a program like ours. Wouldn't it be awesome if the entire class of 2000, nationwide, had a 100 percent graduation rate? Who knows? Maybe it can!

—Jason Summey, 15—

The Leader

If only they knew how hard it is for me.

I'm turning 16, the world I begin to see.

My friends began to change, right before my eyes, and now they seem to laugh, and tell all sorts of lies.

They hang around together in groups of three or four; the language they use… it isn't gentle anymore.

The kids that seem most lonely wind up in their pack, and those that stand alone, they talk behind their back.

Somehow I feel rejected because I don't conform.

Those that step to their own beat don't seem to be the norm. I've watched a few just fade away, with drugs and alcohol; and many more have given up, too many to recall.

Alcohol is an option for everyone in my school.

I've lost a friend to booze again; I will not be a fool.

And sex, it seems so open, for everyone to explore.

Three girls I know that came to school don't come here anymore.

If only I could make a difference, what could I do or say? I would go to school and try my best each and every day. There is one thing I'd like to do before I graduate.

I'd like to touch them one by one before it is too late.

— Tony Overman —

Courage in Action

A couple of years ago, I witnessed courage that ran chills up and down my spine.

At a high school assembly, I had spoken about picking on people and how each of us has the ability to stand up for people instead of putting them down. Afterwards, we had a time when anyone could come out of the bleachers and speak into the microphone. Students could say thank you to someone who had helped them, and some people came up and did just that. A girl thanked some friends who had helped her through family troubles. A boy spoke of some people who had supported him during an emotionally difficult time.

Then a senior girl stood up. She stepped over to the microphone, pointed to the sophomore section and challenged her whole school. "Let's stop picking on that boy. Sure, he's different from us, but we are in this thing together. On the inside he's no different from us and needs our acceptance, love, compassion and approval. He needs a friend. Why do we continually brutalize him and put him down? I'm challenging this entire school to lighten up on him and give him a chance!"

All the time she shared, I had my back to the section where that boy sat, and I had no idea who he was. But obviously the school knew. I felt almost afraid to look at his section, thinking the boy must be red in the face, wanting to crawl under his seat and hide from the world. But as I glanced back, I saw a boy smiling from ear to ear. His whole body bounced up and down, and he raised one fist in the air. His body language said, "Thank you, thank you. Keep telling them.

You saved my life today!"

— Bill Sanders —

Reprinted by permission of Fleming H. Revell, a division of Baker Book House Co. Excerpted from *Goalposts: Devotions for Girls* by Bill Sanders.

Turning Up Your Light

Those who bring sunshine to the lives
of others cannot keep it from themselves.
~J.M. Barrie

More than three decades ago, I was a sophomore at a large high school in Southern California. The student body of 3,200 was a melting pot of ethnic differences. The environment was tough. Knives, pipes, chains, brass knuckles and an occasional zip gun were commonplace. Fights and gang activity were weekly events.

After a football game, I left the bleachers with my girlfriend. As we walked down the crowded sidewalk, someone kicked me from behind. Turning around, I discovered the local gang, armed with brass knuckles. The first blow of the unprovoked attack immediately broke my nose, one of several bones to be broken in the pounding. Fists came from every direction as the 15 gang members surrounded me. More injuries. A brain concussion. Internal bleeding. Eventually, I had to have surgery. My doctor told me that if I had been hit in the head one more time, I probably would have died. Fortunately, they did not harm my girlfriend.

After I recovered medically, some friends approached me and said, "Let's go get those guys!" That was the way problems were "resolved." After being attacked, evening the score became a priority. A part of me said, "Yes!" The sweet taste of revenge was clearly an option.

But another part of me paused and said no. Revenge did not work. Clearly, history had demonstrated time and again that reprisal only accelerates and intensifies conflict. We needed to do something differently to break the counterproductive chain of events.

Working with various ethnic groups, we put together what we called a "Brotherhood Committee" to work on enhancing racial relationships. I was amazed to learn how much interest fellow students had in building a brighter future. Not all bought in to doing things differently. While small numbers of students, faculty and parents actively resisted these cross-cultural exchanges, more and more individuals joined in on the effort to make a positive difference.

Two years later, I ran for student body president. Even though I ran against two friends, one a football hero and the other a popular "big man on campus," a significant majority of the 3,200 students joined me in the process of doing things differently. I will not claim that the racial problems were fully resolved. We did, however, make significant progress in building bridges between cultures, learning how to talk with and relate to different ethnic groups, resolving differences without resorting to violence and learning how to build trust in the most difficult of circumstances. It's amazing what happens when people are on speaking terms with one another!

Being attacked by the gang those many years ago was clearly one of my toughest life moments. What I learned, however, about responding with love rather than returning hate has been a powerful force in my life. Turning up our light in the presence of those whose light is dim becomes the difference that makes the difference.

— Eric Allenbaugh —

Broken Wing

You were born with wings.
Why prefer to crawl through life?
~Rumi

Some people are just doomed to be failures. That's the way some adults look at troubled kids. Maybe you've heard the saying, "A bird with a broken wing will never fly as high." I'm sure that T. J. Ware was made to feel this way almost every day in school.

By high school, T. J. was the most celebrated troublemaker in his town. Teachers literally cringed when they saw his name posted on their classroom lists for the next semester. He wasn't very talkative, didn't answer questions and got into lots of fights. He had flunked almost every class by the time he entered his senior year, yet was being passed on each year to a higher grade level. Teachers didn't want to have him again the following year. T. J. was moving on, but definitely not moving up.

I met T. J. for the first time at a weekend leadership retreat. All the students at school had been invited to sign up for ACE training, a program designed to have students become more involved in their communities. T. J. was one of 405 students who signed up. When I showed up to lead their first retreat, the community leaders gave me this overview of the attending students: "We have a total spectrum represented today, from the student body president to T. J. Ware, the boy with the longest arrest record in the history of town." Somehow, I knew that I wasn't the first to hear about T. J.'s darker side as the first words of introduction.

At the start of the retreat, T. J. was literally standing outside the circle of students, against the back wall, with that "go ahead, impress me" look on his face. He didn't readily join the discussion groups, didn't seem to have much to say. But slowly, the interactive games drew him in. The ice really melted when the groups started building a list of positive and negative things that had occurred at school that year. T. J. had some definite thoughts on those situations. The other students in T. J.'s group welcomed his comments. All of a sudden T. J. felt like a part of the group, and before long he was being treated like a leader. He was saying things that made a lot of sense, and everyone was listening. T. J. was a smart guy and he had some great ideas.

The next day, T. J. was very active in all the sessions. By the end of the retreat, he had joined the Homeless Project team. He knew something about poverty, hunger and hopelessness. The other students on the team were impressed with his passionate concern and ideas. They elected T. J. co-chairman of the team. The student council president would be taking his instruction from T. J. Ware.

When T. J. showed up at school on Monday morning, he arrived to a firestorm. A group of teachers were protesting to the school principal about his being elected co-chairman. The very first communitywide service project was to be a giant food drive, organized by the Homeless Project team. These teachers couldn't believe that the principal would allow this crucial beginning to a prestigious, three-year action plan to stay in the incapable hands of T. J. Ware. They reminded the principal, "He has an arrest record as long as your arm. He'll probably steal half the food." Mr. Coggshall reminded them that the purpose of the ACE program was to uncover any positive passion that a student had and reinforce its practice until true change can take place. The teachers left the meeting shaking their heads in disgust, firmly convinced that failure was imminent.

Two weeks later, T. J. and his friends led a group of 70 students in a drive to collect food. They collected a school record: 2,854 cans of food in just two hours. It was enough to fill the empty shelves in two neighborhood centers, and the food took care of needy families in the area for 75 days. The local newspaper covered the event with a full-page article the next day. That newspaper story was posted on the main bulletin board at school, where everyone could see it. T. J.'s picture was up there for doing something great, for leading a record-setting food drive. Every day he was reminded about what he did. He was being acknowledged as leadership material.

T. J. started showing up at school every day and answered questions from teachers for the first time. He led a second project, collecting 300 blankets and 1,000 pairs of shoes for the homeless shelter. The event he started now yields 9,000 cans of food in one day, taking care of 70 percent of the need for food for one year.

T. J. reminds us that a bird with a broken wing only needs mending. But once it has healed, it can fly higher than the rest. T. J. got a job. He became productive. He is flying quite nicely these days.

— Jim Hullihan —

Passing the Dream

She sat on the bench, feeding the birds.
Just throwing crumbs, not saying a word.
I sat down with my beads and braids,
Proclaiming what a mess her generation had made.
I spoke of poverty, and the war in 'Nam.
What is the use of going on?

She replied softly:

"All my life, I have worked for change.
Today, I give you my dream."
You can make a difference, with the small things you do.
The future is entirely left to you.
If things go wrong and you feel down,
Open your eyes and look around.
Don't look for someone to blame.
Search for an inspiration, to rise again.
The changes you make may not always be seen.
But perhaps you can give a child the chance to dream.
So get to work, and maybe find a small solution to help humankind.
All my life, I have worked for change.
Today I give you my dream."

Today I decided to take a walk.
I passed a teen loudly playing his boom box.
He turned his music down low
And we chatted for a minute or so.
He spoke of the homeless, and the streets filled with crime.
Couldn't my generation have found the time
To ease some of this discord
By feeding the hungry, and housing the poor?

I replied softly:

"All my life, I have worked for change.
Today, I give you my dream.
I hope you make our world a better place.
But you must work diligently; just keep pace
With the changes and dreams of the generation to come.
But with a little luck, a small battle may be won.
Someday, we will merge. And in time you will be
The older generation looking back to see
How you have answered all these questions you ask.
Fixing tomorrow is now your task.
All my life, I have worked for change.
Today, I give you my dream."

— Penny Caldwell —

Chapter
8

Going for It

*Having a dream isn't stupid, Norm. It's not having
a dream that's stupid.*
~Cliff Clavin, Cheers

Dear Young Black Child

*You are growing into consciousness, and my wish for
you is that you feel no need to constrict yourself to
make other people comfortable.*
~Ta-Nehisi Coates

Dear young Black girl,
troubled times lie ahead.
What a world we live in
when a woman is murdered asleep in her bed.
You'll be told you aren't enough,
not smart nor pretty.
They'll try to call you unprofessional and loud.
Though, you're the brightest in the room,
no matter the crowd.

Dear young Black boy,
I know life is not easy.
The world has put labels on you far too soon,
they call you a thug, a criminal, a coon.
It will only worsen as you grow, unfortunately.
When the whites look at you,
they see failure and crime.
They want to lock you up
though you've done nothing but shine.

Dear young Black child
who's reading this now:
Please don't let the world tear you down.
They wish to clip your wings before you fly
because they're afraid of just how high.
Whatever you do,
don't give in.
You have far too much greatness ahead of you
to let them win.

—Alexandria Rhodes, 14—

Rapid Lessons

*Not everyone's ambitions will be world domination or
Carnegie Hall, but we should be driven beyond what
we know and feel safe doing.*
~Stacey Abrams

During the summer before college, I was offered a free "adventure" that could be used as a PE credit. I was not adventurous, but this free trip could 1) save me from a whole semester of loathsome forced physical activity and 2) reduce my tuition by at least $900.

As a Black, first-generation college student working to put myself through school, the potential for time, money, and energy savings was a trifecta. So I skimmed over the actual details of the trip, chose a week to leave, and signed all the paperwork that said if I died, it was on me. My parents and high school friends all basically said, "Black people don't do that." What did they know? In my somewhat conservative estimation, a week of near-death experiences was totally worth it.

On the day of departure, I was a ball of nerves — especially after I took count of the brown faces; taking count is more like an unconscious reflex that I hadn't realized we do until after it's done. There were four with skin like mine out of the maybe 100 folks. Not great odds, but I didn't know what to do with that information at the time. The folks in charge were super nice and enthusiastic but that didn't help calm me. Nothing could quiet the voices in my head lamenting, "Black people don't do this." Here I was on the way to West Virginia with a bus full of people who don't look like me toward an outdoor adventure that

I knew very little about.

Later, as our leaders shared the daily activity breakdown, I found myself planning exit strategies instead of listening about the week ahead of me. We were in cabins in the middle of the woods on a steep mountain five or six hours from home. The only way through this was actually through it. Go figure.

Day one: Whitewater rafting. I was too small for the smallest adult life jacket so I had to wear a child-size one and keep my elbows down so the jacket wouldn't rise. "Is this safe?" I asked as sirens went off in my head to abort mission. "Sure!" was the eager reply. I pressed on.

The lead told us the rules — have fun, listen, never tuck your feet into the raft, and curl into a ball if you pop out. He said the first few rapids were easy and then elaborated on the scale: level 3 rapids we'd feel but aren't powerful enough to pop anyone out of the raft, level 4s required more caution because the possibility of pop-out is increased, and level 5s were doozies but he'd warn us before we got there. Easy enough, I thought to myself, amid the sirens that refused to quiet. I was convinced this was still totally worth it.

The very first level 3 rapid we hit — for which no one should pop out — I popped out of the raft. Immediately. I tucked my legs, closed my eyes, and curled into the tightest ball I could. I imagined this is what being in a toilet was like. When I suddenly stopped swirling, it felt like a weight was on top of me. I opened my eyes to find my balled-up self completely eclipsed by our big yellow raft. I could hear them asking where I was. That I should have been where the raft was. They yelled my name.

I panicked. How would they find me before I ran out of air under the raft? I wasn't a strong swimmer and my life jacket didn't fit right. But I couldn't die — I hadn't lost my virginity, started college, or even turned eighteen yet. Plus, my mom would be livid that I signed those papers saying if I died, it was on me. It wasn't! The raft was! Maybe this wasn't worth it after all.

Then, I got out of my head and back into my body. I did what has always worked. I agitated — poking their feet through the bottom of the raft until they felt me. I broke the rules and spread my whole body, pressing on the raft with every part of me until they saw me. My group formed a human chain to reach under the raft to pull me out.

When they finally got me up, I was spitting and gasping for air. They cheered that I'd made it back on board, that they'd finally found me. "Are you okay?" they asked. I nodded yes, even as my chest heaved and my nose leaked. "How long were you down there?" I stared in bewilderment. I wanted to say it felt like forever, but I still couldn't speak. Some tried to get back into the rhythm of paddling while others looked at me with shock and concern. One leader joked to try to break the ice, "I guess you're a little lighter than most adults... kinda messed up my calculations."

"No kidding!" I blurt angrily.

"There she is!" Another leader exclaims. "Anything you wanna say? What's on your mind now that you've lived to tell the tale?"

"I'm. Not. Getting. Back. In that water." I sputtered, still gasping between my words. They laughed heartily.

Later, we hit a class 5 rapid that had the raft moving so quickly, the leader's directions couldn't keep up with the raft's movement. I broke the rules again, dug my feet into the raft, grabbed hold of each of the handles and held on for dear life. The raft flipped ten or twelve times; once it stopped, I helped each of my group members and our leaders back into the raft.

"You're surprisingly strong," a leader noted.

Other things happened that week that taught me more about me — the uphill bike ride in the pouring rain, the caving experience where I almost slipped into a sinkhole, the sunburned thighs, ears, and nose that surprised even me (because Black people don't get that, I'd been told), the ride home during which Mom said I smelled like a goat. I was just grateful to be able to be offended — but that very first day was what set the stage for that week of learning.

I don't think of that time on the rapids nearly enough. The memory should come any time I don't feel like I belong, or I wish I could backtrack a decision, or someone laughs at or questions my resolve. Any time I question if breaking the rules to ensure my survival is okay, that memory should remind me that I am where I am supposed to be, doing what I'm supposed to, being who I ought to. And I don't have to second-guess how capable I am. Any time I must remind myself that Black people can do any and everything they choose to, that memory will resurface. I'll make sure of it.

— Kamala Reese —

Hitting My Stride

Run when you can, walk if you have to,
crawl if you must; just never give up.
~Dean Karnazes

W hen the COVID-19 pandemic reached my home city of Milwaukee in mid-March, I watched in shock as the pillars of my life began to topple like a line of dominoes. First, my university classes transitioned to online instruction, then my senior track season was canceled, followed closely by a postponed graduation. With my cap and gown still hanging hopefully on the back of my bedroom door, I received an e-mail requesting that I specify the address I'd like my diploma shipped to.

During all of the changes, the only constant I could cling to was a daily run. Using a bandana as a makeshift mask, I laced up my shoes each morning to spend an hour or so away from the chaos. As the lockdown stretched into April, then May, I craved more and more miles, eventually surpassing fifty-mile weeks and finishing my first few twenty-mile runs.

Running for fun, without a key goal or race on the horizon, was new for me. For the past eight years I was always in season for either track or cross country, which meant racing every weekend and crushing workouts during summer and winter. For those quiet, quarantine months, I ran purely for the joy of it.

One Saturday in August, I was about four miles into my daily run when a thought popped into my head. What if I ran a marathon that day? I mulled it over for a few miles, half-heartedly trying to talk myself out of it — 26.2 miles would be a huge jump from twenty, my longest run at that point, plus I was recovering from a two-week setback due to a bout of plantar fasciitis. But once I started thinking about it, I couldn't get it out of my mind.

At fourteen miles I was still feeling pretty good. I looped back to my apartment to grab a glass of water and a grape popsicle — the only semi-reasonable mid-run fuel I had on hand. As the sun started to drift below the skyline, I put on a fresh pair of socks and my favorite playlist and set out for the second half of the run. With four miles to go, the lack of fuel, hydration and proper training started to catch up to me. My happiness and motivation were faltering, so I reached out to the only person I knew could help.

"Mom," I texted. "I could really use some encouragement right now."

"That's what I'm here for," she replied.

My mom has completed over 100 marathons herself and has always been my role model in all aspects of life, including athletics. I told her my situation, strategically choosing to omit that I had chosen a popsicle as my only fuel for a 26.2-mile effort. While the risk of spreading the virus prevented her from coming to coach me in person, she advised me to take it one mile at a time, or even half a mile.

"Just put one foot in front of the other and keep moving forward," she said. "You can and you will do this."

The final miles were agonizing, unlike any running experience I've had before. My legs burned, my stomach growled, and my feet felt hot and swollen. Despite everything I'd heard about marathons, the pain still surprised me, but I took my mom's advice and kept moving, thinking of her and my other idols with every step. The miles slowly melted away, and suddenly I could see my apartment in the distance. My GPS watch hit 26.0, then 26.1 and finally 26.2.

I stopped, breathing hard, and looked around grinning, half expecting someone to jump out and cheer for me. But for everyone else, I realized, it was just 5 p.m. on a Saturday. I felt like I had a secret. Unbeknownst to the people on their evening stroll or commute from work, I had just accomplished a lifelong goal. I made eye contact with a woman driving by and gave her an excited smile. She half-waved, eyebrows raised, probably trying to remember if she recognized this tomato-faced, sweaty girl. She didn't, but I was happy to see her anyway. A split-second celebration with a stranger was the perfect, out-of-the-ordinary way to cap my perfect, out-of-the-ordinary mid-pandemic marathon.

— Sophie Bolich —

Nobody Can Take What's Mine

If you're stuck in a situation that's painful...
it can enable you to step back from your own
experience of it and realize that this is just a
part of what it is to be human.
~Joan Osborne

There I was, a last-minute addition to the weekly performance night at a sleepover summer arts camp in upstate New York, and I blew everybody away with my singing. I can't tell you how proud I was when I sang like my life depended on it: "It don't even matter now, nobody can take what's mine!"

I had just turned thirteen and that performance was by far one of the most triumphant moments of my childhood.

Growing up different can be rough. I've struggled with autism, mental illness, and bullying, and on top of that, I realized early in my teenage years that I was gay, so school was never easy. But I'm grateful to say that I had a couple moments in my adolescence when I really got to shine, and one of those times was at that arts camp, which I had found online.

My camp experiences had their ups and downs. Some kids there turned on me, which was painful, but I also met counselors who became friends and stayed in contact with me for years. One was a theatre counselor whom I connected with around my love of music and the arts. I first talked with her around a campfire, singing James Taylor's "Sweet Baby James" and playing it on guitar for her. I still remember that warm, magical moment when I felt I was understood by someone else and vice versa.

That night when I triumphed was an affirmation that I needed during a miserable time. I changed what people thought of me. I had come off as extremely weird to my bunkmates and fellow campers until then. What did I sing? I started with Joan Osborne's "Ladder" and eventually morphed into "Dracula Moon," augmented with a long high note that made the crowd go wild. After that, I added a bridge that Joan Osborne had added when I'd heard her sing "Ladder" on an episode of *Austin City Limits*, culminating with that defiant line, "It don't even matter now, nobody can take what's mine!"

When I was done with the song, the audience — at least a couple hundred campers and staff — stood up and cheered loudly. And that night, my bunkmates told me how they were bowled over by my performance, admitting that it changed their perception of me. I felt something new: pride. For once in my childhood, nobody could take what was mine.

At the end of the session, a counselor I admired wrote in my camp yearbook, "You're going to be a famous musician someday" and "Thanks for being who you are." I can't tell you what that meant to me at a time when I felt alone in the world.

And what I learned from these experiences is that, whether or not I realized that I was good or that my playing music was special to others, expressing myself creatively has made a world of difference in my life. Without it, I likely would not still be here.

My life has come a long way in the years since. Today I have a TEDx talk about creativity and autism and a wide circle of friends and community. I'm very lucky, but while I couldn't have accomplished this much alone, I also couldn't have accomplished anything had I not been willing to take risks.

May you always know that you are loved and that you are not alone and that whatever risks you take do not make you any less worthy and valid as a human being. These are lessons that I had trouble internalizing as a teenager, so I hope me passing them on helps you now. And may nobody take what's yours.

—Josh Friedberg—

The Girl Next Door

Do you remember
Many years ago
When we were young,
How we used to play together
Every day?

It seems like yesterday—
The childhood world
Of clowns and cotton candy
And summer days
That never seemed to end
When we played hide 'n' seek
From four o'clock till dusk
Then sat outside on someone's stoop
And listened to the crickets
And slapped away mosquitoes
And talked about our dreams
And what we'd do when we grew up
Until our mothers called us in.

And do you remember
That one winter when it snowed
For days and days on end
And we tried to build an igloo
Like the Eskimos?
Or when we made a game

Of raking leaves
All up and down the street
Until we'd made the biggest pile
The world had ever seen
And then we jumped in it?
Or how about the time
We gathered honeysuckle
From your yard
And sold it to the neighbors?
And the grand day when finally
The training wheels came off our bikes
And we were free
To explore the whole world
In an afternoon
So long as we stayed
On our own street.

But those days passed by furtively
And we grew up, as children do
Until we reached a day when we
Assumed that we were too grown-up
To play amid the trees on summer nights…
and when I see you now
You've changed in ways I can't explain
You're like a rose that blooms before its time
And falls a victim to
The February frost.

Because the waist on your jeans is getting tight
Symbolic of a youth that's not your own
And your face is pale and green —
You don't look well.
I see you scowling at the street
From the window in your room,
It's so rare to see you smiling anymore.

And when a car pulls up outside
You run downstairs and out the door
With a suitcase in each hand
And the car speeds away
And the girl next door is gone.

And I long once more
For the summer days
When I stood on your porch
And banged on your door
And bade you come outside to greet
the afternoon's adventures.

Won't you come out to play, once more?
For we are still so young…

—Amanda Dykstra, 14—

I'll Be Back

Although the world is full of suffering,
it is also full of the overcoming of it.
~Helen Keller

L inda and Bob Samele braced themselves as they approached the door to the hospital room. *Keep calm,* Linda told herself as she reached for the knob. *You don't want to upset him any more than he already is.*

That sleety December afternoon, their 15-year-old son, Chris, had been riding with five friends from the Sameles' hometown of Torrington, Connecticut, to nearby Waterbury. Suddenly, the teenagers' laughter turned to screams as their car skidded on an icy patch and slammed into a guardrail. Three of the kids, including Chris, were catapulted out the rear window. One died instantly, another was seriously injured.

Chris had been found sitting on the median, staring with dazed eyes at a torrent of blood gushing from his left thigh. Twenty feet away was his left leg, severed through the knee by a guardrail cable. He was rushed to Waterbury Hospital for surgery. His parents had to wait almost seven hours to see him.

Now Linda's eyes filled with tears at the sight of her son in the hospital bed. Bob, a Torrington letter carrier, took Chris's hand. "Dad, I lost my leg," the young man said softly to his father. Bob nodded and squeezed his hand tighter. After a brief silence, Chris added, "What's going to happen to my basketball career?"

Bob Samele struggled to control his emotions. The game had been Chris's passion since early childhood, and already he was becoming a local legend. The previous season, as an eighth grader at St. Peter's, he had compiled a remarkable 41-point average. Now a freshman at Torrington High, Chris had scored a total of 62 points in two junior-varsity games. "Someday I'm going to play at Notre Dame in front of thousands," Chris would say to his parents with a grin. "And you'll be there to watch me."

Looking down at his son, Bob Samele searched for words. "You know, Chris," he managed at last, "there's a big group of people in the waiting room, including Coach Martin."

Chris's face brightened. Then, with a determined voice, he said, "Dad, tell Coach I'll be back next season. I'm going to play basketball again."

Chris underwent three more operations on his leg in seven days. From the start, his surgeons saw that the jumble of torn nerves, arteries and muscles made it impossible to reattach the severed limb. Chris would need a prosthesis.

During his three-and-a-half-week hospital stay he had a steady stream of visitors. "Don't feel bad for me," Chris would say whenever he sensed pity. "I'll be just fine." Behind his strong spirits lay an indomitable will forged by religious faith. Many of his doctors and nurses were uncomprehending.

"How are you dealing with all this, Chris?" a psychiatrist asked one day. "Do you ever feel sorry for yourself?"

"No," the boy replied, "I don't see where that is going to help."

"Don't you feel bitter or angry?"

"No," Chris said. "I try to be positive about it all."

When the persistent psychiatrist finally left his room, Chris told his parents, "*He's* the one that needs help."

Chris worked hard in the hospital to recover his strength and coordination. When he was strong enough he would flip a Nerf ball through a hoop that a friend had attached to the wall alongside his bed. His demanding therapy included upper-body exercises for crutches and workouts to improve his balance.

Two weeks into his hospital stay, the Sameles gambled on an additional therapy: They took Chris in a wheelchair to a Torrington

High basketball game. "Keep a close watch on him," the nurses warned, concerned about his reaction.

The boy remained unusually quiet when he was wheeled into the noisy gym. As he passed before the bleachers, however, friends and teammates began calling out his name and waving. Then Frank McGowan, Torrington High's assistant principal, announced over the public-address system, "We have a very special friend here tonight. Everyone, please welcome back Chris Samele!"

Startled, Chris looked around and saw that all 900 people in the gym had risen to their feet, cheering and applauding. Tears welled up in the boy's eyes. It was a night he would never forget.

In January, not quite a full month after the accident, Chris was able to return home. To keep up with schoolwork, he was visited each afternoon by a tutor. When he wasn't studying, he was being driven back to Waterbury Hospital for more therapy. Physical pain — sometimes searing — was part of his daily life. At times, watching television with his parents, he rocked back and forth in silent reaction to the ache radiating from his stump.

Then one frigid afternoon, Chris struggled onto his crutches and hobbled around the corner to the old garage where he had learned to shoot. Putting the crutches down, he picked up a basketball and glanced around to make sure no one was watching. Finally, hopping about on his right leg, he began tossing the ball at the hoop. Several times he lost his balance and slammed down on the asphalt. Each time he picked himself up, hopped over to retrieve the ball and continued shooting. After 15 minutes he was exhausted. *This is going to take longer than I thought,* he said to himself, as he began the slow walk back into the house.

Chris got his first prosthetic device in March, on Good Friday. Excited by the new limb, he asked Ed Skewes, director of the hospital's prosthetic and orthotic department, whether this meant he could begin playing basketball right away. Surprised to see Chris serious, Skewes replied, "Let's take this a day at a time." The doctor knew that it's usually about a year before a person can walk comfortably with a prosthesis, let alone play sports.

In the basement at home, Chris spent long hours learning to walk with his artificial leg. Hard as it was to shoot baskets on one leg, he found it even more difficult with the prosthesis. Most of his shots were way off the mark, and he often crashed to the pavement.

In his darkest moments, Chris remembered a conversation with his mother. After a particularly discouraging day, he had asked if she really thought he'd ever play again. "You'll have to work even harder at basketball now," she replied. "But, yes — I think you can do it." She was right, he knew. It all came down to hard work — and refusing to give in.

Chris returned to Torrington High in early April and was immediately one of the gang again — except on the basketball court. After school, Chris's friends would play on an outdoor court. For several weeks, he watched from the sidelines as they flew past. Then one afternoon in early May, he went out suited to play. His surprised buddies made way as he came unhesitatingly onto the court.

From the first, Chris began shooting from the outside, and he felt a thrill whenever the ball swished through the net. But when he tried to drive, hop-skipping toward the basket, or leap for a rebound, he fell to the ground. "Come on, Chris, you can do it!" his friends shouted. But Chris knew the truth: he couldn't do it — not as he used to.

In a game during a summer tournament, he went up hard for a rebound and broke the foot of his prosthesis. As he hopped off the court, he thought, *Maybe I'm just kidding myself. Maybe I'm not up to this.*

Ultimately, however, he told himself there was only one thing to do: push himself even harder. So he began a daily regimen of shooting, dribbling and weight-lifting. After each workout, he carefully removed the artificial leg and four sweat socks he wore over his stump to cushion the prosthesis. Then he showered, groaning slightly as he rubbed soap over the blisters. Before long, the pain was eased by the sense that he was seeing flashes of the old self. *I'm going to do it. And not next year. This year!*

The Monday after Thanksgiving, JV head coach Bob Anzellotti called together the crowd of boys, all nervous and expectant, who were vying for a spot on the Torrington High junior varsity basketball team. His eyes stopped on Chris Samele.

During the two days of tryouts, no one had pushed himself harder than Chris. He dribbled through defenders, dived after loose balls — whatever it took to show everyone he could still play. He even took 10 laps around the gym each day with the others — moving far slower than everyone else, but never failing to finish.

The morning after the last practice, Chris joined the rush to check the roster. *You've done all you could,* he told himself as he peered over the shoulders of others at the list. And there it was — *Samele.* He was back on the squad!

Later that week, Coach Anzellotti called his players together for a team meeting. "Each year's squad has a captain, who is selected for the example he sets. This year's captain will be... Chris Samele." The players erupted with cheers.

On the night of December 15, just eight days shy of a year since the accident, 250 people settled into their seats to watch the game that would bring Chris back to the basketball court.

In the locker room, Chris's hand trembled slightly as he pulled on his maroon jersey. "You're going to be all right, Chris," Coach Anzellotti said. "Just don't expect too much the very first night." Chris nodded. "I know," he said softly. "Thanks."

Soon he was running with his teammates onto the court for pre-game practice. Nearly everyone in the stands stood to cheer. Moved by the sight of their son in a Torrington High uniform once again, Linda and Bob fought back tears. *God,* Linda prayed silently, *please don't let him be embarrassed.*

Despite his efforts to calm down, Chris carried his nervousness onto the court. During warmups, most of his shots clanged off the rim. "Take it easy; relax," Coach Anzellotti whispered. "Don't rush it."

When the players finally came out to the center of the court for the tip-off, Chris was starting at guard. With the opening jump ball, he began playing a tight and awkward game. He managed to keep up, but his movements were jerky, his rhythm off. Several times when he shot the ball, it failed even to touch the rim of the basket. Usually when that happens, kids in the stands taunt, "Air ball! Air ball!" This time, they were silent.

After playing eight minutes, Chris was given a long breather. With two minutes left in the half he was put back in. *Come on, Chris,* he told himself, *this is what you've worked for. Show them you can do it.* Seconds later, he worked himself free 20 feet from the basket, and a teammate whipped him a pass. It was a tough range for anyone — a long three-pointer. Without hesitation, Chris planted himself and launched a high, arching shot. The ball sailed toward the rim — and swished cleanly through the net.

The gym erupted in shouts and cheers. "Thatta way, Chris!" Bob Samele yelled, his voice cracking with emotion.

A minute later, Chris grabbed a rebound amid a tangle of arms. Muscling up, he flipped the ball against the backboard. Once again, it sliced through the basket. And again cheers exploded. By now, tears were streaming down Linda Samele's face as she watched her son hop-skip down the court, his fist raised in triumph. *You did it, Chris,* she kept saying to herself. *You did it.*

Chris continued to go all out, to the delight of the crowd. Only once did he lose his footing and tumble to the floor. When the final buzzer sounded, he had scored 11 points, and Torrington had won.

At home later that night, Chris broke into a wide grin. "I did okay, Dad, didn't I?"

"You did just great," Bob answered, giving his son a big hug.

After chatting briefly about the game, Chris, still wearing a look of joy, made his way up the stairs to his bedroom. In his mind, his parents knew, this night was only the beginning.

As Linda turned out the lights, she recalled an afternoon shortly following the accident when she was driving her son home from therapy. Chris was quiet, staring out the car window; then suddenly he broke the silence. "Mom, I think I know why this happened to me." Startled, Linda replied, "Why, Chris?"

Still looking out the window, Chris said simply, "God knew I could handle it. He saved my life because he knew I could handle it."

— Jack Cavanaugh —

Editor's note: Chris went on to star with the varsity basketball team at Torrington High School during his junior and senior years. He also played both singles and doubles on the school tennis team. He played on the varsity tennis team at Western New England College in Springfield, Massachusetts, and played intramural basketball at Western New England and in summer leagues in the Torrington area.

Just Me

From the time I was little, I knew I was great
'cause the people would tell me, "You'll make it — just wait."
But they never did tell me how great I would be
if I ever played someone who was greater than me.

When I'm in the back yard, I'm king with the ball.
To swish all those baskets is no sweat at all.
But all of a sudden there's a man in my face
who doesn't seem to realize that I'm king of this place.

So the pressure gets to me; I rush with the ball.
My passes to teammates could go through the wall.
My jumpers not falling, my dribbles not sure.
My hand is not steady, my eye is not pure.

The fault is my teammates — they don't understand.
The fault is my coaches — what a terrible plan.
The fault is the call by that blind referee.
But the fault is not mine; I'm the greatest, you see.

Then finally it hit me when I started to see
that the face in the mirror looked exactly like me.
It wasn't my teammates who were dropping the ball,
and it wasn't my coach shooting bricks at the wall.

That face in the mirror that was always so great
had some room for improvement instead of just hate.
So I stopped blaming others and I started to grow.
My play got much better and it started to show.

And all of my teammates didn't seem quite so bad.
I learned to depend on the good friends I had.
Now I like myself better since I started to see
that I was lousy being great — I'm much better being me.

— Tom Krause —

The Gravediggers of Parkview Junior High

*People are always blaming their circumstances for
what they are. I don't believe in circumstances.
The people who get on in this world are the people who
get up and look for the circumstances they want, and,
if they can't find them, they make them.*
~George Bernard Shaw

The most important lessons we are taught in school go beyond answering the questions on a test correctly. It is when the lessons change us by showing us what we are really capable of accomplishing. We can, with the use of band instruments, make beautiful music. We can, with the use of a paint brush and canvas, show people how we see the world. We can, with the hard work of a team, beat the odds and win the game. However, no multiple choice or true/false test will ever teach us the greatest lesson of all: We are the stuff of which winners are made.

Not long after the release of the film *Jeremiah Johnson,* starring Robert Redford, our seventh-grade class was discussing the story. We talked about the fact that this rough and tough mountain man was also kind and gentle. We discussed his deep love of nature and his wishes to be part of it. Our teacher, Mr. Robinson, then asked us a most unusual question. Where did we think Jeremiah Johnson was buried? We were shocked when he told us the final resting place of the great mountain man was about 100 yards away from the San Diego

Freeway in Southern California.

Mr. Robinson asked us, "So, do you believe this was wrong?"

"Yes!" we all chimed in.

"Do you feel something should be done to change it?" he asked with a sly grin.

"Yes!" we replied with an enthusiasm born of youthful innocence.

Mr. Robinson stared at us, and after a few moments of suspenseful silence, he asked a question that would change the way some of us viewed life forever. "Well, do you think you could do it?"

"Huh?"

What was he talking about? We were just a bunch of kids. What could we do?

"There is a way," he said. "It's a way filled with challenge and probably some disappointment... but there is a way." Then he said he would help us but only if we promised to work hard and pledge to never give up.

As we agreed, little did we know that we were signing on to the most adventurous voyage of our lives thus far.

We began by writing letters to everyone we could think of who could help us: local, state and federal representatives, the cemetery owners, even Robert Redford. Before long, we started getting answers that thanked our class for the interest, but "there was absolutely nothing that could be done." Many would have given up at that point.

Had it not been for our promise to Mr. Robinson not to quit, we would have. Instead, we kept writing.

We decided that we needed more people to hear about our dream so we contacted the newspapers. Finally a reporter from the *Los Angeles Times* came to our class and interviewed us. We shared what we had been trying to do and how discouraging it was that no one seemed to care. We hoped that our story would raise public interest.

"Did Robert Redford ever contact you?" the reporter asked.

"No," we replied.

Two days later our story made the front page of the paper, telling how our class was trying to right an injustice to an American legend, and that no one was helping us, not even Robert Redford. Next to the article was a picture of Robert Redford. That same day, as we were sitting in the classroom, Mr. Robinson was called to the office to take a phone call. He came back with a glow on his face like we had never seen before. "Guess who that was on the phone!"

Robert Redford had called and said he received hundreds of letters every day and that ours somehow had never reached him, but he was very interested in helping us achieve our goal. Suddenly our team was not only getting bigger, it was getting more influential and powerful.

Within a few months, after all the proper documents were filed, our teacher and a few of the students went to the cemetery and observed the removal of the remains. Jeremiah Johnson had been buried in an old wooden casket that had been reduced to a few rotted boards, and nothing but a few bones were left of the mountain man. All were carefully gathered up by the cemetery workers and placed in a new casket.

Then a few days later, at a ranch in Wyoming, a ceremony was held in honor of Jeremiah Johnson, and his final remains were placed to rest in the wilderness he had loved so much. Robert Redford was one of the pallbearers.

From then on, throughout the school, our class was referred to as the "Gravediggers," but we preferred to think of ourselves as the "Dream Lifters." What we learned that year was not just about how to write effective letters, how our government works, or even what you have to go through to accomplish such a simple thing as moving a grave site. The lesson was that nothing can beat persistence. A bunch of kids at the beginning of our teenage years had made a change.

We learned that we were the stuff of which winners are made.

— Kif Anderson —

Teenagers' Bill of Rights

With Friends:

We all have the right and the privilege to have friends. We can choose our friends based on our own likes and dislikes. We don't have to like the same people everyone else likes or not like someone because they aren't in our "group." Friendship is a personal thing.

We can ask from our friends that they be trustworthy. If we share something with them and ask them not to tell everyone, we can expect that they will keep it just between us. We will give them the same right. If they don't, they have betrayed our trust and our friendship.

It is okay to be honest with our friends. If they do something that hurts us or concerns us, we can talk to them about it. We will be open to their being honest also. This does not mean it is okay to be mean to each other, just that we can talk honestly about our feelings.

We have the right to be respected for the decisions we make. Some of our friends may not understand the choices we make, but they are our choices. In return, we take responsibility for them.

With Parents and Other Adults:

We have the right to have our feelings respected and not compared to the feelings of puppies… or any other such put-downs. Our feelings are strong and sometimes confusing. It helps if you take our feelings seriously and listen to us before disregarding them.

We feel we have the right to make decisions (some, not all) for ourselves. If we make mistakes we will learn from them, but it is time for us to be more responsible.

Whenever possible, exclude us from your fights. We understand that fighting is part of every relationship, but it is painful for us to be involved. Don't put us in the middle of *any* problem you have with each other.

We agree to treat you with respect and ask that you respect us in return. This includes respecting our privacy.

With Everyone:

We have the right to be loved unconditionally, and our goal is to love you the same.

We have the right to speak our minds, love ourselves, feel our feelings, and strive for our dreams. Please support us by believing in us rather than fearing for us.

— Lia Gay, 16; Jamie Yellin, 14, Lisa Gumenick, 14,
Hana Ivanhoe, 15, Bree Able, 15, Lisa Rothbard, 14 —

The Boy Who Talked with Dolphins

From what we get we can make a living,
what we give, however, makes a life.
~Arthur Ashe

t began as a deep rumble, shattering the predawn silence. Within minutes on that January morning in 1994, the Los Angeles area was in the grip of one of the most destructive earthquakes in its history. .

At Six Flags Magic Mountain theme park, 20 miles north of the city, three dolphins were alone with their terror. They swam frantically in circles as heavy concrete pillars collapsed around their pool and roof tiles crashed into the water.

Forty miles to the south, 26-year-old Jeff Siegel was thrown from his bed with a jarring thump. Crawling to the window, Jeff looked out at the convulsing city and thought of the creatures who mattered more to him than anything else in the world. *I've got to get to the dolphins,* he told himself. *They rescued me, and now they need me to rescue them.*

To those who had known Jeff from childhood, a more unlikely hero could not have been imagined.

Jeff Siegel was born hyperactive, partially deaf and lacking normal coordination. Since he couldn't hear words clearly, he developed a severe speech impediment that made it almost impossible for others to understand him. As a preschooler, the small, sandy-haired child was taunted as a "retard" by other kids.

Even home was no refuge. Jeff's mother was unprepared to deal with his problems. Raised in a rigid, authoritarian household, she was overly strict and often angry at his differences. She simply wanted him to fit in. His father, a police officer in their middle-class Los Angeles community of Torrance, worked extra jobs to make ends meet and was often gone 16 hours a day.

Anxious and frightened on the first day of kindergarten, five-year-old Jeff climbed over the schoolyard fence and ran home. Furious, his mother hauled him back to school and forced him to apologize to the teacher. The entire class overheard. As the mispronounced and barely intelligible words were dragged out of him, he became instant prey for his classmates. To fend off the hostile world, Jeff kept to isolated corners of the playground and hid in his room at home, dreaming of a place where he could be accepted.

Then one day when Jeff was nine, he went with his fourth-grade class to Los Angeles' Marineland. At the dolphin show, he was electrified by the energy and exuberant friendliness of the beautiful animals. They seemed to smile directly at him, something that happened rarely in his life. The boy sat transfixed, overwhelmed with emotion and a longing to stay.

By the end of that school year, Jeff's teachers had labeled him emotionally disturbed and learning-disabled. But testing at the nearby Switzer Center for children with disabilities showed Jeff to be average-to-bright, though so anxiety-ridden that his math test score came out borderline retarded. He transferred from public school to the Center. Over the next two years he became less anxious, and his academic achievement improved dramatically.

At the start of seventh grade he returned, unwillingly, to public school. Tests now showed his I.Q. in the 130s, the gifted range. And years of therapy had improved his speech. But to his classmates, Jeff was still the same victim.

Seventh grade was unfolding as the worst year of Jeff's life — until the day his father took him to Sea World in San Diego. The minute the boy saw the dolphins, the same rush of joy welled up in him. He stayed rooted to the spot as the sleek mammals glided past.

Jeff worked to earn money for an annual pass to Marineland, closer to his home. On his first solo visit, he sat on the low wall surrounding the dolphin pool. The dolphins, accustomed to being fed by visitors, soon approached the astonished boy. The first to swim over was Grid Eye, the dominant female in the pool. The 650-pound dolphin glided to where Jeff sat and remained motionless below him. *Will she let me touch her?* he wondered, putting his hand in the water. As he stroked the dolphin's smooth skin, Grid Eye inched closer. It was a moment of sheer ecstasy for the young boy.

The outgoing animals quickly became the friends Jeff never had, and since the dolphin area was isolated at the far end of Marineland, Jeff often found himself alone with the playful creatures.

One day Sharky, a young female, glided just below the surface until her tail was in Jeff's hand. She stopped. *Now what?* he wondered. Suddenly Sharky dived a foot or so below the surface, pulling Jeff's hand and arm underwater. He laughed and pulled back without letting go. The dolphin dived again, deeper. Jeff pulled back harder. It was like a game of tug-of-war.

When Sharky surfaced to breathe, boy and dolphin faced each other for a minute, Jeff laughing and the dolphin open-mouthed and grinning. Then Sharky circled and put her tail back in Jeff's hand to start the game again.

The boy and the 300-to-800-pound animals often played tag, with Jeff and the dolphins racing around the pool to slap a predetermined point or give each other hand-to-flipper high-fives. To Jeff, the games were a magical connection that he alone shared with the animals.

Even when there were summer crowds of 500 around the pool, the gregarious creatures recognized their friend and swam to him whenever he wiggled his hand in the water. Jeff's acceptance by the dolphins boosted his confidence, and he gradually emerged from his dark shell. He enrolled in a course at a nearby aquarium and devoured books on marine biology. He became a walking encyclopedia on dolphins and, to his family's amazement, braved his speech impediment to become a volunteer tour guide.

In 1983 Jeff wrote an article for the American Cetacean Society's newsletter, describing his experiences with Marineland dolphins. He was unprepared for what followed. Embarrassed by the extent to which he'd been playing with the dolphins without the park's knowledge, Marineland management revoked his pass. Jeff returned home numb with disbelief.

For their part, Jeff's parents were relieved. They could see no benefit to the time their son was spending with dolphins until a day in June 1984 when Bonnie Siegel took an unexpected long-distance phone call. That evening she asked her son, "Did you enter some kind of contest?"

Sheepishly, Jeff confessed that he'd written an essay for a highly coveted Earthwatch scholarship worth more than $2,000. The winner would spend a month in Hawaii with dolphin experts. Now, telling his mother about it, he expected a tirade. Instead, she said quietly, "Well, you won."

Jeff was ecstatic. Best of all, it was the first time that his parents realized he might achieve his dream of someday sharing his love of dolphins.

Jeff spent the month in Hawaii, teaching dolphins strings of commands to test their memories. In the fall, he fulfilled another condition of the scholarship by giving a talk on marine mammals to fellow students at Torrance High School. Jeff's report was so enthusiastic that it earned him, at last, grudging respect from his peers.

After graduation, Jeff struggled to find work in marine research, supplementing the low pay with minimum-wage moonlighting. He also earned an associate's degree in biology.

In February 1992 he showed up in the office of Suzanne Fortier, director of marine-animal training at Six Flags Magic Mountain. Though holding down two jobs, he wanted to do volunteer work with Magic Mountain's dolphins on his days off. Fortier gave him the chance — and was immediately amazed. Of the 200 volunteers she'd trained in 10 years, she'd never seen anyone with Jeff's intuitive ability with dolphins.

In one instance, her crew needed to move a sick 600-pound dolphin named Thunder to another park. The animal had to be transported in a nine-by-three-foot tank. During the journey, Jeff insisted on riding in the truck bed with Thunder's tank to try to calm the anxious animal. When Fortier later called from the cab of the truck to ask how Thunder was doing, Jeff replied, "He's fine now. I'm cradling him." *Jeff's actually in the tank with Thunder!* Fortier realized. For four hours, Jeff floated inside the cool tank, holding Thunder in his arms.

Jeff continued to amaze co-workers with his rapport with the animals. His favorite at Magic Mountain was Katie, a 350-pound, eight-year-old dolphin who greeted him exuberantly and swam with him for hours.

Once again, as at Marineland, Jeff could interact with the dolphins and find affection in return. Little did he dream how severely his love would be tested.

As Jeff struggled to reach Magic Mountain on the morning of the earthquake, freeways were collapsing, and caved-in roads often forced him to backtrack. *Nothing is going to stop me,* he vowed.

When Jeff finally reached Magic Mountain, the water in the 12-foot-deep dolphin pool was halfway down, and more was draining from the crack in the side. The three dolphins there when the quake hit — Wally, Teri and Katie — were in a frenzy. Jeff lowered himself to a ledge five feet down and tried to calm them.

To ease the dolphins through the continuing tremors, Jeff attempted to distract them by playing games, but it didn't work. Worse, he had to reduce their food: The pool's filtration system had shut down, creating the additional risk that an accumulation of their body waste would further contaminate the water.

Jeff remained with the dolphins that night as temperatures fell into the 30s. He was still there through the next day, and the next, and the next.

On the fourth day a road opened, and staffers secured a truck to transfer Wally, Teri and Katie to the dolphin pool at Knott's Berry Farm. But first, someone had to get them into their transport tanks. Transporting a dolphin is normally a routine procedure, after it has been safely guided through a tunnel and hoisted on a canvas sling. But the water level in the connecting tunnel was too low for the animals to swim through. The three dolphins would have to be caught in open water and then maneuvered into canvas slings.

Staffer Etienne Francois and Jeff volunteered for the jobs. As much as he trusted the dolphins, Jeff knew the likelihood of getting hurt or bitten by them in an open-water capture was almost 100 percent.

Wally was easily removed from the pool, but Teri and Katie became erratic. Each time Jeff and Etienne closed in on Katie, the powerful dolphin fended them off with her hard, pointed beak.

For almost 40 minutes the men struggled as Katie butted and whacked them with her thrashing tail. Finally, just before they maneuvered her into a sling, she sank her needle-sharp teeth into Jeff's hand. Ignoring the bleeding, Jeff helped capture Teri and hoist her into the transport tank.

When the dolphins reached Knott's Berry Farm, Katie was exhausted but calm. Later, Fortier told friends that Jeff's courage and leadership had been essential in safely transporting the dolphins.

Today, Jeff is a full-time dolphin trainer at Marine Animal Productions in Gulfport, Mississippi, where he organizes programs for schools.

One day, before he left for Mississippi, Jeff gave a demonstration to 60 children from the Switzer Center at one of the aquariums where he had taught. He saw that a boy named Larry slipped off to play alone. Realizing Larry was an outcast, as he himself had been, Jeff called him forward and asked the boy to stand next to him. Then Jeff plunged his arms into a nearby tank and hauled up a harmless but impressive three-foot horn shark. As the children gasped, he allowed Larry to carry the dripping creature proudly around the room.

After the session, Jeff received a letter reading: "Thank you for the magnificent job you did with our children. They came back glowing from the experience. Several told me about Larry getting to carry the shark. This was probably the happiest and proudest moment of his life! The fact that you were once a student here added to it. You are a model of hope that they, too, can 'make it' in life." The letter was from Janet Switzer, the Center's founder.

For Jeff, that afternoon held an even more gratifying moment. As he spoke, he saw his mother and father in the audience, watching intently. From the look on their faces, Jeff could tell they were proud of their son at last.

Jeff has never earned more than $14,800 a year in his life, yet he considers himself a rich man and an exceptionally lucky one. "I'm completely fulfilled," he says. "The dolphins did so much for me when I was a child. They gave me unconditional love. When I think about what I owe the dolphins…" His voice trails off momentarily, and he smiles. "They gave me life. I owe them everything."

— Paula McDonald —

Reprinted by permission of Paula McDonald. Also reprinted with permission from the April 1996 *Reader's Digest*.

Wild Thing

Face the thing you fear, and you do away
with that fear.
~Author Unknown

With the wind biting my face and the rain soaking though my clothes, it didn't seem like July. I watched a puddle form at the foot of my sleeping bag as the 10-foot plastic sheet jerry-rigged above me gave way to the wind. I hadn't eaten for almost a day, and a rumble in my stomach demanded why I was in the Northern Cascades of Oregon — alone, soaked — in the first place. With two more days alone in the wilds ahead of me, I had plenty of time to think about that question.

I'd always been impressed by people who had been in Outward Bound, basically because I'd always lumped myself in the I-could-never-do-that category. For one thing, I just assumed I was too small and urban; I'm no granola. I also wasn't a big risk-taker. I'd always relied a lot on my family, friends and boyfriend, and I evaluated myself on how well I met their expectations of me.

Signing up for an Outward Bound course the summer after my junior year in high school was a chance to break away from that. After all, the courses are described as "adventure-based education programs that promote self-discovery through tough, outdoor activities." Exactly what I needed; I'd be facing challenges away from my usual support-ers. As the starting date approached, though, I became increasingly terrified. I'd never attempted mountain climbing, white-water rafting, backpacking, rappelling or rock climbing, and I was plagued by fears that I'd fail at one or all of them. I begged my mother to cancel for me. No such luck.

I shouldn't have worried so much. For most of the people on the course, it was their first time with Outward Bound, too. Then again, the course was pretty hard because I had to adjust to a different way of day-to-day living.

For starters, I've always been a big fan of showers. I usually take one a day, and it was tough to forgo this ritual for three weeks. I also never realized how handy toilets were until they disappeared from my life, toilet paper and all. (We used leaves and snow.) On the whole, though, these inconveniences seemed less important as the course progressed. Besides, I was far too busy to sit around and watch my leg hair grow.

The first week, my group rafted 100 miles down the Deschutes River. I was soaked, shocked and exhilarated. Then we climbed Mount Jefferson, the second highest peak in Oregon. Every time I gazed at that snowy, 10,000-foot peak, I felt a combination of panic and delight. The delight faded, however, the first time I strapped on my backpack. It was so heavy that I needed someone to help me put it on. And then I could barely walk in a straight line. Eventually, I got the hang of it and could actually feel myself getting stronger. Somehow, we made it up Mount Jefferson in five days. At the peak, I decided I could do anything I set my mind to, which was good since the solo component of my course — that three-day bonding session with myself — was next.

For solo, my instructors dropped me off in a clearing in the woods with very little equipment and minimal food. I was alone with a pencil, some paper and my thoughts. Sure, I was bored at first and a little scared, but honestly, it was one of the coolest things I've ever done. I realized how little time I actually spent alone, and I kind of enjoyed my own company.

Overall, during the three weeks of my course, I became a new woman. I discovered parts of myself that I had no idea existed. I can't even count the times that I thought I couldn't give anymore, and somehow, I'd find the strength to carry out the task at hand and carry it out well. I loved that feeling, and I didn't lose it. Back home, my grades soared with this realization that personal limits didn't have to exist unless I let them.

My experiences with Outward Bound are invaluable, but that doesn't mean I'm going to give up my dreams of a career (and modern plumbing) and live in the woods. I will, however, forever be grateful for what I got out of the course: Before I went I always thought, *I can't do this*. Now I think, *I'm not afraid to try.*

—Jennifer Philbin—

To Track Down My Dream

I t was the district track meet — the one we had been training for all season. My foot still hadn't healed from an earlier injury. As a matter of fact, I had debated whether or not I should attend the meet. But there I was, preparing for the 3200-meter run.

"Ready... set..." The gun popped and we were off. The other girls darted ahead of me. I realized I was limping and felt humiliated as I fell farther and farther behind.

The first-place runner was two laps ahead of me when she crossed the finish line. "Hooray!" shouted the crowd. It was the loudest cheer I had ever heard at a meet.

"Maybe I should quit," I thought as I limped on. "Those people don't want to wait for me to finish this race." Somehow, though, I decided to keep going. During the last two laps, I ran in pain and decided not to compete in track next year. It wouldn't be worth it, even if my foot *did* heal. I could never beat the girl who lapped me twice.

When I finished, I heard a cheer — just as enthusiastic as the one I'd heard when the first girl passed the finish line. "What was that all about?" I asked myself. I turned around and sure enough, the boys were preparing for their race. "That must be it; they're cheering for the boys."

I went straight to the bathroom where a girl bumped into me. "Wow, you've got courage!" she told me.

I thought, *Courage? She must be mistaking me for someone else. I just lost a race!*

"I would have never been able to finish those two miles if I were you. I would have quit on the first lap. What happened to your foot?

We were cheering for you. Did you hear us?"

I couldn't believe it. A complete stranger had been cheering for me — not because she wanted me to win, but because she wanted me to keep going and not give up.

Suddenly I regained hope. I decided to stick with track next year. One girl saved my dream.

That day I learned two things:

First, a little kindness and confidence in people can make a great difference to them.

And second, strength and courage aren't always measured in medals and victories. They are measured in the struggles we overcome. The strongest people are not always the people who win, but the people who don't give up when they lose.

I only dream that someday — perhaps as a senior — I will be able to win the race with a cheer as big as the one I got when I lost the race as a freshman.

— Ashley Hodgson —

No-Hair Day

Whatever you are doing, love yourself for doing it.
Whatever you are feeling, love yourself for feeling it.
~Thaddeus Golas

f you are turning 16, you stand in front of the mirror scrutinizing every inch of your face. You agonize that your nose is too big and you're getting another pimple — on top of which you are feeling dumb, your hair isn't blond, and that boy in your English class has not noticed you yet.

Alison never had those problems. Two years ago, she was a beautiful, popular and smart eleventh-grader, not to mention a varsity lacrosse goalie and an ocean lifeguard. With her tall, slender body, pool-blue eyes and thick blond hair, she looked more like a swimsuit model than a high school student. But during that summer, something changed.

After a day of life-guarding, Alison couldn't wait to get home, rinse the saltwater out of her hair and comb through the tangles. She flipped her sun-bleached mane forward. "Ali!" her mother cried, "what did you do?" She discovered a bare patch of skin on the top of her daughter's scalp. "Did you shave it? Could someone else have done it while you were sleeping?" Quickly, they solved the mystery — Alison must have wrapped the elastic band too tightly around her ponytail. The incident was soon forgotten.

Three months later, another bald spot was found, then another. Soon, Alison's scalp was dotted with peculiar quarter-sized bare patches. After diagnoses of "it's just stress" with remedies of topical ointments, a specialist began to administer injections of cortisone, 50 to each spot, every two weeks. To mask her scalp, bloody from the shots, Alison was granted permission to wear a baseball hat to school, normally a violation of the strict uniform code. Little strands of hair would push through the scabs, only to fall out two weeks later. She was suffering from a condition of hair loss known as alopecia, and nothing would stop it.

Alison's sunny spirit and supportive friends kept her going, but there were some low points. Like the time when her little sister came into her bedroom with a towel wrapped around her head to have her hair combed. When her mother untwisted the towel, Alison watched the tousled thick hair bounce around her sister's shoulders. Gripping all of her limp hair between two fingers, she burst into tears. It was the first time she had cried since the whole experience began.

As time went on a bandanna replaced the hat, which could no longer conceal her balding scalp. With only a handful of wispy strands left, the time had come to buy a wig. Instead of trying to resurrect her once-long blond hair, pretending as though nothing had been lost, Alison opted for a shoulder-length auburn one. Why not? People cut and dyed their hair all the time. With her new look, Alison's confidence strengthened. Even when the wig blew off from an open window of her friend's car, they all shared in the humor.

But as the summer approached, Alison worried. If she couldn't wear a wig in the water, how could she lifeguard again? "Why — did you forget how to swim?" her father asked. She got the message.

After wearing an uncomfortable bathing cap for only one day, she mustered up the courage to go completely bald. Despite the stares and occasional comments from less-than-polite beachcombers — "Why do you crazy punk kids shave your heads?" — Alison adjusted to her new look.

She arrived back at school that fall with no hair, no eyebrows, no eyelashes, and with her wig tucked away somewhere in the back of her closet. As she had always planned, she would run for school president, changing her campaign speech only slightly. Presenting a slide show on famous bald leaders from Gandhi to Mr. Clean, Alison had the students and faculty rolling in the aisles.

In her first speech as the elected president, Alison addressed her condition, quite comfortable answering questions. Dressed in a T-shirt with the words "Bad Hair Day" printed across the front, she pointed to her shirt and said, "When most of you wake up in the morning and don't like how you look, you may put on this T-shirt." Putting on another T-shirt over the other, she continued. "When I wake up in the morning, I put on this one." It read, "No-Hair Day." Everybody cheered and applauded. And Alison, beautiful, popular and smart — not to mention varsity goalie, ocean lifeguard and now, school president with the pool-blue eyes — smiled back from the podium.

— Jennifer Rosenfeld and Alison Lambert —

I Did It!

The task ahead of us is never as great
as the power behind us.
~Ralph Waldo Emerson

MAY 1989

My high school graduation was only one month away, and I was more determined than ever to roll across the graduation stage in my manual wheelchair. You see, I was born with a disease called cerebral palsy and because of it, am not able to walk. In order to practice for graduation, I began using my manual wheelchair daily at school.

It was very difficult pushing myself around campus all day while lugging four or five schoolbooks, but I did it. During the first couple of days of using my manual wheelchair at school, everyone offered to give me a push from class to class, but after a few times of my teasingly remarking, "I don't need your help or want your pity," everyone got the hint and let me huff and puff myself around school.

I had always received tremendous satisfaction from using my manual wheelchair, but when I began to push myself around school, the personal rewards were far greater than I ever imagined. I not only saw myself differently, but my classmates, too, seemed to view me on a different level. My classmates knew of my perseverance and determination and respected me because of them. I couldn't have been more pleased about the emotional and physical liberation that my insistence on using my manual wheelchair was bringing to my life.

My electric wheelchair was a tremendous source of freedom for me while I was growing up. It gave me the independence to move about in ways that I was not able to do under my own power. However, as I became older, I realized that the electric wheelchair that had once given me so much freedom was quickly becoming an obstacle of confinement. I felt that I was an independent person except for the fact that I was limited by my dependency on my electric wheelchair. The very thought of being dependent on anything for the rest of my life frustrated me.

To me, graduating from high school in my manual wheelchair was a symbolic point in my life. I wanted to enter my future as an independent young man — I was not going to allow myself to be carried across the graduation stage by an electric wheelchair. I didn't care if it took me 20 minutes to push across the stage, I was going to do it.

JUNE 14, 1989

Graduation. That evening all of the graduates marched around the pavilion in caps and gowns and to our seats on the stage. I sat proudly in my manual wheelchair among the first row of my graduating class.

When the announcer called my name, I realized that everything I had striven for as a child was now a reality. The independent life that I had worked so hard for was now within my grasp.

I pushed myself ever so slowly toward the front of the stage. I looked up from my concentration on pushing my wheelchair and realized that everyone on the pavilion was giving me a standing ovation. I proudly accepted my diploma, turned to my fellow classmates, held my diploma above my head, and yelled as loud as I could, "I did it… I did it!"

— Mark E. Smith —

Excerpted from *Growing Up with Cerebral Palsy* by Mark E. Smith

New Beginnings

Dear Graduate,

Well, this is it! Graduation is over and you're ready to begin life's journey! I know you have lots of mixed feelings. That's the weird thing about most of life's big moments — very rarely do they consist of one emotion. But that's okay. It helps to make the good times more precious and the not-so-good times bearable.

I've spent a lot of time trying to figure out what sage advice I could pass along. That's one of the hard parts about being a parent — determining what should be said and what should be left for you to discover. I finally decided just to offer a little insight to life's basic questions. Some people go through their whole lives without ever giving them any thought. Too bad — as you search for the answers, you can make some wonderful discoveries. They can also be frustrating; just when you think you've found the answer, you'll find the need to ask another question. (Which explains why even at my incredibly advanced age, I still don't have any answers!) At any rate, I hope that sharing this little piece of myself and my soul will somehow help to carry you through when the questions come along.

Who? It took me a while to realize that this is probably the most important question of all. Take time to discover who you are and be your own person. Strive to be honest, respectful and happy. When you are at peace with yourself, everything else will fall into place. Just be careful not to wrap your identity in possessions. Allow yourself to grow and change. And remember always that you are not alone — you have your family, your friends, your guardian angel and God (not necessarily in that order!).

What? This is a tricky one, and at first this question had me fooled. I thought the question was, "What will I do today?" However, I found that things really got interesting when I instead asked, "What is my passion?" Discover what it is that burns inside and keeps you going, then nurture it. Take it apart and build it back together. Do whatever you want with it, but never let it from your sight. Do it because that's what you love to do. The joy it brings you will keep you going through some of the doldrums of life.

When? This is the sneaky one. Do not ignore it. It will keep you balanced. Some things are best done now. Procrastination usually just creates more work. But keep in mind that there is a season for everything, and some things are better left for another day. As hard as it may be, remember to take time to rest and enjoy the miracle of each new day. With practice, you will learn the pleasure of doing some things now and the unique delight of waiting and planning for others.

Where? Surprisingly, this is the easiest one. You will always have the answer with you if you keep your home in your heart and put your heart into wherever you call home. Be an active part of your community and you will discover the special charm that will endear it to you. Remember always that the simplest act of kindness can make an enormous difference, and that you can change the world.

Why? Never stop asking this one. It's the one that will keep you growing. Let it. Let it challenge you when you've become too complacent. Let it shout at you when you are making decisions. Let it whisper to you when you lose sight of who you are or where you want to be. But you also need to be careful with this one. Sometimes the answer does not come for years, and sometimes it doesn't come at all. Recognizing that basic fact can keep you sane and allow you to move on.

How? Ah, this is the one on which I can't advise you! This is the one you will answer in your own special way. But you've come so far in the past few years, I know that you'll do fine. Just remember to believe in yourself and in miracles. Remember that the greatest discoveries come after stumbling over questions. And please remember— always—that I love you.

Congratulations on your new beginning.

Love,
Mom

— Paula (Bachleda) Koskey —

We are pleased to introduce you to the writers whose stories appeared in the original *Chicken Soup for the Teenage Soul*. These bios were the ones that ran when the stories were originally published. They were current as of the original publication date in 1997.

Meet Our Original Contributors

Dr. Eric Allenbaugh is a management consultant, a national keynote speaker and bestselling author of *Wake-Up Calls: You Don't Have to Sleepwalk Through Your Life, Love or Career*. Eric has been a guest on nearly 300 television and radio talk shows regarding leadership and life issues. His seminars are frequently described as "life changing." He can be reached at Allenbaugh Associates, Inc., in Lake Oswego, OR, at 503-635-3963 or via e-mail at eric@allenbaugh.com.

Kif Anderson is establishing a reputation as a unique speaker who blends magic, motivation and merriment to lift his audiences to new heights of inspiration. He writes a monthly column for the on-line magazine *Lighten Up! America* and is an author of many works on magic. Kif is presently working on his first major book, titled *Reaching Beyond Perceived Realities*. In 1991 he was honored with the distinguished Comedy Magician of the Year Award. Kif can be reached at P.O. Box 577, Cypress, CA 90630, by e-mail at magicalmotivator@themall.net, or by calling 562-272-7363.

Jack Cavanaugh covers sports for *The New York Times*. He also has written extensively for *Sports Illustrated* and a number of other national publications, including *Reader's Digest*, the *Sporting News, Golf Digest, Tennis* magazine and *American Way*, the in-flight publication of American Airlines. As a sportswriter, he has covered hundreds of major sports events, including the Olympics, the World Series, the Super Bowl, scores of title fights, the U.S. Open tennis and golf tournaments, the Masters golf tournament, and the Davis Cup. During a breakaway period from print journalism, he was a news reporter for ABC News for six years and, later, for CBS News for two years. Cavanaugh has taught writing courses at the University of Connecticut and at Norwalk Community and Technical College in Norwalk, CT. His book *Damn the Disabilities: Full Speed Ahead* was published in 1995. He lives in Wilton, CT.

Diana L. Chapman has been a journalist for more than 11 years, working for such newspapers as the *San Diego Union, Los Angeles Copley Newspapers* and the *Los Angeles Times*. She specializes in human interest stories. Diana was diagnosed with multiple sclerosis in 1992 and is currently working on a book involving health issues. She has been married for eight years and has one son, Herbert "Ryan" Hart. She can be reached by calling 310-548-1192 or writing to P.O. Box 414, San Pedro, CA 90733.

Nick Curry III was born in Korea and then adopted by an American family when he was four years old. This all-American boy was president of his class, played soccer and baseball, and "will golf for food!" He attends school in Orlando, FL.

Amanda Dykstra has always wanted to be a writer. This is her first published poem. She can be reached at Minerva382@aol.com.

Melissa Esposito wrote this essay while in high school in 1992. She was 16 at the time. Today Melissa is a sophomore in college. She misses her two little sisters, Emma and Kathryn. Kathryn was born after Melissa wrote the essay, and Melissa welcomed her into the family without the anxiety Emma originally created.

Charles C. Finn wrote this poem as a first-year high school teacher in Chicago in 1966. He now lives with his family in southwest Virginia and splits his time between counseling and writing. His website (www.poetrybycharlescfinn.com) has further information on "Please Hear What I'm Not Saying," including the unedited, original version of the poem, as well as his books of poetry.

Jennie Garth has been playing the role of "Kelly" in Fox Television's *Beverly Hills, 90210* for seven years. Among its ensemble cast, Jennie has since become one of the break-out stars of one of the most success-ful series ever for the Fox network. She began starring in telefilms in 1993, such as Danielle Steel's *Star* and also starred in and was executive producer of *Without Consent* for ABC. She went on to produce her most recent project, *A Loss of Innocence*. Jennie was born in Champaign, IL, moved to Phoenix when she was 13, and at 15 moved to L.A. with her mother to pursue Jennie's dream of acting.

Lia Gay is a 16-year-old high school student who lives in Santa Monica, CA. She loves to write stories and poems, and plans to pursue writing as a career. She played a large part in developing the concept and compiling the stories in this book, and plans to join the author for portions of the book tour. You can reach her through Kimberly Kirberger at 310-573-3655.

Stacia Gilmer received her Bachelor of Arts, with honors, from Carroll College in 1993. She is a Behavior Specialist in East Texas. Stacia is married and has four beautiful children, Victoria, Antonio, Wesley and Taylor. She plans to write more short stories. Please reach her at jgilmerl33@hotmail.com.

Lisa Gumenick is a 15-year-old freshman in Pacific Palisades, CA. She lives with her mom, dad and sister. Her older brother attends Brown University. Lisa loves friends, talking, dancing and drawing.

Andrea Hensley has worked for the Salvation Army Camps, a program that reaches out to children, for five summers. Currently, Andrea works as a substitute teacher in the Renton School District. Andrea can be reached at 12037 64th Ave. South, Seattle, WA 98178.

Jennifer Love Hewitt stars as Sarah Reeves on the Golden Globe-winning FOX drama series, *Party of Five*. She can be seen on the big screen in three new films this year: *I Know What You Did Last Summer*, *Trojan War* and *Telling You*. A gifted vocalist, her latest album on Atlantic Records, *Jennifer Love Hewitt*, was released in 1996.

Ashley Hodgson, age 15, began her writing career with a winning personal hero essay in fifth grade. Her writing achievements sparked ambition in other areas: academics (4.0 GPA), speech, track (she has run since sixth grade) and science projects.

Jim Hullihan is an internationally recognized film producer and leadership retreat designer whose motivational media assemblies' programs annually appear before 4 million people. As the creator of America's first CD-ROM magazine for teens entitled *Sweet! Digizine*,

Jim is the leading motivation expert in U.S. secondary education. He can be reached at 148 S. Victory, Burbank, CA 91502, or by calling 818-848-1980.

Kaleel Jamison worked as an organization development consultant until her death in 1985. She wrote numerous articles on leadership, human interactions and empowerment. Her work is being carried on by The Kaleel Jamison Consulting Group, Inc., 500 Federal Street, Troy, NY 12180; phone: 518-271-7000, www.kjcg.com.

Randal Jones is a professional speaker and resident of Re: Think. He teaches seminars on thinking skills and personal management, helping people live and work deliberately for maximum effectiveness and satisfaction. He can be reached at 4307 Lealand Lane, Nashville, TN 37204, or by calling 615-292-8585.

Mary Ellen Klee is an acupuncturist working in Santa Monica, CA. Since 1971, she has been a student and teacher of the Arica method and practice developed by Oscar Ichazo. She has had a home in Big Sur, CA for over 30 years and is a trustee of the Esalen Institute. Starting with a teenage diary, writing has been a hobby and refuge for most of her life.

Paula (Bachleda) Koskey is the happy mother of two wonderful hormone hostages (a.k.a. teenagers), HopeAnne and Luke, and one post teen (whew!), Jesse. She would like to thank her children for all their inspiration and encouragement — and Clairol for covering the gray. She maintains her balance by writing, walking, eating chocolate and believing in miracles. Paula is the author of a children's book entitled *Secrets of Christmas*. She can be reached by writing 1173 Cambridge, Berkley, MI 48072, or by calling 810-542-0376.

Tom Krause has been an educator/coach in Missouri for the past 18 years. His many experiences with students of all ages have led to a collection of short stories and poems. You can contact Tom at P.O. Box 274, Aurora, MO 65605, or call 417-678-4904.

Chris Laddish is a freshman in San Rafael, CA. He has always enjoyed writing and has won first place in the Philips Literary Writing contest two years in a row. He hopes to become a screenwriter or journalist. Chris enjoys mountain biking, in-line skating and exploring the Internet. He is the youngest of six children and has lived in San Rafael his entire life.

Alison Lambert is a member of the class of 2000 at the University of Pennsylvania in Philadelphia. She is a certified emergency medical technician with the Newtown Square volunteer fire company #1 in Newtown, Pa. Ali is also an ocean lifeguard in Long Beach Township, NJ. She can be reached by e-mail: alambert@sas.upenn.edu.

A. J. Langer is best known for her role as Rayanne Graff on the groundbreaking ABC drama series *My So-Called Life*. Her story is dedicated with all her love and appreciation to her friends, her kindergarten group.

James Malinchak, age 27, is the author of two books for students: *Teenagers Tips for Success* and *From College to the Real World*. He specializes in motivational and inspirational presentations for teenagers and college students worldwide and is being called "America's #1 Teen Motivator." For information on his talks or books, contact him at P.O. Box 3944, Beverly Hills, CA 90212, or call 954-796-1925, or e-mail JamesMal@aol.com.

Paula McDonald has sold over one million copies of her books on relationships, and has won numerous awards worldwide as a columnist, inspirational feature writer and photojournalist. She writes regularly for *Reader's Digest* and other magazines, and has been a guest on many major U.S. television shows, such as *The Today Show* and *Larry King Live*. For Paula, life is an endless adventure to be lived to the fullest. She resides happily on the beach in Rosarito, Mexico. Paula is available as a speaker or writer, and can be contacted through Creative Consultants, 417W. San Ysidro Blvd., Suite L724, San Ysidro, CA 92173, phone/fax: 011-52-66-313173.

Rick Metzger is a nationally recognized speaker who focuses on how to be the best using the abilities and talents that we each possess. From professional athletics to his current world and national power lifting championships, he understands motivation and setting goals and shares messages with millions. Reach him at 33 N. Melody Lane, Waterville, OH 43566, or at 1-800-215-TALK (8255).

Kent Nerburn is an author, sculptor and educator who has been deeply involved in Native American issues and education. He has served as project director for two books of oral history, *To Walk the Red Road* and *We Choose to Remember.* He has also edited three highly acclaimed books on Native American subjects. Kent won the Minnesota Book Award in 1995 for his book *Neither Wolf Nor Dog: On Forgotten Roads.* The story "Like People First" appeared in Kent's book *Letters to My Son.* Kent holds a Ph.D. in Theology and Art and lives with his family in Bemidju, MN.

Tony Overman is a nationally known motivational youth speaker. He founded the National Youth I Care Hotline and produced *Teen Talk*, a nine-part video series. Tony conducts training workshops for teachers and motivational assemblies for schools. He can be reached at 18965 F.M. 2252, Garden Ridge, TX 78266, phone: 800-487-8464.

Theresa Peterson is a high school student and an active member of her church. Her spare time is spent reading, writing and having fun with her friends. She is a warmhearted person whose loyalty to her friends and family is admirable. She can be reached at P.O. Box 366, Woodstown, NJ 08098.

Daphna Renan is currently a freshman at Yale College. She moved six times before she entered sixth grade, and it was during these early years that she learned the significance of deep and enduring friendships. Daphna would like to thank those who have filled her life with love, laughter and learning.

Sheila K. Reyman is a certified community college instructor. The consultant/trainer for a family child care program, Sheila presents workshops throughout the state. She has also been invited to speak with teens regarding goal-setting and positive attitudes. She can be reached at P.O. Box 20987, Mesa, AZ 85277, or by calling 602-807-1965.

Jennifer Rosenfeld is a career counselor and is currently authoring *Building Your Yellow Brick Road: Real Women Create Extraordinary Career Paths.* She would love to hear more inspiring career profiles and can be reached at 212-794-6050.

Bill Sanders makes a dynamic impact on the lives of teenagers through his nationwide speaking ministry. He is the author of 13 books and numerous cassette programs, and currently writes two books each year. Bill Sanders and his family live in Kalamazoo, MI.

Jack Schlatter is a well-known speaker, writer and recording personality. A frequent contributor to *Chicken Soup for the Soul* books, he can be seen and heard on the video and audio versions of the *Chicken Soup for the Soul* series. He stars in the bestselling *Gifts by the Side of the Road* by Career Track. Jack is listed in *Who's Who Among Teachers in America*, and his talks are filled with humor, wisdom and inspiration. He can be contacted at P.O. Box 577, Cypress, CA 90630, phone: 714-879-7271, e-mail: jackschlatter@themailnet.

Veronica A. Shoffstall is a member of the Baha'i faith, which teaches that all people are from one race and have been created noble by one God. She has been trying to make sense of the world through words all her life. Now in her mid-40s, she is trying to recapture the wisdom of her youth and learn the lessons expressed in her poem "After a While," which she wrote at the age of 19. She can be reached at 229 East 25th Street, #4D, New York, NY 10010.

Mark E. Smith is an author and sought-after inspirational speaker. He shares the priceless lessons he's learned from living with cerebral palsy with thousands each year. For Mark's autobiography ($11.95 + $3 S&H), or to inquire about having him speak at your function, write: 27 Goree, Martinez, CA 94553, or call 510-228-8928.

Jason Summey is a 14-year-old high school freshman who handles himself in front of audiences like a 40-year-old pro. He speaks regularly about his "Be Cool, Stay in School" program and is currently writing a book on the subject. Reach him at P.O. Box 16844, Asheville, NC 28816, or call 704-252-3573.

Andrew Tertes authors enchanting books, stories and poetry intended to inspire passion for one's own personal journey. For news on Andrew's upcoming books for adults and children, write to Unicorn News, P.O. Box 3164, San Rafael, CA 94901, or call 888-434-6789.

Terri Vandermark graduated from Johnson City High School in 1983. She spent her first five years after graduation as a PCA for the elderly and continues to enjoy helping others. Today she works full-time as parts crib attendant for Felchar Mfg., a division of Shop Vac Corp. She enjoys writing, reading *Chicken Soup for the Soul* books, being in love with Randy and spending time with her special friend, Tonya. Her latest dream has come true — getting her story published in *Chicken Soup for the Teenage Soul.*

Glenn Van Ekeren is a dynamic speaker and trainer dedicated to helping people and organizations maximize their potential. Glenn is the author of *The Speaker's Sourcebook, The Speaker's Sourcebook II* and the popular *Potential Newsletter.* Glenn has a wide variety of written publications and audio and video presentations available. He can be reached at People Building Institute, 330 Village Circle, Sheldon, IA 51201, or by calling 1-800-899-4878.

Sarah Vogt was born and raised in Columbus, IN. Currently, she resides in South Florida and works as a PC/network analyst for a major corporation. Sarah has an undergraduate degree from Florida Atlantic University in business administration. Computers are her hobby and her livelihood and writing is her passion. She can be reached at 80 Catalpa Way, Columbus, IN 47203.

Mary Jane West-Delgado is a physical therapist and author of short stories and cartoons. She is president of Toe Bumpers, Inc., creating fun and decorative safety products for the home. You can reach Mary Jane at 805-688-1372 or by e-mail at delgado@terminus.com.

Sharon Whitley is a former bilingual grade-school teacher who has also taught high-school special education. Her work has appeared in *Reader's Digest* (including 18 international editions), *Los Angeles Times Magazine, Guideposts* and the *San Diego Union-Tribune.* She can be reached at 5666 Meredith Ave., San Diego, CA 92120, phone: 619-583-7346.

Amy Yerkes is currently a student at University of Maryland, College Park. She is planning a career in public relations and enjoys writing poetry in her spare time.

Bettie B. Youngs, Ph.D., is one of the nation's most respected voices in youth and parent education. She is the author of 14 books published in 30 languages, including *Values from the Heartland, Gifts of the Heart: Stories That Celebrate Life's Defining Moments* and *You and*

Self-Esteem: A Book for Young People, from which this piece is excerpted. Contact her at 3060 Racetrack View Dr., Del Mar, CA 92014.

Meet Our New Contributors

Gloria Ahn goes by "Glo" because her mom says she glows like the stars. Her next goal is to matriculate in a writing Ph.D. program near LA/Hollywood in order to continue pursuing comedy, dance, modeling, and acting. The quote that would best sum up her life story is: "If you think my hands are full, you should see my heart."

Malaysia Barr is a current student at Clemson University, working toward a Bachelor of Arts in Communication, with a minor in English. She is the oldest of three and enjoys reading, writing, singing, and listening to jazz. Malaysia plans to publish urban Christian young adult fiction in the future.

Sophie Bolich is a Milwaukee-based bilingual journalist, poet, and all-around creative. She is always on the go and loves to spend time outside running, biking, skateboarding and walking. She is always happiest when surrounded by friends, great views, and with a cup of coffee in hand.

Odelia Chan is a Christian, writer, singer, teacher, and avid reader. She holds a B.A. in Communications and is also a Certified Holistic Nutritionist. She is the author of *Obstacles: One God. One Team. One Vision*, a Christian novel for young people. Odelia lives with her wonderful family in Canada.

Stacia Datskovska is a seventeen-year-old journalist and NYU student. She has previously published in places like *USA Today*, *Baltimore Sun*, *HuffPost*, *POPSUGAR*, and more. When Stacia is not writing, she enjoys cooking, reading, spending time in nature, and traveling.

Amara Dynes is a junior in high school. She grew up always reading books, which turned into a love for writing. Amara loves to spend her time with family and friends, watching *Gilmore Girls*, and traveling. For college, she hopes to attend a HBCU and study political science/policy.

Alexis Farber is a high school sophomore in New York City. She enjoys writing and has had two poems published in *Poetic Power*. In addition to writing, she has taken up lyrical dance after being a competitive gymnast for many years. She hopes to pursue a psychology major at UCLA.

Lindsay Freiberger is a high school senior in Pasadena, CA. She competes for the water polo and swim team and enjoys the outdoors. She recently became president of the school's Environmental Club and is passionate about writing. Lindsay hopes to pursue a college degree in fashion journalism in 2022.

Josh Friedberg is an author, TEDx speaker, music historian, and singer-songwriter who lives in Chicago. He has a master's degree in English from Northeastern Illinois University and has published many articles at PopMatters, Good Men Project, and other publications. E-mail him at joshfrmusic@gmail.com.

Katie Greenan, Ph.D. is an Assistant Professor of Communication at the University of Indianapolis. She received her Doctorate and Bachelor of Arts degrees from Purdue University and Master of Science degree from Syracuse University. Family, health, and education are Katie's chief values. E-mail her at katiegreenan@gmail.com.

Grace Hanna has a Bachelor of Science degree from Florida State University. She currently lives in Tallahassee, FL and is pursuing a career in the field of health and human services.

Kayleen Kitty Holder is the fourth-generation editor of a weekly newspaper, *The Devine News*, which has served the community for over 124 years! She began writing a column at sixteen. Kayleen and husband Daniel have two children. Her beautiful daughter A'Dell, son Tucker, and goddaughter Audrey are the inspiration for most of her stories.

Emily Jones is a student in Suffolk, working in English and Humanities, who has been writings short stories since she could hold a pen. She hopes to go on to publish novels or write screenplays, balancing her love for creativity with school and work. E-mail her at emilyjones161003@gmail.com.

JS is a high school student, studying visual arts. Their hobbies include filmmaking and watching films, video games, and torturing their sister. They plan to be a producer/director someday.

Michael I. Mason is an honor roll student maintaining a 4.2 grade point average. He is a poet and has participated in poetry slam competitions. Michael enjoys roller skating, reading and writing.

Baylie Jett Mills is the author and illustrator of *The Adventures of Max* children's book series and has previously been published in the *Chicken Soup for the Soul* series. She is an accomplished pianist and plays the guitar, ukulele, and harmonica. Baylie loves reading, writing, and spending time with her family and four adorable dogs.

After surviving whitewater rafting, **Kamala Reese** went on to earn a B.A. in Communication and an M.S.Ed. in English. She is a mentor and former high school teacher who is living a life teenage her would be pleasantly surprised by — filled with love, laughter, and persevering against the odds.

Alexandria Rhodes is a literary arts major at a Regional Governor's School for the Arts. She comes from a very supportive, and large, family. She has had a love for writing ever since elementary school.

Alyssa Rodriguez received her Bachelor of Arts and Science in Philosophy, with honors, from the University of San Diego. She is a part of the Los Angeles Acting Studio SD and is working toward a career in screenwriting.

Keeana Saxon has a B.A. from Spelman College and a J.D. from Western New England University School of Law. She is now a commissioner with the city of Boston, a piano teacher, and the Founder and Executive Producer of Kidogo Productions, a multimedia company for preschoolers. She is working on a set of children's poems.

Maisha Sheikh was born in Bangladesh and raised in New York. She is currently a student at Brooklyn Technical High School and plans to attend college in New York City this fall. When she's not scrolling through her Twitter feed, she can be found watching shows with her siblings and crocheting for hours on end.

Stephanie Simmonds works in the mental health field as a psychiatric attendant. Stephanie will be celebrating her second anniversary to Johnny this August. This is her first time being published. Stephanie enjoys attending church, reading, writing and traveling.

Julia Tilson has lived in Muskoka all her life, where her hobbies include writing, canoeing, painting, and dancing. She can usually be found sitting in an old oak tree searching for wild animals and thinking about stories. She is currently editing three of her own books, including two fantasy novels.

Rylee Toole is an upcoming junior in high school, aspiring to pursue a major in English after graduation. She loves telling poorly constructed jokes, naps, her cat Minerva, her friends and family, and this really cool guy named Roman. Feel free to e-mail her at retoole714@ gmail.com.

Thomas E. Turner received his Associate of Arts from Jones County Junior College in 2017. He has one son and is a veteran of the United States Navy. Thomas enjoys reading, writing, jiu-jitsu and nature. He dedicates this particular work to his father, Eddie Turner, and his sister, Kristin Turner-Plunkett.

Brooke Wallace received her dual Bachelor of Arts in Elementary/ Special Education and Master of Special Education from Ball State University in 2013. She has been a special educator for eight years, where she currently is a Director of Special Education. Brooke has devoted her career to fighting for inequities within education.

Dallas Woodburn is a bestselling author and book coach. Her debut novel *The Best Week That Never Happened* won first place in The YA Book Awards and her next novel is forthcoming in 2022. She has also written extensively for newspapers and magazines. Dallas lives in the San Francisco Bay Area with her husband and daughter.

T.C. Zimmerman is a web developer who received her Bachelor's of Science in Computer Science from Jackson State University, but has always had a passion for writing stories and poetry. She currently resides in Central Mississippi with her fiancé.

We are pleased to introduce you to the writers whose stories appeared in the original *Chicken Soup for the Preteen Soul*. These bios were the ones that ran when the stories were originally published. They were current as of the original publication date of that book in 2000.

Meet Our Contributors from Chicken Soup for the Preteen Soul

Brandi Bacon is a sixteen-year-old sophomore in Kentucky. She is a cheerleader and has recently returned from Germany where she was a foreign exchange student. Brandi has been writing since she was in the second grade and hopes that her story will help other kids who are facing difficult situations.

Raegan Baker is a freshman in college majoring in communications. She enjoys reading, writing and spending time with friends and family. Raegan loves children and would like to one day work with children and teenagers who suffer from OCD. You can reach her via e-mail at RWB7and18@aol.com.

Justin Day is a sixteen-year-old from Oklahoma who lives his life playing soccer and is interested in playing for a pro club. He enjoys going on dates and playing video games. He also enjoys writing poems and short stories in his spare time. Justin wrote his true story "April Morning" because he wanted to write something that came from the heart.

Tiffany Jacques is a high school sophomore in Montana. She is very close to her family. The things she loves most are children, the color yellow, butterflies, and having fun with her friends and boyfriend. Tiffany plans to go to college and would like to be a physical therapist, get married and have lots of beautiful children.

Scott Klinger is an eighteen-year-old film student in Laguna Beach,

CA. He has written several television commercials, comic strips and a screenplay. He is also a published photographer and just launched a film production company called Effusions Films. In his free time he likes to snowboard and travel. You can reach him at 273 Cajon St., Laguna Beach, CA 92651, by phone at 949-376-7150 or via e-mail at effusionfilms@aol.com.

Jarod Larson enjoys driving since he just got his driver's license. He also likes fishing, swimming, basketball and hanging out with friends. He wants to attend Fresno State Collage. He is very close with his mom, Susan, and sisters, Alana and Adena.

Beverley Mitchell was discovered by a talent agent when she was only four years old while throwing a tantrum at a mall. She booked her first job acting in a commercial for AT&T and the rest is history. Aside from working on the hit television show, *7th Heaven,* Beverley enjoys hanging out with her friends, shopping, going to the beach, snowboarding, photography and making scrapbooks. She has two dogs, Dakota and Trixie, and two cats. Beverley is the winner of the Young Artist Award for Best Actress in a Television Drama Series (*7th Heaven*) in both 1996 and 1997.

Nicole Peters is a sixteen-year-old from Oklahoma. Her goal in life is to continue writing and earn a Master's in Psychology so that she can help others. She is active in her Christian youth group and enjoys being a teenager.

Lauren Wheeler is twelve years old and enjoys going to camp, hanging out with her friends and playing tennis. She loves making new friends online with people from diverse backgrounds. She is on a swim team that has been undefeated for two years.

Xiao Xi Zhang, age eighteen, moved to the United States from China at the age of twelve. His experiences of sadness, loss and success in this country led him to write his story for *Chicken Soup for the Preteen Soul.* He can be reached at xzhang2000@aol.com.

Thank You

We owe huge thanks to all our contributors and fans. Barbara LoMonaco, D'ette Corona and Laura Dean read the original book to familiarize themselves with this wonderful title. Editor Laura Dean read all of the new submissions and narrowed down the selection for Associate Publisher D'ette Corona and Publisher and Editor-in-Chief Amy Newmark.

Amy edited the new stories and shaped the final manuscript, as D'ette Corona continued to be Amy's right-hand woman in working with all our wonderful writers. Barbara LoMonaco, Kristiana Pastir, and Elaine Kimbler jumped in at the end to proof, proof, proof. And yes, there will always be typos anyway, so please feel free to let us know about them at webmaster@chickensoupforthesoul.com, and we will correct them in future printings.

The whole publishing team deserves a hand, including our Senior Director of Marketing Maureen Peltier, our Vice President of Production Victor Cataldo, our Executive Assistant Mary Fisher, Editor Jamie Cahill, and our graphic designer Daniel Zaccari, who turned our manuscript into this inspirational, supportive book for teenagers.

Sharing Happiness, Inspiration, and Hope

R eal people sharing real stories, every day, all over the world. In 2007, *USA Today* named *Chicken Soup for the Soul* one of the five most memorable books in the last quarter-century. With over 100 million books sold to date in the U.S. and Canada alone, more than 250 titles in print, and translations into nearly fifty languages, "chicken soup for the soul®" is one of the world's best-known phrases.

Today, twenty-eight years after we first began sharing happiness, inspiration and hope through our books, we continue to delight our readers with new titles, but have also evolved beyond the bookshelves with super premium pet food, television shows, a podcast, video journalism from aplus.com, licensed products, and free movies and TV shows on our Popcornflix and Crackle apps. We are busy "changing your world one story at a time®." Thanks for reading!

Share with Us

We all have had Chicken Soup for the Soul moments in our lives. If you would like to share your story or poem with millions of people around the world, go to chickensoup. com and click on Submit Your Story. You may be able to help another reader and become a published author at the same time. Some of our past contributors have launched writing and speaking careers from the publication of their stories in our books!

We only accept story submissions via our website. They are no longer accepted via mail or fax. Visit our website, www.chickensoup. com, and click on Submit Your Story for our writing guidelines and a list of topics we are working on.

To contact us regarding other matters, please send us an e-mail through webmaster@chickensoupforthesoul.com, or fax or write us at:

Chicken Soup for the Soul
P.O. Box 700
Cos Cob, CT 06807-0700
Fax: 203-861-7194

One more note from your friends at Chicken Soup for the Soul: Occasionally, we receive an unsolicited book manuscript from one of our readers, and we would like to respectfully inform you that we do not accept unsolicited manuscripts, and we must discard the ones that appear.

Paperback: 978-1-61159-996-1
eBook: 978-1-61159-296-2

More insp

Chicken Soup for the Soul

for the Soul®

Tough Times for Teens

101 Stories
about the
Hardest Parts
of Being a
Teenager

Jack Canfield,
Mark Victor Hansen,
and Amy Newmark

Paperback: 978-1-935096-80-1
eBook: 978-1-61159-199-6

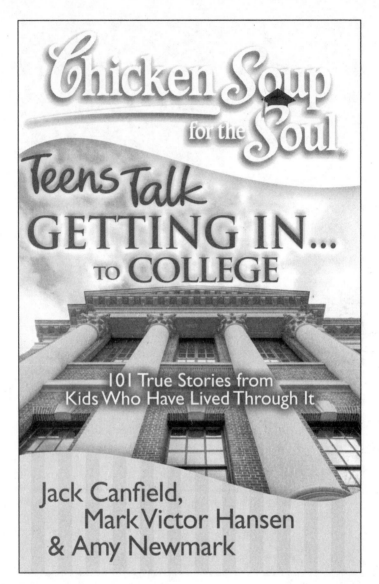

Paperback: 978-1-935096-27-6
eBook: 978-1-61159-153-8

More

Chicken Soup for the Soul®

for the Soul

Campus Chronicles

101 Inspirational, Supportive, and Humorous Stories about Life in College

Jack Canfield,
Mark Victor Hansen,
Amy Newmark & Madeline Clapps

Paperback: 978-1-935096-34-4
eBook: 978-1-61159-152-1

life

Changing lives one story at a time®
www.chickensoup.com